It's Upside Down

A heart-wrenching and humorous journey through assisted living

By Susan Richard

Susan M Richard

Dedicated with love to my parents who blessed me with a childhood as it should be.

Contents

This is based on the true story of my parents' journey through assisted-living. The names of the facilities and many of the characters have been changed.

The group placed their order while George flirted with the waitress. She arrived with pints for everyone except Thelma who ordered Pepsi. Thelma grasped the straw in her gnarled hand, shakily unwrapping it by ripping small shards of paper off. By the time the plastic straw was revealed, a pile of paper resembling a mouse's handiwork lay on the table. The others were in conversation but quietly eyed Thelma as she struggled to place the straw in the icy Pepsi. She slowly lowered the straw, quivering as it neared the rim of the tumbler, somehow missing the glass every time by an inch. No lid covered the beverage, allowing her a four-inch opening for a bull's eye, but every time she closed in on success the straw veered off to the right. Ken and Stu made eye contact but said nothing, and George watched with a grin just under the surface. Thelma continued unsuccessfully for over twenty minutes, until finally with no apparent deviation from previous attempts, the straw slid into the glass. Thelma was unfazed and not the least bit frustrated.

Without missing a beat George said, "Hey Thel, the straw's upside down." She immediately withdrew the straw in an attempt to insert it the other way around. Ken and Stu howled with laughter, not at their mother's struggle but at George's quick wit. Thelma, oblivious to the entertainment she was providing, continued on her mission for another twenty minutes.

4 Years Earlier May 2007

Chapter 1 The Stroke
Did you hear about the boy who ran through the screen door?
He strained himself.

Today life changed. George did not know things were going to change as he lifted the rusty lid on the charcoal grill looking out over his apple orchard. It was early May in western Vermont's Champlain Valley. The apple blossoms were in full bloom blanketing the rolling hillside with a sea of white and pink. George was content. Life had been good to him and Thelma, and now he was living out his retirement dream of being a gentleman farmer. Thelma had been slow to get on board with country living, especially with the forty-five minute drive back into Burlington. She eventually came around with the help of friends, therapy and drugs.

Tonight they were entertaining a few local ladies with a mildly competitive game of croquet, unlimited cocktails and George's famous Cornell barbecue chicken recipe grilled over charcoal, never gas.

"Jesus George, you're tracking dirt across the kitchen," Thelma complained as he left a trail of dirt and grass clippings.

"Thel, it's clean dirt," he reminded her.

It was a conversation they had had countless times over their fifty odd years of marriage, both recognizing neither one would ever change, but still hoping for a miracle. Thelma moved around the kitchen assembling potato salad and her prized homemade baked beans. She hesitated every now and then as if lost in thought as she moved from task to task. She sensed things took her longer now and wondered why it was so much more difficult to follow a recipe or make an entry in the checkbook. She fixed herself a perfect Manhattan with a drop of dry vermouth and a twist before joining the others on the croquet court.

The croquet court was perfectly manicured to regulation size, framed with a four-inch high border of grass clearly marking its boundaries. The sun was casting magic light just over the top of the mountains as it spilled across the orchard on a perfect spring evening.

Ada and Helen were the honored guests. Both ladies had been born and raised in Monkton, married local farm boys and then stayed to raise their own families. Like any self- respecting Vermonter, they had been suspicious and stand offish of George and Thelma when they first arrived to the country from the big city of Burlington twenty years earlier. After all, George was a college professor and Thelma a housewife living in the suburbs where women joined bridge clubs and lived in the fast lane. It only took a couple games of croquet, a few cocktails, Thelma's cooking and George's jokes to win over the locals. Thelma, Ada and Helen quickly became walking buddies. Every morning they strolled the dirt roads gossiping about their husbands and laughing until they nearly peed their pants. It was better and cheaper than any therapy.

The game of croquet was nearing its conclusion with both Ada and George poison. Neither one was playing chicken, things were getting serious. Thelma and Helen watched with amusement hollering advice to both players. Ada spread her short eighty-five year old legs lining up the mallet end with her red ball. She eyed George's yellow ball with the precision of a hawk going in for the kill. She smacked the ball with as much force as she could muster and watched her ball bounce over the grass rolling with enough energy to create a small clink as it tapped George's ball. Ada was champ.

They moved inside to the sunroom for dinner. The ladies cackled over silly stories about their husbands while George interjected jokes whenever he could get a word in. Conversation lingered well into the evening covering all manner of topics from spraying the orchard, to a moose sighting in the cornfield, to the trailer trash neighbors in the beat-up single-wide and impending old age.

George cut in, "Thel, if I'm ever in a nursing home or about to be put in one, use my shotgun. It'll only take one shell. You know I keep the gun next to the bed and ammunition is in my nightstand."

"Oh George, I'm not going to shoot you," Thelma automatically responded, knowing George was only half joking. Thelma knew he wanted nothing more than to live out his final days on his orchard.

The evening continued with friendly banter and the warmth of friendship. Empty cocktail glasses littered the table as the ladies said goodnight with plans to walk at 7am sharp the next morning. Life was good.

Thelma began to clean up the kitchen while George closed up the garage for the night. George retired to his blue leather recliner to catch the 11 o'clock news before bed. Thelma continued picking up the debris from the night's festivities but had trouble focusing on getting everything tidied up. She uncharacteristically left empty glasses and dessert dishes in the sunroom for later. Not long ago, Thelma would never have left a single dirty dish out overnight but things were changing. Thelma bid George and the 11 o'clock news goodnight and headed straight to the bedroom. She crawled between crisp sheets and clicked on the television perched on the bureau. The background noise helped her fall asleep, although after a couple cocktails, sleep would not be an issue. She never heard George come to bed.

Thelma was startled awake by a loud thud. "George, George, George…what was that?" She repeated her frantic call, "George? Are you all right?" There was no answer. She was becoming more alarmed and struggled to find the light switch next to the bed. Her heart started racing as anxiety blossomed.

"George? Where are you? Oh shit, Oh my God, George!" she screamed when she saw him lying in a pool of blood next to the bed. His eyes were wide open. He had evidently fallen out of bed and hit his head on the corner of the night stand. "Oh George, can you get up? George, why aren't you moving? What should I do? I'm calling 911," she announced.

"Don't call Thel, just leave me here. I'll be fine in a minute." She hesitated but hurried into the bathroom to grab a towel for the bleeding. As she wiped away the dark blood from his forehead she realized he was not able to move his left side. He made no effort to get himself up.

"You have to try and sit up George. Oh Jesus, what do I do? Let me try and help you," but her tiny frame was no match for George's two hundred pounds of dead weight.

"Just leave me alone, Thel. I'll be fine." Thelma was becoming more distraught and confused, not knowing what to do and not able to move him. Time passed. Precious time passed with no phone call to 911. Thelma was rattled, and after an unknown amount of time managed to find the phone next to her bed and dial 911. She had not yet made the upgrade to a cell phone.

"What is your emergency?"

"Oh, oh, oh, my husband fell out of bed and he's bleeding and he won't get up."

"Is he conscious? Is he talking?"

"Yes, oh please hurry and help us."

"Can you tell me the address?"

"Oh, it's Monkton. Oh, I can't remember, please hurry."

"It's ok ma'am. We have your address and an ambulance is on the way."

While waiting for the ambulance to arrive, Thelma scurried around the house collecting the partially drained cocktail glasses and assorted dishes from the night before and placed them in the refrigerator. She worried what the paramedics might think if they saw the kitchen was not in pristine condition.

The rescue team arrived after what seemed an eternity to Thelma. They quickly assessed George and prepped him for the ride to the hospital. "Thelma, you can ride with us to the hospital."

"Oh, no I can drive," she responded with a shaky voice.

"Thelma, listen, I think George would like to have you with him in the ambulance. I think it's best if you ride with us." She wandered around the kitchen lost in thought when the EMT guided Thelma to the ambulance after helping her gather up her purse and address book.

Thelma's world was turned upside down. She had never dealt with a life-or-death situation before, especially with George or with any of her four children. How she wished her children lived closer so they could be here and join her at the hospital. She sat quietly in the waiting room perched in a chair like a frail bird. The nurses offered her coffee and soothing small talk but she was not listening. George was quickly tended to by ER doctors who were immediately concerned about a stroke and ordered a battery of tests. The doctors confirmed he suffered a massive stroke on the right side of his brain, compromising the left side. Only time would tell what the real damage was.

With the help of a kind nurse, Thelma called her housecleaner whom she regarded as part of her family since her kids all lived away. Kathy worked several jobs, had derelict children and a deadbeat husband, but somehow managed to maintain a kind heart and genuinely loved Thelma and George. Kathy didn't hesitate, she jumped in her car to come sit with Thelma at the hospital.

Kathy embraced Thelma's tiny shaking body, "Thelma, let me just give you a hug."

"Oooh Kathy, it's just awful. You have no idea how awful this has been."

"Thelma, can you tell me what happened? How is George?" But Thelma was unable to relay any real information and sat quietly staring. "Who would you like me to call?"

"Can you call Sue?" she managed to whisper. Kathy located the number for Thelma's daughter who lived in Maine, and who was the closest as the other three children lived in Florida.

Sue quickly made arrangements for a sub to cover her fourth-grade classroom for the upcoming week and headed to Vermont, a long five-hour drive. She called her siblings in Florida to deliver the news and was barraged with questions: *How bad was the stroke? How long had he been on the floor before 911 was called? How much damage was done by the stroke? Can he walk? Can he talk? Will he survive? Will he be able to live at home again? What hospital? What did the doctors say? Did they give him the TPA drug?*

Sue finally arrived at the hospital midafternoon, after a drive that allowed her thoughts to run wild about her parent's future and their lack of a plan in the event of a catastrophic illness. How many times had they brought up the subject of a "plan" in case something happened? Just last year the kids had convinced them to place a deposit on a house in a beautiful 55-plus community in Maine, but George got cold feet and pulled back his deposit. Thelma was crushed, and now they were back to no plan.

"Hey Mom, I'm here," Sue whispered in her mother's ear. Thelma glanced up confused at first but then recognition flooded her face. Relief spread through her knowing she no longer had to endure this by herself, even though Kathy had selflessly stayed with her all day. There was no replacement for family. Kathy quietly hugged Thelma and said goodbye to Sue.

"Oh Sue, I'm so glad you're here. You don't know what I've been through. It's been awful."

"What have the doctors told you?"

"They're still working on him but he fell out of bed and hit his head, it was terrible."

Sue was confused, "I thought he had a stroke?"

"Oh no, he fell out of bed. He must have tripped in the dark and then hit his head on the nightstand," Thelma quietly explained.

"But when Kathy called me this morning she told me dad suffered a stroke."

They were called into George's room where he was being prepped for a move to an intermediate care room. She was shocked. He looked as though he had aged fifteen years since she had last seen him two weeks earlier. They confirmed George had indeed experienced a stroke. The left side of his face drooped and his voice was very weak. At least he had a voice. She knew strokes often meant the loss of speech, which would be a devastating consequence for her father–but since the stroke was on the right side, his speech was thankfully unaffected.

Sue was on the phone with her brother Stu, a physical therapist, with years of experience working with stroke patients. Stu gave her instructions, "have Dad squeeze your hand with both his right and then left hand."

"OK, he's able to squeeze with his right hand. Nothing, absolutely nothing from his left hand." Clearly an indication of stroke.

After disconnecting from Stu she looked at her mother, "Mom, does Dad know what happened? That he had a stroke?" Sue gently pushed her mother for understanding.

"Oh no, he didn't have a stroke. Why are you saying that? The doctors haven't said anything about a stroke," Thelma responded. "You can't say anything to him about a stroke, it will upset him." They walked quietly down to the cafeteria to kill time while

George was transferred to his room. Thelma was shaky from the ordeal and had not eaten anything since the night before.

"Oh Sue, I'm not hungry," Thelma claimed.

"Mom, you have to eat something. How about I buy you a bag of chips, a bottle of water and a chocolate ice cream." Thelma sipped the water and inhaled the ice cream but the chips remained untouched. "Mom, I need you to understand that Dad had a stroke and things are going to be different now. Do you understand?" Sue was hoping Thelma would start talking.

"Oh Sue, this is so awful." And with that the conversation was stonewalled. After they sat with George for a couple hours watching him sleep through a barrage of medical checks, they both needed a break. He barely acknowledged their kisses as they said goodnight with promises to return first thing in the morning.

Arriving back at the house in Monkton without George felt to Thelma like a betrayal. He had only spent one night in the hospital in all their years of marriage and it was for a knee replacement. He had been so anxious to leave the hospital after his knee surgery, he shocked his doctors by proving he could walk up the three-step ladder less than a day after surgery. It was well known among his friends, if they unfortunately found themselves in the hospital, George would not be up to visit them. He avoided hospitals at all costs, finding any flimsy excuse. He did not even visit Thelma's mother during her last days at a nursing home. Whether it was leftover trauma from his time in WWII or just an aversion to hospitals, he never said.

Sue helped settle Thelma into her bed, turned on the television in the bedroom for white noise and closed the door before calling her siblings. She began with her sister.

"Hey Karen, it's been a long day and Mom's in bed. I'm really worried about her because she is not herself. I know she's been slipping lately but it's definitely getting worse. As for Dad, they're still running tests and will know more tomorrow."

"Well I'm calling his doctors directly in the morning to get information." Karen was a nurse practitioner and also their medical power of attorney.

"Perfect, you clearly understand the medical information better than I do. I'm trying to keep mom calm, fed and with a dose of reality. She doesn't believe dad had a stroke and doesn't even want me to mention the word. It's crazy." After they finished their conversation she spoke with both her brothers. Both wondered if they should fly up but Sue advised they wait to see how things played out. There were still too many unknowns. They all agreed a tag team effort might be best considering they all had to juggle work schedules, kids and travel. Even with George's immediate crisis, Sue had an uneasy feeling regarding her mother.

The next morning was a brilliant but windy May day with a biting chill. On their way to the hospital Sue suggested they grab cash from the bank. Sue pulled up to the

ATM machine. "Oh Sue, I don't know how to use that thing. I've never used one before. Just pull up to the window and I'll talk to the girl."

"Why don't you learn how to use it? I'll show you and then you can grab money anytime you want without worrying if the bank is open." Sue knew her mother needed to be a little more independent with George now out of commission.

During their marriage, George had always handled the finances but Thelma had a handle on what was available for groceries, lessons for the kids, clothes and her weekly hair appointment. On a professor's salary they were not rich but they lacked for nothing. When the kids were young, payday at the university was on the 25th of the month and that's when Thelma stocked up at the grocery store. It was always a happy day at the MacCollom house.

Inside the ATM kiosk Thelma looked at Sue, "What do I do now?"

"You slide your card into the machine." Sue watched in utter amazement as Thelma tried to push her ATM card straight into the glass screen. When that failed she tried jamming the card into the crevices of the screen where there was clearly no slot. Sue stepped back, took a long slow breath. "Mom, do you see the slot right here?" she said, pointing to the spot and demonstrating. Her hopes of Thelma being a quick study were dashed, Thelma could not do it. Sue was suddenly embarrassed for her mother and thankful no one else was in the ATM lobby to witness this clear mental decline. Sue had been well aware Thelma's mind had been slipping, but this behavior was a whole new level. It was scary. She hoped it was caused in part from the incredible stress of the last two days.

All four kids had noticed things with their mother's memory over the last few years. Thelma had always been the consummate hostess—so when, on several occasions, not enough food was cooked for the family it was a sign. She struggled to write checks and often made mistakes while trying to follow a recipe. But the most obvious was during their famously competitive Hearts games around the family dining table. More and more frequently Thelma would play the wrong suit or place the kitty in her hand, forcing a misdeal. Although everyone noticed the change, they just chalked it up to having a few drinks.

"Here Mom, let me show you how to do it." Sue gently guided her mother's hand through the steps of withdrawing money. She noticed her father had taped the PIN number to the back of the card. He clearly knew more than he had let on.

Walking into the hospital room they were assaulted with the odor of plastic, disinfectant and bad food. George sat slumped in the partially raised bed. This was a man bearing no resemblance to the man who always had a smile, a joke or advice to Thelma not to worry. He looked like he had survived a street fight with a nasty bruise and stitches on his forehead, a drooping left side and the inability to move himself. Sue bit her lip while watching as her mother gently kissed her father. They made what small talk they could with George between visits from various nurses and medical personnel.

Rubbery yellow eggs and gelatinous oatmeal sat uneaten on his tray. "Dad, would you like me to get you something else to eat?"

"A jelly donut and coffee," he managed to whisper with a slight grin from the right side of his mouth. Sue checked with the nurse to make sure it was permissible, not knowing if there was some restricted diet.

The nurse explained, "That is fine as long as you break the donut into very small bite-size pieces. We don't want George to choke." Sue left Thelma sitting quietly in the chair next to the bed as she made a donut run, grateful for a few minutes alone.

Growing up, every Sunday morning George made a trip down to Twitchell's, the corner store, to buy a half dozen donuts. This was their treat before heading off to church. The paper bag always contained a sweet combination of jelly donuts and glazed donuts.

Together Thelma and Sue situated George into a sitting position where he could be fed. Sue carefully broke off a tiny piece of the sugary donut and placed it in George's mouth. "Geez, Dad you swallowed that whole piece without chewing!" He opened his mouth for another bite just like a baby bird. Within five minutes he had consumed the entire donut with the exception of the powdery white sugar outlining his mouth. He then took a sip of coffee, heavy on the cream and sugar, while Thelma held the cup for him. She seemed pleased to be doing something to help him.

By the following day it was determined George would be moving to rehab for three weeks to recover strength and mobility. Stu and Karen both warned the rest of them there were no guarantees when it came to stroke rehab. Stu was a physical therapist who worked with stroke patients and Karen was a nurse. Much depended on George's willingness to work and how quickly he started the work. He was 81 years old and time was of the essence.

Thelma and Sue fell into a routine of sitting with George during the day, making a food run midday before stopping for a bite to eat on the way home as neither one had the energy or desire to cook. "Mom, you understand Dad has a lot of work to do in order to recover from his stroke, right? He's going to be in a rehab facility for at least three weeks."

"Oh Sue, it's just the injury to his head. I don't know why he needs to go to rehab."

"Mom, he had a STROKE. He is paralyzed on his left side and he can't get up or walk on his own right now. This is going to require a lot of work from both of you."

"I don't remember the doctors saying anything like that." Sue decided to drop the subject for now. She wanted to talk with her siblings and tell them how Thelma would still not allow herself to say that George had a stroke. It was almost as if saying the words would make them true.

Thursday afternoon was the designated moving time. George was being transferred to rehab by ambulance while Thelma and Sue met him there. They gathered up a few things from home they knew George would want while at rehab: razor, comb, comfy blankets and his partial bridge. He would also need pajamas, but he had never worn pajamas in his entire life and insisted he was not about to start now. Rehab required him to have pants with an elastic waist for easy on and off. They shopped for loose-fitting pajama pants and loose-fitting t-shirts. George appeared to be insulted or maybe embarrassed by the fact he had to wear elastic waist pants. This was the least of his problems.

The staff at the rehab center sat down with Thelma to explain the seriousness of the stroke and the immense effort and life changes facing them both. Thelma was weepy and unsure how to react as her life crumbled around her. Holding her mother's hand, Sue listened but it was doubtful Thelma heard anything the nurse was saying. She was withdrawn and shaky. They toured the facility, met a multitude of therapists and reviewed George's daily schedule. Learning how to feed himself, how to walk again, how to dress himself and how to get to the toilet was his assignment. Thelma was required to attend the sessions in order to help support his recovery.

Thelma moved through the next few days in slow motion as if in a daze. Time slowly ticked by, making every day feel like a week. George made minimal progress but his attitude was good. He was notorious for his positive attitude, if not always realistic. One of George's graduate students had said George always did everything in his power to not be an asshole. Thelma might have disagreed on occasion.

"Mom," Sue started. "Have you thought about when I leave in a couple days? How do you feel about staying here alone and getting yourself back and forth to rehab every day?" Sue was trying to figure out what changes needed to be in place for Thelma and knew her mother was in no condition to stay alone and get herself safely to the hospital. Time was running out before Sue had to return to Maine.

"Oh, I can do it," she said with no confidence.

"I spoke with Karen, Stu and Ken last night because I have to go home on Sunday. Ken and Stu are flying up next weekend which means you will be alone during the week." She paused waiting for a reaction that did not come. "I think it will be best if you stayed with friends this week because it's a 40-minute drive to rehab and things are really stressful right now. If I arrange for you to stay with a different friend each night and have them deliver you to rehab everyday, would you be ok with that?"

"Really Sue I don't need you to do that." Thelma sat down on the couch with an exhausted sigh, crying softly, hoping Sue would not notice.

Observing her mother from across the room for several minutes was heartbreaking. Thelma sat with her eyes closed, clearly struggling to keep it together. Her mother appeared to have shrunk into an old lady in just the last week. Had she been like this but with everyone so busy, no one noticed—or was her mother declining as quickly as her father? Sue spent hours the following day arranging for a different friend to host Thelma each night, which included a ride to rehab.

Luckily Thelma had a large network of friends. She, of course, had her Monkton walking buddies but she also had decades old friends from their early days in Burlington and close friends from Laurel Hill where they raised the family. In the twenty years living in Monkton, Thelma had never been comfortable spending the night alone. In fact, she always arranged to have one of the kids visit or she would go to a friend's for the night when George was out of town. She was now even more uneasy about staying alone.

Thelma began to fuss. "There are just so many pills and I don't think these are the right pills."

"Here Mom, let me help you with these." Sue took the pill box color coded by day and clearly marked with the day of the week and showed her mother how to open the compartments. "OK Mom, you try it." Thelma stared at the pill box and made no effort to open the one labeled Thursday. "Mom, do you know what day it is?" Sue gave it a few minutes and showed her the Thursday section. She pulled out her mother's pills and laid them on the table with a glass of water. For the next forty minutes Thelma struggled to swallow her pills. She placed a pill on her tongue slowly sipping water until the pill dissolved in her mouth. The once clear glass of water was now a milky concoction of pharmaceuticals. She wondered how much of her medications were actually being ingested. Her grandson, Charlie, had once sat with her for over an hour demonstrating how to swallow pills by using mini M&Ms, but to no avail.

Sitting in the sterile rehab room in a straight-back chair, Sue watched the nurses help George out of bed and into the bathroom by supporting his weight while issuing instructions on how to move his left leg. He dragged the left leg as if the leg were not even attached to his body. This was a man who had been riding his John Deere tractor while spraying his orchard less than a week earlier. Sue felt overwhelming sadness knowing this was not what her father had envisioned for himself.

Although plans were in place for Thelma to be supervised and chauffeured around the next week, Sue felt real trepidation saying goodbye to both parents. She honestly was not sure whom she was more concerned about. It appeared her father had a good chance of partial recovery but her mother seemed to be slipping away mentally by the day. After a tearful goodbye she left her parents to make the long drive back to Maine.

Chapter 2 Coming Home

Have you seen the new movie called "Birds of a Feather"?
It stars Walter Pidgeon and John Sparrow.

"Oh boys," Thelma fretted as they were brewing coffee in the morning. "I'm so glad you're here. This is so hard for your father, it's been awful. They make him work so hard and I'm afraid they're hurting him. You know he gets tired very quickly." Thelma was thrilled to have her two sons in town from Florida for the week.

Stu and Ken, were up to assist with the transition home. Seeing their father so vulnerable took them by surprise, but they rallied with a brave face for the sake of their mother.

Stu lived in Florida with his wife Elaine and three teenaged children on the Gulf. They owned their own home healthcare business and were both licensed physical therapists. Ken was the youngest of the four children and also lived in Florida with his wife Marie and their two young sons. Ken was an attorney who had decided to hang a shingle after encountering the frustrations of working for others with an unbearable corporate mentality. He had a passion for music and auto racing.

"OK Mom," said Ken. "You ready to head to rehab to visit Dad? Stu is going to stay here to take care of a few things before Dad gets released, so it's just you and your favorite son." Ken grabbed the keys and began the painfully slow process of guiding Thelma to the Explorer.

"Oh Ken, why do *you* have the keys? I am perfectly fine to drive, you know."

Ken hesitated, "Are you sure Mom, I am happy to drive."

"You people keep telling me I shouldn't drive and I really resent it!"

"Fine Mom, you can drive." Ken handed her the keys and looked at Stu, who raised his eyebrows but said nothing. Getting into the vehicle, down the driveway and to the main road took an agonizing ten minutes. Ken was securely strapped in and watched Thelma carefully because he had real doubts about her driving. On the winding country roads Thelma was going at least 15 mph below the speed limit, but Ken kept quiet. At least they weren't speeding. When they approached the four corners intersection in Hinesburg Ken saw the light turn red, but no signs of Thelma slowing down.

"Red light, Mom, it's a red light!" But it was too late and they breezed through the intersection and by the grace of God there were no other cars coming. "Mom, you just blew through a red light, we could have been killed!"

"Oh, I didn't see it. We're fine," she replied. Ken gripped the handle on the door, deciding then that this was the last time she would be driving. When Thelma had picked them up at the airport, she waited in the car but the boys noticed she had parked at an angle taking up almost three parking spots. Ken had quickly offered to drive home from the airport, so this was his first experience with Thelma behind the wheel in the last year. The next day Ken drove.

The following day Thelma, Stu and Ken were awaiting orders and release papers at the rehab facility.

"Okay George," the nurse said. "Are you ready to make the trip back home to your house and precious apple orchard? We're going to miss you flirting with us, but we're not going to miss your nasty cigar dottle you leave everywhere!" George grinned, but now had to prove he could dress himself. George laid the t-shirt on the bed with his one working hand while he carefully slid the shirt up his weakened arm and over his head with the good hand. A task that used to take mere seconds now required significant concentration and at least five minutes. The urge to help him was palpable but they knew their father had to do it himself. Everything took longer, a lot longer. He never complained, he simply joked with whomever was nearby.

They began the long trek down the hallway.   "George, be careful," Thelma warned as she tried to stay close with her hands in position to catch him if he fell. She didn't have a chance in Hell of catching him.

"Thel, just walk ahead," George grumped. "I'm good."

"Dad, you're looking a little gimpy there." Stu directed. "Lift your left foot." He was analyzing his father's gait from a physical therapist's point of view. The walk down the corridor took fifteen agonizing minutes, the loading of the car took another ten minutes and the drive back to Monkton Valley Orchard took the usual forty minutes.

George was quiet during the drive home sitting in the passenger seat in the front of the Ford Explorer, a seat he rarely sat in. He looked forward to the day when he would drive again. While Stu drove, Ken and Thelma sat in the back seat chatting about the changes made at the house to accommodate George. There were handicap rail bars in the bathroom, rails on both entrances, a toilet extender and bars to prevent him from rolling out of bed. They meandered down the back road towards the house, finally making the slow approach up the dirt drive. George stared out at his apple trees dotting the hillside. The odor of freshly spread manure permeated the air that George breathed in like sweet perfume. "Tomorrow I need to get out there and spray the trees, it's already a week overdue."

"Stu, I think he's asking you to spray tomorrow!" Ken teased.

"You're the one with all the experience Ken, so I think it's up to you because I have to supervise Dad's exercises."

The vehicle pulled to a stop in front of the garage. Thelma took several minutes to figure out how to undo her seatbelt while the boys scurried to George's side of the car. He sat there with a limp left arm as they unfastened him and gave orders on how to shift his body to safely extricate him from the car. He struggled to maneuver his left leg but Stu was there to physically support him. This process took ten minutes and by now Thelma was waiting and watching and ready to catch George if he fell.

With George and Thelma safely settled in the house, Stu and Ken found the vodka, tonic and cranberry juice. They prepared Thelma a very weak highball with Crown Royal, water and a lot of ice. George was already asleep in his recliner.

Ken looked at his parents and then at Stu. "How the hell are they going to stay here by themselves?"

"We have to start looking at assisted living facilities in town," Stu said. "But first we have to line up people to come in everyday to help dad. Mom clearly isn't going to be able to help much, she seems to be in a fog." Stu drained his first drink. "She should definitely NOT be driving."

Thelma didn't seem to hear the conversation. The events of the day had drained all energy to make dinner, the grocery store was a half hour away and there was no delivery out this far in the country. They rummaged through the freezer locating a bag of homemade meatballs and sauce when they heard a knock on the door. A steady stream of neighbors noticed the activity at the house and began delivering well wishes and casseroles. Thelma fussed over them by offering appetizers and cocktails but they all politely declined, they just wanted to check in. She loved nothing more than having people in the house to talk with, wait on and now to distract her from the harsh reality of her future.

In her day, she was the consummate hostess, lying in bed at night planning the menus for her coveted dinner parties. She even had a notebook where she diligently recorded menus from past parties so as not to repeat a single dish. Every detail of the party was planned from the hors d'oeuvres to the color of the cloth napkins to the guest list. Hosting a dinner party these days was beyond her capabilities.

"Dad, what's your plan?" Ken asked. "What if staying out here in Monkton doesn't work? You can't drive right now, Mom probably shouldn't be driving and you're a long way from town. Who is going to mow the lawn, spray the trees and pick the apples? What happens this winter when it snows and the drive needs to be plowed?" This was not the first time the questions had been asked but now there was an urgency.

George responded, "I'll just ask some friends to do it until I'm back in action."

"You can't ask your friends to do all this work all summer Dad," Stu pointed out. "It's like a full-time job."

Out of the blue Thelma snapped, "I resent the fact that you don't think I should drive!"

"What if Dad falls and it's only you and him out here?" Stu ignored her comment, knowing exactly where this conversation was headed.

"I'll call 911 and they'll come help us."

Ken cut in, "Tomorrow we want to look at a couple places in Burlington that can give you support and will allow you to be closer to town."

"Your father does not want to be in a nursing home. And neither do I."

"Boys," George said. "We're fine here, don't worry. I'm not going to a facility. I told your mother to shoot me if it comes to that. I plan to die right here in Monkton."

"Dad, if you fall and break a hip," Stu explained, "it's directly to a nursing home. And besides, the places we want to show you are independent living facilities where you have your own apartment, your own furniture and you come and go as you please. They are not nursing homes."

"Sounds like prison to me." George said.

Ken and Stu toured four different facilities the next day and both agreed Champlain Waters was their first choice—their only choice, really. The four facilities had shockingly different approaches. One upscale facility required the residents to sign over all assets to the facility in return for lifelong care. It came with an arrogant attitude from the staff. The other two facilities felt and smelled distinctly like nursing homes and appeared tired and worn. Champlain Waters was a relatively new complex with a large U-shaped building surrounding a lovely courtyard. All apartments were well lit with abundant windows, new carpet and well designed layouts. The boys were able to get George and Thelma on the waiting list for a one-bedroom.

"Two to three months?" Stu wondered out loud as they walked back to the Explorer. "What the hell are we going to do with them until then?"

"I spoke with Karen last night," Ken said. "She's bringing Anna, who has the summer off between semesters. I guess Karen somehow convinced Anna to stay with Mom and Dad for a month."

"Is she nuts?" Stu said. "What twenty-one-year-old wants to spend the summer bathing their grandfather?"

Ken posed the question, "Do you have a better idea? They can't live alone, Dad can barely walk and Mom is so confused she doesn't even know what day it is half the time. And every place we've checked has a waiting list."

While enjoying beverages in the sunroom, they watched as a UPS truck created a cloud of dust as it made its way up the dirt drive. Ken jumped up to meet the driver to intercept the delivery. He returned to the sunroom with an Oreck box for the big reveal. They asked George and Thelma what it might be but neither one had any idea. Ken carefully lifted out a beautiful new high-tech air filter. This triggered George's memory, "Oh I remember. When I was in rehab I ordered it off the TV with my Amex card." He was quite proud of himself.

"How much other shit did you order, Dad?" Ken asked. The answer was unclear. George had a tendency to order things, and during the last year Ken had to take legal action to get their money back from a cruise George had booked which they were never going to take.

Ken and Stu returned to Florida a few days later, leaving George and Thelma sitting in the Explorer with Thelma behind the wheel. This was not ideal, but they had limited options and she insisted she was fine to drive home. Both boys were visibly upset bidding goodbye to their parents. Stu sobbed as they walked away, a reaction Ken had never seen from his older brother before. Coming to terms with their parents' mortality was not easy.

They all kept their fingers crossed George and Thelma could make it through one night alone without incident. Stu had reviewed and monitored George's ability to get up with his walker and make it to the bathroom. Karen and Anna were flying up the next day, so the dynamic duo would be on their own for about eighteen hours. George was a fall risk and Thelma insisted on helping by trying to hold him up despite the one hundred pound difference. Ken made sure there was a prepared meal ready for them which only required a quick microwaving, and he set up the coffee maker so all they had to do was depress the start button. Fingers were crossed and prayers sent. They survived.

Karen and Anna decided the best plan of action was to rent a car and spare everyone the nightmare of George and Thelma trying to get to the airport on time. Entering the house, they realized they had arrived in the nick of time. One lone glass sat in the sink, both parents were wearing dirty wrinkled clothes and George was resting in his recliner with Fox News recycling stories. After welcome hugs, Karen quickly assessed her parents and began taking charge. "Mom, let's get you into clean clothes."

"What's the matter with my clothes? Oh Karen, I'm so glad you're here, you just don't know how awful it's been. Your father is working so hard and I am trying to help but it's so hard."

"I know. Mom, let's get you something to eat." Karen noticed they had not eaten since her brothers had left the day before; even the coffee pot was still ready to go. She planned to give Anna a crash course on nursing. Anna was not a nurse and had no intention of ever becoming a nurse, but was evidently going to be one this summer.

Anna looked at her mother in horror, "Mom, it's not right that I have to see Gramp naked and wash his privates. I thought I was just going to cook for them, drive them around and help Gramp walk."

"Welcome to reality Anna," Karen replied with a grin. Anna was the oldest of three girls and a senior at the University of Florida, where she was studying food packaging and struggling to pass organic chemistry. She was a beautiful girl with a kind soul. The month in Vermont as a nursemaid would be life changing.

The next day Karen drove Thelma to visit an adult daycare center offering activities and a place to go a few days a week. There was even bus service that would pick her up and deliver her to the front door in Monkton. Thelma was unimpressed. "Oh Karen, these people are all a little crazy and this is not for me. I don't know why you keep trying to send me to these horrible places. I don't like it."

"I was thinking it might be good for you to get out and socialize, and there's even a bus that will pick you up."

"Well, I resent the fact that you kids keep telling me that I can't drive. I am perfectly fine and I get out plenty. I don't need to go to some nursing home with half-crazy drooling old people for the day." Thelma was getting worked up. Wisely, Karen let it go, but informed her siblings the adult daycare was an option. Karen and Anna spent the week finding their groove and a new normal. George needed assistance getting in and out of his chair, help getting to the bathroom and help getting dressed, but things were slowly improving. Thelma fretted over George but the enormity of the situation seemed too much for her at times. Anna quickly realized Thelma needed as much assistance as George but in a different way. Pills were especially confusing.

"Good morning Gram," Anna said. "Have you had breakfast yet?"

"No honey, I can't eat until I take my pills. I've been looking at my pills and I think they're mixed up, they don't look right to me. Why do they keep changing my pills?"

"Here Gram, let me help you." Anna carefully laid out a colorful assortment of blood pressure, anti-anxiety and cholesterol medicines for her grandmother. Thelma spent the next forty minutes swishing, swallowing and examining her pills and still they weren't all swallowed. Finally, with coaxing from Anna, she chugged the last of the milky chemical concoction from the bottom of the glass.

"We're on our own today Gram, now that mom's gone back home. What would you like to do? We have to wait until after Gramp finishes his physical therapy, but then we can go out to the grocery store if you want. What would you like for dinner? Because I'd love to cook for you."

"Oh whatever you want. It's so good to have you here." Thelma responded by giving Anna a hug and gentle kiss on the head.

Anna settled in with her grandparents, but after only one day it seemed a month would be an eternity to the twenty-one-year-old on summer break from college. It was surprising to Anna how much help her grandparents needed, considering they had been living on their own just a few weeks earlier. There was very little downtime between assisting George with daily hygiene, dressing and eating, keeping the house in order and calming Thelma down between daily meltdowns.

One morning after Anna had patiently assisted Thelma with her pills and reassured her they were in fact the correct pills and no one had mixed them up, Anna walked past George and caught the unpleasant aroma of body odor. She had not yet found the courage to bathe her grandfather but decided she now had no choice.

"Hey Gramp, I'm going to start the bath water for you. Do you like your water really hot or just warm? Anna knew they were both embarrassed and uncomfortable.

"Warm is good, Anna," he replied as Anna made her way into the small bathroom off the bedroom. Anna felt dread at the prospect of bathing her grandfather when she suddenly formulated a solution.

"Hey Gram, I have Gramps in the bathtub sitting on his special chair, he's all undressed but needs help. I've soaped up the washcloth and you have to wash him well in those places he can't reach. It's your job Gram!" Anna sounded more confident than she was feeling. Thelma made no argument, happily taking the wash rag. She started singing *rub-a-dub-dub* while she washed George. Anna quickly walked away.

Anna was feeling a little panicky as bedtime approached and wanted a plan because the night before she had not slept well at all. She decided to have Thelma come wake her if George fell or needed to use the bathroom. George was not stable enough yet to maneuver on his own and Anna did not want a fall on her watch. Thelma, thankfully, agreed to the plan.

Anna slept fitfully all night, suffering from vivid nightmares of George succumbing to another stroke and falling while Anna was there by herself. She awoke to brilliant sunlight streaming through the white shades and listened for any movement in the other room, relieved she had only been dreaming. She heard only silence, so laid quietly nestled in a mound of blankets before facing another day with her grandparents. She eventually dragged herself out of bed hoping to have a few minutes to herself. Upon entering George and Thelma's bedroom, she saw the bed was empty and caught sight of George in the bathroom. He was in the bathroom shaving.

"Gramp, what are you doing? I told you not to get up without my help. Where's Gram?" Anna was clearly shaken. She thought her plan was foolproof but now realized a Plan B was in order. "Let me help you, Gramp." She grabbed the special belt apparatus which allowed her to hold him up from behind preventing a fall. George just smiled.

"Grandma, why didn't you come wake me up like we discussed last night? I was supposed to come help Gramp out of bed so he doesn't fall." Anna tried to remain calm but was frustrated at her lack of control.

"Oh Anna, he said he could do it and I watched him. He is working really hard, you know." Thelma was completely oblivious to Anna's concerns.

"OK, but we're trying a new plan tomorrow because if Gramp falls, he's going back to rehab or to a nursing home. Is that what you want?" She was desperately trying to put the fear of God into them. "I found some walkie talkies and we're going to practice using them so tomorrow morning when you need to get up, you call me and I'll come right over."

"Sounds like a plan, Anna," George replied, quite relaxed about the situation. After a few minutes of squawking noise and channel surfing they found a common channel. For the next hour they practiced the art of pushing, talking and listening.

Later that afternoon George's friend Hugh came over to help spray the orchard for George. It was a task not suited for the faint of heart or the environmentally conscious. Hugh loaded the 50-gallon tank precariously secured to the back of the Ford Ranger with a mixture of pond water and Malathion. George had the truck rigged so the driver steered with the right hand while the left hand guided a sprayer out the driver's side window. One had to make sure the wind was blowing in the correct direction or risk being showered with a toxic mix of chemicals. An issue George never concerned himself with.

Hugh had been a friend for years ever since they met in the neighborhood of Laurel Hill. Both men had attended Cornell following the war, both had worked at UVM, although Hugh had moved on to other endeavors. Both men also shared a love of the Lake Mansfield Trout Club. Hugh had an extremely high opinion of himself, but was a good friend and sincerely cared about George.

Following the successful spraying of the orchard, Hugh was invited to stay for drinks and dinner. Anna, of course, was charged with kitchen duty, an assignment she relished because she loved cooking and it afforded her a few minutes of peace and control. Anna decided to pull together chicken breasts stuffed with a combination of feta cheese, spinach and garlic, rice and sauteed green beans fresh from Hugh's garden. Just as Anna was rinsing the beans under the tap, Hugh strolled into the kitchen looking to refill his Manhattan. Before Anna had the chance to say anything, she felt his hand on her ass.

"You can be my nurse anytime," Hugh whispered next to Anna's ear, sending shivers of disgust down her spine. She did not know what to do; she couldn't tell her grandparents and she was there alone. She moved away from him and decided to walk into the living room on the pretext of checking on George and Thelma. Hugh followed and sat across from George where they started bantering. Anna returned to the kitchen completely unnerved. She did her best to steer clear of him for the remainder of the evening by rearranging the kitchen and taking a walk. Hugh finally made his departure following dinner, sensing George was losing steam. She was not sad to see him leave.

"OK Gram and Gramp, here is the plan for tonight: if you need to get up, Gramp, you have to tell Gram and she'll call me on the walkie talkie. I will come immediately. Let's try this one more time." Anna handed a walkie talkie to Thelma. Thelma held it upside down looking confused for a moment but then Anna calmly showed her the talk button and demonstrated how to call, again. After a few tries Thelma seemed to have the knack of it. "Now just leave this next to your bed, Gram, and only push the talk button if you need me. Don't turn any other knobs, OK?"

"OK, I think I have it Anna," Thelma said. They hugged goodnight but Anna stayed up and watched a movie while sprawled on the couch trying to relax and savor the quiet. When she finally retreated to her room on the other side of the living room, she was dogged with nightmares once again. Morning arrived without a call from the walkie talkie, causing Anna to proceed across the living room with trepidation. Knocking softly, she entered her grandparents' bedroom only to find both of them in the bathroom.

"What happened to our plan?" Anna asked, clearly frustrated by the lack of compliance. "I thought you were supposed to call me as soon as Gramp needed to get up. Now he's in the bathroom teetering and could very easily fall and then we would have a big problem!"

"Oh, I tried, Anna, but the walkie talkie wasn't working and I didn't want to wake you up. George said he could do it and I walked right behind him so he wouldn't fall." Anna checked the walkie talkies only to find them set to the incorrect channel and turned off. She needed a Plan C.

The day was packed with appointments around town with Anna as driver and tour guide. Anna prodded her grandparents through their morning routines, but even with prodding and encouragement, it took them two hours before they were ready to buckle up. By the time they finished with George's doctor appointment, it was already lunchtime. Anna had a craving for Al's French Fries, a greasy hamburger institution in South Burlington. They waited in a line zig zagging past the cashier who immediately recognized George from his days of eating Al's after his lunchtime handball games. The cashier asked if he wanted his "usual." Anna questioned her grandfather as to just how often he had frequented Al's. Anna kept a close eye on her grandfather, ready to catch him if necessary. They all enjoyed their hamburgers and a pint of fries cooked to greasy perfection. The malt vinegar was the crowning touch.

Their next stop was the grocery store to stock up on Pepsi, Cabot Seriously Sharp Cheddar, bananas, whole milk and whiskey. George insisted on coming in the store with Thelma and Anna. He carefully shuffled along using his cane but not picking up his left foot as he had been repeatedly instructed to do. He appeared quite unsteady after the long day. Anna stayed close to George's side, leaving Thelma master of the shopping cart. Thelma was nervous George might fall and desperately wanted to walk beside him. Anna convinced her pushing the cart was her job. They neared the liquor aisle with a wine display at the far end. Bottles of an inexpensive merlot were stacked perilously in pyramid style. George, unsteady on his feet, took the corner too sharp, grazing a lower bottle of wine. And just like a set of dominoes, the entire display came crashing down. George just smiled. Anna reacted quickly grabbing the back of his belt to prevent a fall. Feeling frazzled and overwhelmed, Anna ushered her grandparents out of the grocery store as soon as they had paid and drove directly back to Monkton.

After the fiasco at the grocery store Anna wanted to use every precaution to get George back inside without incident. There was a new handrail on the front porch specifically built for George to help him ascend the three steps. It was much easier than navigating through the garage with numerous hazards.

"Gram, can you go into the house and unlock the front door so it will be open when I get Gramp there?" Anna asked, thinking it was a simple request.

"Sure, I can do that." Thelma made her way through the cluttered garage and into the kitchen. George was becoming more and more unsteady after the busy day. He was barely shuffling his left foot. Anna's right hand clenched the back of his belt in anticipation of a fall, a scene she did not want played out. They slowly maneuvered up the three front steps with George slowly moving one foot at a time.

"We're almost there, Gramp, and then you can relax in the recliner. I'll even put Fox News on for you!" encouraged Anna, looking to see if the front door was unlocked yet. They inched closer and could clearly see both doors still closed. Anna opened the storm door with one hand while holding George up with the other. She tried the front door but it was locked and there was no sign of Thelma. Anna knew at least ten minutes had passed since disembarking the Explorer. Anna knocked but no response. She could not ask George to walk back to the garage and she did not know how long he could stand there. Anna spotted a couple of porch chairs tied to the railing to prevent the gusty winds from blowing them away. After easing George carefully into a chair, she set off to find Thelma.

"Gram? Gram?" no answer as Anna entered through the kitchen. "GRAM? Where are you? Are you in here?" Anna yelled louder as panic began to set in.

"I'm in here," came a muffled voice from the bathroom in the master bedroom.

"Gram, you didn't unlock the front door like I asked you to. We've been waiting outside for ten minutes," blurted Anna in frustration.

"Oh, I guess I forgot," Thelma responded, completely unaware of her assigned task. Anna moved to the front door to relocate George to his recliner.

"Hey Anna, before I sit down, I need to use the bathroom." It was going to be a long month.

"OK you two, tonight we need to try Plan C because you're not following directions well," announced Anna holding two bright orange survival whistles in her hand. "Tonight Gram, you're going to put this next to your bed on the nightstand and when Gramp needs to get up, you *have* to blow into it hard. I'll hear it and I'll come right over because we do not want Gramp to fall. I have one for you too, Gramp, but it might be hard for you to reach with your left hand."

"Oh, this could be fun, Anna," Thelma remarked as she placed the wrong end of the whistle in her mouth. Anna calmly rotated the whistle without saying a word. Thelma practiced blowing enough air into the whistle until she finally produced the ear piercing beckon Anna was hoping for. If this did not work, she was at a loss for what to try next. In the morning Anna was jerked awake from a dream by a shrill whistle that pierced the morning peace. She realized Plan C was working.

Meanwhile, George and Thelma's four adult children agonized over the fact none of them lived in Vermont, and their parents were quickly developing the need for greater and greater assistance. Anna would only be there for one month and the assisted living facility had no openings for another 2-3 months. They needed a plan, and fast.

Even if they could find a local person to come into the house once a day, it would not be enough for George and Thelma. They required almost 24-hour care at this point. Back in Maine, Sue scrambled to look at a few assisted living facilities in her area but needed to find one with immediate availability. As luck would have it, her friend Lisa was an Activity Director at Sun River Villas, a beautiful new two-story assisted living facility housing both independent and assisted care apartments. There was a small one-bedroom, very small, available in one week, but the price was steep. After numerous conference calls with her siblings, they all agreed it was the best move for the moment. Now to inform George and Thelma they would be moving to Maine, a plan they would not like, but better than their current plan. Their current plan was non-existent.

Chapter 3 The Kidnapping

I'm going to put the cat out.
I didn't know it was on fire.

"Hey Mom, this is Sue," Thelma listened as she placed the receiver near her ear. "What do you think about moving to Maine? We found a nice apartment with lots of help for Dad, meals will be cooked for you every day and you would be near me. Norm and I will only be a twenty-minute-drive away, rather than a five-hour drive. What do you think?"

"Oh honey, I don't know. I need to discuss this with your father," Thelma replied as if it were not an urgent matter.

"Mom, I've spoken with Karen, Stu and Ken and we all think this is the best move for you and Dad right now, at least until Dad gets back on his feet. You guys cannot stay alone in Monkton." Sue continued. "Anna is only going to be with you a few more weeks and then she has to go back to Florida. You guys did not have a plan in place and now we have to make a plan for you." Sue thought again about how many times they had asked George and Thelma to make a plan in the event of a crisis.

"I don't know Sue." Thelma replied calmly. " I don't know why you kids all think we can't take care of ourselves."

"Mom, you know Dad needs a lot of help right now and it's too much for you to lift him. This way someone will cook your meals, clean your apartment and help Dad with anything he needs. They'll also help you with your pills every day."

"I don't need help with my pills," Thelma snapped.

"That's not what Anna tells me," said Sue immediately regretting the words. Thelma started weeping as the enormity of the situation swept over her. "I know this isn't what you want Mom, but it's the best plan we can come up with right now and it's not forever. Do you remember my friend Lisa? Well, she works at a place called Sun River Villas, and we can get you in there. She'd be there every day to keep a close eye on you, and I'll be close by." Sue was calm but firm. "What if Dad falls? What are you going to do, who is there to help you? How are you going to get Dad to the doctor's office by yourself?" Sue felt a crack in mother's defenses, so she asked to speak to her father. After a long conversation with George (long for George was all of two minutes), he grudgingly agreed Maine might be the best option for now. Sue quickly put plans in place to move them out the following weekend with the help of her husband Norm, son Charlie, Anna, brother in-law Ray and with the blessing of all her siblings.

The mission began on a Friday night following a long week at work with the five-hour drive to Vermont. Piled in the Silverado were Norm, Sue, Ray and Charlie. Charlie was Sue's youngest son and a sophomore in high school. He adored his grandmother and idolized his grandfather. He had spent innumerable hours on his grandfather's orchard burning brush piles, learning how to drive a pickup truck even before his feet could touch the pedals, shooting targets with his Gramp's guns when the gun weighed as much as he did, and driving the go cart with his brother and cousins until the tires were worn bare. Thelma had spoiled Charlie rotten whenever they came to visit by introducing him to lamb chops and filet mignon. His parents informed him on more than one occasion that lamb chops were not in their budget.

The thought of the two days ahead was overwhelming. Everything George and Thelma would need in Maine had to be packed up, including furniture, clothes, medicine and personal items.

Halfway through the drive to Vermont, Sue's phone rang. "Hello."

"Hi Aunt Sue, this is Anna. Are you guys on your way?" she asked with a hint of desperation.

"Yeah, we're about an hour and a half away. Is everything ok?" Sue asked, feeling a knot forming in her stomach.

"Well, Gram's been crying for an hour and I don't know what to do."

"Why is she crying?" Sue asked.

"She says it's all too much and we don't understand what they're going through. She doesn't want to go to Maine, she says they're being forced against their will and Gramp just wants to stay in Monkton." Anna sounded exhausted.

"Will she get on the phone with me?" Sue wondered.

"No, she doesn't want to talk with anyone right now."

"OK, hang in there Anna. We'll be there soon and then you'll have reinforcements. You do know you're going to Heaven for everything you've done this past week?" Sue half joked. As they passed through Hinesburg, the last little bit of civilization before reaching Monkton, Norm pulled into the local IGA for a few supplies. Once they reached the house it was tough to run out to the store again. They all ran in and grabbed necessities: beer, wine, chocolate and Vitamin water for Charlie. Arriving at the house they filed into the kitchen one at a time and made their way down the long galley kitchen with outdated pink wallpaper. As they rounded the corner to the living room, they saw George reclining in his blue chair with a cigar hanging from his mouth and Fox News blaring. Thelma was napping on the couch and Anna was on her phone. Anna broke into a smile when she saw the calvary.

"Oh my God, I'm glad to see you guys!" Anna cried out, disconnecting from her phone. They all hugged and introduced Ray to George, Thelma and Anna. George did not get up from his recliner but he was clearly happy to see everybody and hugged them with his right arm. Thelma started drink orders and inquired if anyone was hungry. The verdict was drinks only, for now. Ray declined a drink.

"So how are you feeling Dad?" asked Norm observing the changes in George. The last time Norm had seen his father-in-law was before the stroke.

"It's coming along slowly, I can get around with my cane now but I don't think I'll be taking Thel dancing this weekend," he joked. "My left arm needs some work but I'll be playing handball again soon and beating you turkeys at croquet." Norm noticed George physically moving his left arm with his right hand and wondered if would ever have use of his left arm or hand again. Sue sat next to Thelma and talked about everything except the elephant in the room, moving to Maine.

"We have a big day tomorrow because we have to decide what you'll need in Maine, organize it, pack it and then load up on Sunday, drive back to Maine and move you into your new apartment on Monday." Sue braced for the inevitable resistance.

"Well I don't know if this is what we want Sue," Thelma said calmly. "We're doing fine here and your father does not want to leave Monkton. I just don't see how we can make him move."

"Mom, we've been over this and you and Dad cannot stay here alone. Anna will only be up here a few more weeks and then you'll be completely on your own. I'm a five-hour drive away so if something happens, I can't just pop over." Sue reiterated this for the hundredth time.

"Your father and I feel as if you're taking us away without our permission. This is really hard on us Sue, you just don't understand." Thelma started to weep.

"Mom, I know this is hard. This is hard for us too! I know this is not ideal and not what you would have chosen in a perfect world, but what other choice is there? You cannot stay here alone right now, Champlain Waters has a waiting list, you tried Florida last year and you both hated it. What other options are there?" Sue was getting frustrated and knew this conversation was going to be on repeat this weekend.

In the morning Sue awoke to a symphony of chirping birds and wind whistling down the valley straight through the open window. She silently crept through the living room, stepping over the bodies of Ray and Charlie who were camped out on the floor and the couch. The coffee maker had a built-in grinder capable of producing industrial-level decibels. She struggled, briefly, with whether or not to run the grinder and risk waking the others. Coffee won and with the coffee brewed, she sat down to compile a "to do" list for the day. Slowly, everyone made their appearance and declared their plan for the day, with the exception of George and Thelma. They would require special supervision.

Ray was in his glory when assigned the task of mowing the fields with George's tractor. This chore would keep him busy most of the day and away from developing family drama. Ray was Norm's older brother, and had a myriad of mental health issues that prevented him from maintaining lasting relationships with family and friends. He was the life of the party with his guitar and beautiful voice, but as soon as alcohol was involved, things turned dark. Typically, after a day with Ray, everyone was ready to part ways. He had promised to be on his best behavior this weekend.

Charlie began moving and tagging furniture under the watchful eye of his grandmother. He appeared to have things under control and was very gentle with his grandmother when he disagreed with her opinion. He had his grandmother wrapped around his little finger. Knitting had been a passion of Thelma's and one Christmas she had knit a sweater with a polar bear for Charlie, his favorite animal. He possessed a passion for living and always had ideas and solutions. If there was a job to be tackled, Charlie was your man. While Norm drove into town to rent a U-Haul, Sue and Anna began organizing clothing for the deployment to Maine. George remained parked in his chair.

"Hey Mom, come help me with your underwear drawer. I don't know what you want to take with you because you have a lot here," Sue called to her mother.

"I'll be right there," she replied. "I'm looking through some old cards deciding which ones to keep." Thelma had kept every greeting card, Christmas card, obnoxious holiday letter and photo sent to her over the last ten years. This included the envelope.

Sue opened the second drawer to sort through more underwear, throwing old granny panties in one pile, slips and bras in another when she pulled out a black lacy one piece camisole adorned with garters and strategically placed lace. Sue held it carefully from the delicate straps so Thelma and Anna had a proper view of the garment.

"Oh MY GOD Gram, what is that?" asked a horrified Anna.

Thelma laughed, "Oh, your grandfather always bought me new things whenever we went away. He loved shopping at Frederick's of Hollywood. He liked me to dress up in sexy outfits." She was grinning from ear to ear.

"TMI, TMI Gram!" screeched Anna.

They pushed forward and only found a few more risqué pieces of lingerie, which were quickly placed in the "leave in Vermont " pile, figuring there wouldn't be a need for them in the assisted living facility. In the last drawer, Anna and Sue pulled out a pile of old photographs and were scanning them when they both stopped simultaneously on one particular photo. Thelma was sitting in a hot tub next to another man, clearly not George, and both appeared to be naked. Thelma's hairdo reflected a 1970's vibe and was grinning at her tub mate.

"What is this, Mom? What is happening?" Sue asked. " Who is this guy and where exactly was Dad?"

"Let me see. Oooooooh, I remember now." With a twinkle in her eye she said, "This was a party up at John Taggart's house when we went fiddle heading. It was a good party."

"Fiddle heading? Why are you naked?" asked Anna.

"Why do you think?" Thelma matter of factly replied. Sue decided she honestly did not want to know any more about the photo, the party or her parent's sexual exploits. She glanced at Anna, who was desperately trying not to laugh. Her parents were known for their parties in the 70s and 80s. On several occasions, Ken and Sue had arrived home during their teen years mid party to find couples making out on the stairs who were not married to each other.

Next they moved over to George's bureau, working from the bottom up sorting through countless t-shirts, a drawer full of shorts, one full of socks and finally a drawer full of tighty whities and white t-shirts. Anna and Sue were just about finished emptying the underwear drawer when they pulled out a bottle of Viagra tucked away in the corner.

"Oh my God Aunt Sue, old people aren't supposed to act like this!" Anna stood there with her mouth open and the beginnings of a smile.

"God only knows what else we're going to find," Sue commented, holding the bottle of little blue pills wondering what to do with them. She knew George wouldn't need them any time soon and dropped the bottle into the bathroom waste basket. It was hard to unsee but at least it would make a good story.

Later in the day everyone was scurrying around the house trying to make a plan for loading the U-Haul. George was safely in his recliner and Thelma was perseverating over her pills in the kitchen. Sue and Norm were in the bedroom, eyeing the contents and trying to decide which pieces were appropriate for the move. Space was limited. Sue spotted the shotgun in the corner of the room and moved close to Norm so George would not overhear.

"Norm, we have to take Dad's guns and keep them at our house, because they can't stay here. I'm pretty sure they're not allowed at the assisted living facility and Dad keeps talking about having Mom shoot him," Sue said. "I really think this is a safety issue." Sue was feeling the switch from being a daughter to now being a parent to her parents. "Will you please gather up all his guns and take them back to our house? We won't say anything to him because it will definitely upset him."

Norm frowned, "I'll only do it if you check with Karen, Stu and Ken and you're all in agreement."

"Fine, I'll call them all right now. He can have them back when things settle down but he can't even hold the gun right now. And with all his joking about having Mom shoot him, we can't leave guns in an empty house." The siblings all readily agreed this was the best plan for now.

The next morning several pots of coffee were brewed and consumed before the loading commenced. George was politely thrown out of his recliner while Norm, Ray and Charlie loaded up. Thelma wandered around making comments on every piece of furniture being loaded. George and Thelma looked lost. Sue quietly observed them talking softly to each other with heart-wrenching sadness. It was tearing Sue up to see her parents uprooted so abruptly, but what other choice was there? Last-minute checks were made by Anna and Sue.

"Mom, what are you doing?" Sue asked.

"I'm just going through some of my clothes." Sue watched as Thelma unloaded a suitcase.

"Mom, those clothes were all packed and ready to go. Why are you unloading them? We went through all your clothes yesterday and you agreed to everything we packed." Sue tried to hide her frustration.

"We did? Well I thought I would look through them. I don't know what I'll need."

Sue stepped closer, "here Mom, let me help you reload the suitcase and then I need you to come have some breakfast and load up your pills. We're leaving for Maine this morning."

"I am really upset about this Sue. Your father and I were talking last night in bed and we do not want to go to Maine. We're just fine here," repeated Thelma.

"Mom, we've been over this. You cannot stay here. It's not safe and there isn't any family around to help you. Also, it's not forever, it's just until Dad gets back on his feet and has use of his hand again." Sue felt like she was stuck in the movie *Groundhog Day*. "You know, it might only be for a few months and there will be lots of help for you guys at Sun River Villas. Dad needs help right now."

Thelma would not let it go. "We have friends who can help us."

"Mom, your friends are all in their 80s and they probably need help too!" Sue said, noting the conversation was not headed anywhere constructive.

After several double checks, the three vehicles were ready to start the journey to Maine. Norm and Charlie would be driving the U-Haul, Anna had the pleasure of driving the Explorer with George and Thelma, while Sue drove the Silverado with Ray as co-pilot. Everyone was buckled in, when George decided he needed to use the bathroom. Norm was in the running for son-in-law of the year as he escorted George to the bathroom. Twenty minutes later the caravan pulled down the dirt drive heading east.

Chapter 4 Sun River Villas
I'd rather owe it to you than cheat you out of it.

The five-hour drive took closer to eight hours once they counted bathroom breaks, refueling and lunch. The one thing everyone learned was nothing happened quickly. Even the simplest task now took twice as long. Ordering lunch at Panera, for example. In the past, everyone would read the extensive menu board behind the counter, place their order and eat. These days George really didn't feel like reading the menu, which required someone to read it aloud, item by item. Thelma looked lost, not able to follow the menu and had not listened to the first reading of the menu—which required someone to read the menu again. Choosing a table took a few minutes because it needed to be large enough for the group, and George needed to be able to maneuver into a chair. Once seated, George needed help to unwrap his sandwich, open the bag of chips and untwist his bottle of Pepsi. And then there was the requisite trip to the restroom. Anna bought George a jelly donut to enjoy later during the drive. As they were cruising down Interstate 89 through New Hampshire, George struggled to free the donut from its brown paper, loosening a cloud of powdered sugar all over the front seat. He carefully took a large mouthful of jelly donut using his right hand when a gush of artificially red goo squirted out, fell on his lap, the seat belt and the upholstery. He began wiping it up with a confiscated napkin from Panera but only achieved in making a bigger mess. It was smeared all over the front of the Explorer.

The apartment at Sun River Villas was not available for move-in until the following morning. The caravan pulled into Sue and Norm's driveway just as the sun was setting low in the pale sky. An afternoon sea breeze had kicked in, dropping the temperature at least fifteen degrees. Rocky, Sue and Norm's black terrier mix, welcomed them with frantic barking and a few howls for good measure. Thelma was scared of the dog and refused to get out of the Explorer until Rocky had been contained. Luckily, Anna and Sue had the foresight to pack a small overnight bag for George and Thelma, eliminating the need to rummage through the larger suitcases.

Everyone settled into the house where football quickly appeared on the TV, wine was uncorked for Anna and Sue, while whiskey was poured for Norm, Thelma and George. Charlie was sent into town to pick up pizza for dinner as there was no delivery out where Sue and Norm lived. Sue and Norm gave up their bedroom on the first floor for George and Thelma. The staircase up would be too much for George's current handicap. Sue and Norm happily crashed on the sofas and Anna was assigned Henry's room upstairs.

The morning arrived bringing ominous gray clouds and suffocating humidity. They braced themselves for one more emotionally and physically draining day. George and Thelma arose with little enthusiasm and a lot of attitude about the current situation they found themselves in.

"Good morning, Mom," greeted Sue. "Did you sleep ok?"

"I don't know why you brought us here, we want to be home in Monkton. Your father did not sleep well last night and we talked about things. We want to go home. You just don't understand what we're going through."

Sue bit her tongue, knowing that rehashing the conversation would get them nowhere but frustrated. She explained the plans for the day to her parents, who received them with little excitement. Once everyone was showered, dressed and fed, they loaded up for the last leg of the journey.

"Will you be leaving the Explorer at the apartment?" George wondered.

"Yes, but we thought Anna could use it while she's here to get back and forth between Sun River and our house," Sue said.

"Isn't Anna staying at the apartment with us?" Thelma asked. Anna's mouth dropped open but no sound emerged.

"We thought Anna would stay with us Mom. She doesn't get to see Charlie and Henry very often and your apartment is only one bedroom. Anna will have the Explorer and come visit you everyday." Anna mouthed an emphatic *THANK YOU* behind Thelma's back. "Charlie still has a few weeks of school left, Norm and I both have work, but Anna will be around for a few more weeks to help out and make sure you guys are behaving. She'll come back here and spend evenings with us. Also, Henry will be coming home from college next week." Henry was Sue and Norm's oldest son.

The parade of vehicles arrived at Sun River, a new two-story white building consisting of two wings and a pond out back. It was situated on a relatively busy road but close to shopping, the hospital and only a twenty-minute drive to Sue's house. All the apartments opened onto wide hallways with common areas throughout the facility. It emanated a homey feel, with plush leather and solid wood furniture. It did not feel like an assisted living space, and certainly did not smell like a nursing home. Sun River was created to allow independent and assisted residents to live together; there were no separate units for those requiring more assistance. Couples who were dealing with one spouse in the throes of Alzheimer's could still live together.

With four capable adults, the move was quick. George and Thelma were parked on a comfortable sofa outside their apartment where they supervised the activity.

"Looks like a lot of folks here are using walkers and canes," George commented. "We won't be here long because we're heading back to Vermont soon." It was clear George had no self-awareness.

Within a couple hours the apartment was set up, with familiar photos hung and the bed made up with a new comforter and pillows. Unfortunately, it was a very small space and only a fraction of the items lugged from Vermont were going to fit. Their couch was not going to fit in the living room, so the decision was made to place two recliners side by side facing the television. The remaining furniture quickly went to storage in the basement of Sun River.

The group ventured downstairs to the dining room at 5 o'clock sharp for dinner. They entered the large room encased by windows overlooking the pond, searching for an available table. Most tables were already filled with gray-haired ladies and the occasional gentleman who all watchfully checked out the newcomers as if they were fresh meat. It was always a big event when new blood arrived. It threatened to upset the social dynamics of who sits with whom. Sue and Norm spotted an empty table and laid claim to it wanting to keep the first meal with just family. George and Thelma could deal with the social dilemma tomorrow. Dinner was served by a cute high school girl who took George's flirting with good nature. Dinner passed approval by George and Thelma, and they felt a sense of relief after all the complaining. Back up in the apartment, they sat around and enjoyed an evening cocktail before everyone left for the night. George regarded the apartment as if looking for something.

"Hey, have you seen my guns?" he asked.

"Dad, you're not allowed to have guns at Sun River," Sue answered, quickly shooting a glance at Norm.

"When we left Monkton, my guns were not in my room where I left them. Where are they?" George persisted, very out of character.

"Dad," Sue replied. "I asked Norm to store them at our house in his gun cabinet for safe keeping."

"I want my guns," George said. "I did not not give them to you."

"We didn't want to leave the guns at an empty house in Monkton and you cannot have guns here at SunRiver, it's not allowed." Sue started gathering her things, knowing it was time to go home. "Dad, you can have your guns back at any time. We're just keeping them in a safe place."

They left Sun River after a strained goodbye, feeling George's uncharacteristic angst with them over the guns. Upon arriving home, they settled in for a debriefing before heading to bed. It had been a long stressful day, and tomorrow was the beginning of a work week for Sue and Norm.

Lisa, the Activity Director and a good friend of Sue's, welcomed George and Thelma first thing in the morning. Lisa had been in a car accident years earlier that had left her in a coma for several weeks. As a result, she found her empathy and passion suited her perfectly for working with the older crowd. She patiently gave George and Thelma a tour of the facility, pointing out the exercise room, the hairdresser, the Bingo room and the card tables where regular games of bridge were played. Both George and Thelma only showed mild interest in joining a game later that day. Thelma signed up for an exercise class with Lisa, but had no luck talking George into participating. Time would ultimately reveal he had basically given up, but would never admit it.

Just before lunch Thelma and George decided to head down to the dining room on their own. There was an elegant menu board placed by the entrance indicating entree choices, vegetable and starch options as well as desserts including the sugar-free variety of chocolate cake. They walked and shuffled into the dining room, scanning to see where they might like to sit. They spotted a table with two elderly ladies closely watching them as they approached.

"Hello ladies, can we join you for lunch?" George pleasantly asked with a grin.

"This table is full, our friends are not here yet," snipped the woman, whose mouth appeared to be sucking a lemon.

"Come on George, we don't need them." Thelma pulled his arm. A few tables over, two women and a small bald-headed man waved their arms in an effort to attract George and Thelma's attention. The two made their way across the dining room dodging parked scooters, walkers and the occasional cane positioned perfectly as a tripping hazard. All eyes watched and a few residents were heard whispering, *they must be new.*

"Would you like to sit with us for lunch? You started with the wrong table, they're a bunch of bitches over there," the bald man stated. "You must be new residents here?"

The experience was reminiscent of being back in high school, where cliques ruled the day and where one sat for lunch had everything to do with social status. They had an informative lunch receiving the ins and outs of life at Sun River.

Alice, a wheelchair-bound resident, who was loud, funny and entertaining, offered the most critical advice. "You must arrive early in order to secure your table of choice and save seats for your friends. Also, another bit of advice is to avoid Peter. He's that nasty man over there with the big belly and ugly brown cardigan sweater. He's a creep and a predator." Alice continued with her slate of things to know about Sun River. "I hope you two understand Sun River is like a prison," Alice continued. "One must sign in and out of the facility and there is absolutely NO drinking in the dining room. Thankfully there is a counterculture of drinking in the conference room after hours." George and Thelma made note of this information.

As they were leaving the dining room, George was pulled aside by another resident who wanted to fill his ear. "You must never ever leave Alice alone in your apartment, or you're sure to be missing items of value. I am not joking." Thelma noticed a small frail woman sound asleep on the sofa right outside the dining room. "Just leave her be, that's Lillian and she's 104 and naps there every day."

George and Thelma slowly settled into their new routine; they were not happy about it and quite vocal. Thelma was confused and scared. The move had happened with such speed it left her feeling as though she had been kidnapped. "I don't know George, I don't think I can stay here much longer," she complained. " I am so mad at Sue."

"We'll be back in Vermont soon Thel, I just need to get my arm and leg working a little better and we're out of here," George reassured.

Thelma left the apartment and wandered downstairs to where Lisa ran activities. She spotted Lisa sitting alone in her office and entered tentatively. Lisa quickly welcomed her to take a seat. As Thelma situated herself in one of the two chairs, Lisa noticed her hands shaking.

"Hi Thelma, you're looking lovely today. How are things going?"

"I am so mad at my daughter Sue. I don't know how she could do this to us. She took us away from Vermont, our house and our friends without our permission. I am so mad at her. I hate her for this." Thelma was getting worked up and had never in her life spoken about her children like this.

"Oh Thelma, Sue has done everything out of love for you and George. She wants you to be safe." Lisa was getting worried about the direction of the conversation, and was in a tough spot as Sue was one of her close friends.

"She had NO RIGHT!" yelled Thelma.

Lisa listened like a pro and said what she could to alleviate Thelma's anxiety, painfully aware she was stuck in the middle of a family feud. Thelma eventually wandered back upstairs to her apartment.

Back in the apartment, Thelma's landline rang. "Oh Stu, it's so good to hear your voice. This place is awful. There are nurses who just come right into the apartment thinking they know what medicine I take. I really resent this. The food is horrible and last night the menu said we were having prime rib. What a joke, it tasted like shoe leather and we couldn't even cut it with a knife. Your father and I want to go back home. We have to get out of here." And then Thelma was weeping into the phone. Stu listened patiently, thinking his mother sounded rather lucid with her remarks against Sun River. George took the phone for a grand total of thirty seconds before returning to the TV. Similar phone calls occurred on a daily basis between Thelma and both Ken and Stu. The boys began to second-guess the decision to move them to Maine, because they were absolutely miserable and sounded in control of their situation. Reality was a different story.

Sue stopped by SunRiver one Saturday morning to take Thelma out shopping, hoping a change of scenery would help. Anna had been spending every day with George and Thelma and deserved a break. As they left the apartment, Thelma shakily tried to place the key in the lock by inserting the key every conceivable way but nothing worked. Sue watched with increasing concern as a simple task was not so simple any longer.

"Here let me help you Mom."

"I don't need your help, you've done enough," Thelma stormed. "Your father and I are very upset about being here and we want to go home." Her tone was nasty and it was an attitude Sue had never experienced from her mother. "Everyone just keeps telling us what to do. I know what to do!" Thelma had rarely, if ever, spoken a cross word to Sue her entire life, and had always been the June Cleaver type of mother. Thelma's advice to her kids when they were growing up was, *you should always be yourself because what a boring world it would be if everyone was the same.*

Sue let her mother struggle with the key, knowing nothing would help at this point. Later, upon returning from the shopping trip, Thelma stopped at the mailboxes in the lobby to retrieve her mail. This required Thelma to insert a small key to open their box. Same story, Groundhog Day, and Sue remained quiet because any efforts to help would be met with displeasure. Both mother and daughter were feeling sadness at the current situation and the crumbling relationship.

"I can't wait to get out of this place and back to my own house. The food here is awful. Last night they served us sirloin steak and I'll tell you what, it was no sirloin steak. It was as tough as rawhide," Thelma ranted. Sue, Norm, Henry, Anna and Charlie had stopped by on a Friday night to take them out to dinner at a local BBQ restaurant. Anna was heading back to Florida the following morning after spending a month tending to her grandparents. It was a summer she would not soon forget.

"Thel, just walk ahead of me," George instructed, concentrating on carrying his cane while moving down the hallway.

"I'm trying to protect you if you fall."

"I don't need your help Thel, just walk ahead," he repeated. As he took a step into the hallway he lost his footing and went down like a slow-motion ballet move. Norm quickly stepped in to help him up, physically unhurt but suffering bruised pride. George proceeded as if nothing had happened and he playfully poked Thelma in the rear end with his cane as she walked in front of him.

The group was sitting in a booth waiting on their meals with awkward conversation. George and Thelma were emitting a frosty vibe towards Sue and Norm even as Henry and Charlie joked with their grandparents. In the past, any meal out with this group was lively, loud and laughter-filled.

"Do you still have my guns?" inquired George, knowing full well where the guns were. "I want them back," he continued with the unfamiliar hostile attitude. Norm was immensely hurt because they had always had a good relationship.

"Dad, Norm didn't steal your guns," Sue explained. "I asked him to grab them when we left Vermont because we couldn't leave an empty house with guns, and you can't have them in the assisted living facility. It's the law." Dinner proceeded with conversations directed at the boys and Anna, in an attempt to stay away from talk of guns, Sun River and Monkton. They escorted George and Thelma back to their apartment so they could say their goodbyes to Anna before making a quick exit.

Life at Sun River continued for the next month in much the same manner. Thelma constantly complained about the food and that someone had messed up her pills, while George was making minimal progress. He still needed a cane to walk, had very limited use of his left hand and was focused on Norm stealing his guns.

Sue was at home when her phone rang. "Hey Sue, it's Stu. Elaine and I decided we are flying up to Maine in a couple weeks to move Mom and Dad back to Monkton." He waited but heard nothing. " Ken and I have talked and they are absolutely miserable.

It sounds to us like they're doing much better and they assured us they can handle living in Monkton on their own. I feel we owe them the chance to try." He paused again and waited for Sue's reaction.

"Stu, bad idea. I will not support the move back to Monkton, because they cannot take care of themselves. I know they've told you how wretched Sun River is and how poorly they're being treated, but they are in a safe place and I'm able to check on them because they're only twenty minutes away. Monkton is a five-hour drive for me. Who's going to watch them, drive them to the doctor, how are they going to get to the grocery store and what happens when the snow comes?" Sue sighed and continued. "Mom is in no mental condition to drive and Dad can barely walk, in fact he falls a lot. Even though his walking is improving, his left arm does not work. Who is going to cook, clean and shop?"

"They're really unhappy and we can set up a support system in Monkton. They call us every day telling us how badly they want to go home. Mom cries on the phone every time we speak so Elaine and I have decided to make it happen." Stu paused again for a reaction.

"Well, Norm and I will not help with the move because we cannot support it and it is not in their best interest right now. You aren't with them, you don't see what goes on and how confused they are." Sue was frustrated with the situation. "What happens when Dad falls or Mom wants to drive somewhere and how are they going to get to the doctor? You really need to spend some time with them to understand. I get it that Mom can fool you over the phone."

The call ended abruptly without the usual pleasantries. Stu and Elaine booked flights, reserved a moving truck complete with movers, and then delivered the happy news to George and Thelma. They were being sprung from the Sun River prison. Stu's point of reference was simply the daily phone calls begging for parole. Without ever seeing the facility or experiencing a day with George and Thelma, it was impossible to grasp the reality of the situation. Sue and Norm remained firm in their position of not supporting the move. Karen supported Sue's line of thinking and Ken was somewhere in the middle, not wanting to subject himself to more chaos in his life. The once-close siblings were beginning to feel a divide.

Moving day arrived, again. Stu and Elaine flew into Portland the night before the move. Sue and Norm picked them up and they all enjoyed a night out in the Old Port of Portland, adeptly avoiding any discussion of the elephant in the room. They all knew where the other stood. They had argued their points on the phone with heated exchanges, but were now making a mature effort to get along despite their disagreements.

Early Saturday morning Elaine and Stu supervised the rapid pack-and-load of George and Thelma's apartment by Anderson's Movers out of Burlington, Vermont. Sue and Norm remained true to their word and observed from the overstuffed leather chairs, refusing to lift a finger for the doomed move. George and Thelma sat with them in the common area, but the tension was thick between them. Within a few hours, everyone and everything was loaded and ready to go. They would be traveling in the Ford Explorer with Stu and Elaine back to Monkton. Pulling out of Sun River with Johnny Cash playing on the CD player, George and Thelma were happy–happy for the moment.

Chapter 5 The Return
This shirt's a little tight around my broad shoulders and loose around the middle.

George and Thelma were ecstatic heading home to Monkton, allowing Stu and Elaine to feel good about their decision. Why shouldn't their parents be allowed to live out their lives in a place of their own choosing? Stu drove with George as copilot, while Elaine and Thelma occupied the backseat. Thelma napped on and off for most of the trip with her head bobbing as the Explorer traveled Interstate 89 and winding New England country roads.

The movers arrived in Monkton just ahead of them and made quick work of unloading. Stu and Elaine were now faced with a mountain of work as George was predictably parked in his recliner. Unfortunately for George, the cable had yet to be reconnected so he decided to supervise. Thelma was wandering around the house transferring items from one spot to another. Elaine was frantically getting their bedroom set up so they could sleep in the old familiar bedroom. Stu was setting up the assorted handicapped equipment of raised toilet seat, bathtub seat and bed rails.

"Come on Dad, I'll help you get ready for bed," Stu suggested, but saw no movement on his father's part. "Dad, push yourself up and out of the chair so we can walk into the bedroom."

George slowly transported himself to the bedroom with Stu hovering right beside him holding tight to the back of his belt. The bedtime routine crawled along slowly as Stu assisted with the clothing change despite the occupational therapist insisting George do it himself. Upon removing his dirty underwear, George tossed them directly onto the bedroom floor.

"Jesus George," Thelma reprimanded. "You're going to trip on those. Put them in the hamper." But her words fell on deaf ears. Stu and Elaine fell into bed completely drained. George tossed and turned for about ten seconds, while Thelma laid awake for hours worrying about everything—and worries always expanded in the quiet of the night. She eventually dozed off for a fitful night's sleep. Hours later as the sun streaked across the floral wallpaper of their bedroom, she was aroused by movement in the bathroom. She quickly got out of bed to investigate.

"Shit George!" she gasped. "What happened? Let me help you."

"No Thel, I'm fine," he responded, sprawled on the bathroom floor unable to get himself up.

"I'm going to get Stu." She rushed off to the other bedroom and knocked softly on the door. "Your father fell and needs help. I tried but I can't lift him."

Stu and Elaine jumped out of bed, making quick eye contact with each other. It took Stu several minutes to get George upright and examined for any injuries. Stress filled the room as reality set in. The reality of their ability to live independently was now being questioned. Stu and Elaine would only be in Monkton for a few more days, and then what?

"These pills aren't right," Thelma grumbled. "Someone mixed them up and I am not taking them. I have never taken a yellow pill before." Thelma sat at the kitchen table playing with her pills. "Oh I hate that place in Maine, they were always giving me the wrong pills."

"Thelma," Elaine said. "I'm going to organize all your pills today so you'll be good for a couple weeks and all you have to do is open the pill box for the correct day." Elaine realized the meds were yet another issue to deal with.

"Stu, did you bring my guns back from Maine?" George randomly asked.

"No, Norm is holding on to them until you're able to load them yourself."

"I can load them now and I want them back. Norm stole my guns," George insisted. "I did not give him permission to take them."

"I'll talk with Norm about the guns, but he did not steal them, he's just keeping them safe. As soon as you can load, aim and shoot the gun with your left arm, you can have them back." George did not respond, leaving an awkward silence in the room.

Stu and Elaine found a few moments alone to talk and soon arrived at the same conclusion, living on their own in Monkton was not going to work. Even with support staff coming in a few hours a day, it would not be enough. They were at the point where they really required 24-hour care. Stu and Elaine were mature enough to admit their mistake and understand just how convincing George and Thelma had been on the phone. It had not taken long. They decided to spend the day taking a second look at the assisted living facilities in Burlington and getting a deposit down as soon as possible. Just as before, Champlain Waters turned out to be the most appealing, with an anticipated opening for a one-bedroom apartment within three weeks. They immediately added George and Thelma to the wait list, left a deposit and prayed. Later that day they returned with George and Thelma for a tour of the facility. They were less than impressed.

There was little choice at this point. Stu contacted his siblings and all were in agreement that staying alone in Monkton was not an option. Sue was already well aware. Champlain Waters looked to be the best solution. George had been repeatedly told to make a plan, a plan in the event of catastrophic illness or circumstance. Make a plan or someone else might have to make a plan for you and you might not like their plan. That day had arrived and George did not like the plan.

Champlain Waters confirmed an opening for the one-bedroom apartment for the second week of August, leaving George and Thelma to fend for themselves for about three weeks. Arrangements were hastily made to have a combination of friends and paid help come in daily to check on them. Ken and Karen were rearranging schedules to make room for trips to Vermont and Sue volunteered to move them into Champlain Waters when the time came. Somehow they managed to survive the three weeks without incident, thanks in large part to the steady stream of friends and family, but it was exhausting.

Yet another moving day arrived and they all hoped this was the last move. Sue made the trek over to Vermont and relished the solitude of the ride before facing a deluge of stress. Because she was a teacher, she had the summer off, allowing her the freedom to take time to help her parents. Norm had to work and her boys both had summer jobs, so this was a solo trip.

The last few months had been difficult with her mother complaining about the alleged kidnapping and giving her the cold shoulder. Her father would not let go of the gun issue, and Sue felt bad because Norm was taking the brunt of George's wrath, even though it was all her idea to take the guns. She had always had a close relationship with her parents so these past few months were distressing. Stu had assured her the movers would pack everything and the actual move would be a piece of cake. Sue walked into the house to find piles of papers, dishes and clothes scattered all over the house, nothing was packed, nothing was organized, and her parents were confused.

"OK Mom, we have to decide what you want to take to Champlain Waters and remember we can always come back for anything you forget because it's only a 30-minute drive. Whatever we pack, you are not allowed to remove it or think twice about it. We have a lot to do and no time. Plus, I'm here by myself so I really need your cooperation!"

In 1969, the family went on an adventure. George took a sabbatical to Australia for one year and Thelma had done all the packing for that trip. There were thirteen suitcases, four kids ranging in age from 4-13 and to make matters even crazier, Thelma had a broken wrist when they left. Thelma was a trooper and seemed to have a super power to get everything organized and everyone where they needed to be. The only snafu on that trip was when Ken got lost on Waikiki Beach. He was found unfazed, unharmed and sunburned.

Sue and her parents spent the day packing, organizing and deciding which pieces of furniture made the cut. Anderson's Movers arrived and instantly recognized George and Thelma from their recent move back from Maine. They quietly nodded understanding to Sue.

Upon entering the house they glanced around at the chaos. "There doesn't appear to be anything packed and ready to go."

"Don't worry about any of the little stuff," Sue said. "I'll get all that myself. Just move the big stuff and get the bed set up at Champlain Waters, and I'll be there to tell you where to place the other furniture." She rubbed her hands through her hair and audibly sighed.

The hired move was relatively fast, with four strong experienced young men and only large pieces of furniture to move. Sue, Thelma and George followed the movers with the Explorer full of linens and clothing for their new destination. Thankfully their new apartment was on the ground floor and had an outside entrance accessed from a paved walkway straight from the parking lot. No elevators or stairs required. The sun shone through the double windows, giving their new apartment a cheery lightness. The apartment had an open plan with a kitchen/living area, a short hallway leading to a bathroom and a large bedroom. The other entrance led to a long hallway resembling a hotel corridor. The only exception: The doors were decorated with wreaths and knick knacks depicting their resident's personality—or perhaps aiding the residents who had memory issues to identify their door. George decided to hang a large plastic insect from the door. He had been affectionately referred to as a bug doctor during his tenure as an entomologist at UVM.

Although most of their furniture was moved in, many of their personal items were not yet packed or organized, despite Stu's reassurances. They grabbed a bite to eat at an Italian chain restaurant, where George grumbled about not liking ethnic food but managed to finish an entire portion of spaghetti and meatballs, salad, breadsticks and a couple beers. They headed back to Monkton for the night.

With George and Thelma settled into the guest room as their bed was at Champlain Waters, Sue scrounged up some lounge cushions for a makeshift bed in the living room. Sunrise cued the group to arise and get moving. Sue brewed fresh coffee and performed an inspection of the refrigerator, knowing it would need a good cleaning out. She discovered eggs, cheese, mushrooms and tomatoes, perfect for breakfast. Thelma played with her pills while George drove up to the mailbox for the morning paper. Sue was uneasy about him driving but figured he was only traveling one tenth of a mile.

"OK Mom, can you carry these things out to the driveway and make a pile? I'll start loading everything if you can keep things coming." Sue desperately tried to find a task to keep her mother occupied while George walked around the property looking lost. It was going to be a hard day for him, for all of them.

"Mom, where is the pile of stuff we started?"

"I've been organizing things," Thelma responded. Sue went into the house only to discover Thelma unpacking things that were all ready to go.

"Mom, come here. I have an important job for you." Sue sat Thelma down in the sunroom with a pile of old photographs to sort through, hoping to keep her busy long enough to get the kitchen cleaned and the car packed. It was exhausting trying to get things accomplished, corralling Thelma and finding small jobs to keep her busy, while George continued to roam the orchard. It was like watching toddlers.

After several trips between Monkton and Champlain Waters, hours of work and an aching back, the apartment was coming together. George and Thelma were not impressed.

"Are we going back to Monkton?" George asked. "I have a few things I need there." Sue knew there really wasn't anything left to do in Monkton but her father really needed one last night in his precious orchard.

"Sure Dad, why don't we spend one more night in Monkton and then tomorrow night we'll sleep at Champlain Waters." Sue managed to settle them into the guest room one last time while she lay in the middle of the empty living room with the screen door open, allowing the sound of peepers to waft over her. Sleep did not come, hard as she tried. The longer she lay there, the more wild her thoughts were. Finally, sometime in the wee hours her body gave out and she slept, not a restful sleep.

George was quiet as they pulled out of Monkton one last time, and no one spoke during the thirty-minute drive to their new home. In the apartment, the day passed quickly. Getting the television hooked up to cable was of the utmost importance but it would take time. George would just have to survive one night without Fox News. There were countless phone calls to be made, addresses to be updated and the facility to explore.

"We can eat dinner here in the dining room," Thelma suggested, much to Sue's surprise.

"I was thinking it might be nice to get out of here for a change of scenery." Sue was not in the mood to eat with six other elderly residents and make small talk. "What do you guys feel like eating?"

"Not Olive Garden," George replied.

"How about Applebee's, you can both find something you like there."

"Well, we haven't eaten at the Rotisserie in a long time," Thelma suggested. Sue dreaded the dark and dated interior but knew they both loved it.

"That sounds great," George agreed and it was settled. They were seated in a booth at the front of the dark paneled room with small windows barely letting in enough light to read the menu. Drink orders were placed by Sue and George.

"Oh, I would like a very dry Manhattan with Crown Royal, a twist, up with a side of ice," recited Thelma. The waitress frantically scribbled the drink instructions while groans were heard from both George and Sue. The drinks arrived and immediately Thelma spotted a cherry in her cocktail.

"I just don't understand why they can't make my drink the way I ask," she sputtered. When the waitress returned to take their dinner order, Thelma explained the error of the bartender and expressed her desire for a new drink. They feasted on the typical Rotisserie meal of French onion soup and a hot roast beef sandwich. Thelma barely touched her sandwich but finished off her soup and her properly made cocktail. Thelma recounted the story of how the Rotisserie used to be a post office when they lived on Davis Parkway. In 1956 George and Thelma purchased their first home for $18,000. Thelma remembered pushing Karen in the stroller to mail letters to her mother in Ithaca, New York. It may have been the fifteenth or fiftieth time Sue had heard this story, but she patiently listened. She realized the hostility of the last few months was dissipating. They returned to Champlain Waters for their first night.

With only one bedroom, Sue crashed on the couch and fell into a deep sleep, completely exhausted. In the morning she finished up a few last details and phone calls before heading back to Maine. The apartment would be cleaned once a week including clean sheets, three meals a day were served in the dining room, there were countless activities and Sue had arranged Thelma's pills for two weeks. The Explorer was parked in a resident spot and George insisted he was able to drive despite having only one working arm. Life as they all knew it was changing, and Sue was thankful her boys had had the opportunity to spend time at the orchard.

Stu called a few days later to check in and received an earful. "It's okay, I guess. It sure isn't Monkton. Everyone here is gimpy and either using a walker, a cane or a wheelchair. They're all a bunch of old folks waiting for their maker," George complained. Stu silently wondered if George had looked in the mirror lately.

"You wouldn't believe it, Stu," Thelma started. "Breakfast is at 8:00 am sharp and people line up at 7:45 outside the dining room doors blocking the elevator, and you better watch your toes or they'll run right over you with their scooters. It's very dangerous." Thelma continued. "It really isn't a very good breakfast either, because they only put out a few stale muffins and pastries and a pitcher of juice."

"You know," Stu reminded them. "You guys complained about the food at Sun River and they cooked whatever you wanted for breakfast."

Chapter 6 Life at Champlain Waters

Did you see the movie The Broken Leg?
It has a large cast.

George and Thelma reluctantly settled into a routine at Champlain Waters. They tolerated the nuisances of assisted living, although technically they were considered independent. Despite what the four children thought, George and Thelma truly believed they would be moving back to Monkton in the near future.

With the past squabble behind them, the four kids spoke frequently over the phone piecing together their parents' wellbeing, as none of them were close by. They wisely decided to take turns visiting Vermont each month to check in. Sue volunteered to drive up first and the others would fly into Burlington for future weekends. They were foolishly hopeful George would make more progress with his recovery, but they all understood Thelma's mental condition was unlikely to improve. Since the night of the stroke it became obvious George had been covering for her lapses in mental acuity. Champlain Waters offered increasing levels of assistance simply by writing a hefty check each month. Currently they were receiving two meals a day in the dining room, house cleaning services once a week and upkeep of the apartment. This was the basic package. One of the best aspects of Champlain Waters were their friends who also resided there, offering constant social interactions. Something Monkton lacked.

Ken's turn arrived in early September, and he was shocked to see both parents awaiting his arrival at the base of the escalator at the Burlington airport. He thought the plan was for one of their friends to pick him up.

"How did you guys get here?" Ken wondered as he leaned in to hug both parents.

"I drove the Explorer, how do you think we got here?" answered George. Ken decided to let it go. Thelma could not stop touching Ken's arm as they walked through the airport to the parking lot.

"I'll drive now," Ken offered. "Do you guys want to grab a bite to eat before we head to Champlain Waters?" Ken jumped in the Explorer and then realized both parents needed assistance buckling their seat belts. He took a calming breath, unfastened his seat belt, and climbed out to help Thelma buckle up before shutting her door. Next he went around to the passenger side to get George scooted properly on the seat and buckled. George still could not lift his left arm without using his right hand to physically move it. Ken knew patience would have to be his mantra for the weekend.

"Were you guys buckled in when you drove over here?" They ignored him so he moved on. "OK, where do you two want to eat?"

"Ribeye Ranch!" suggested George.

"I am not eating there, it's filthy and you know they just shut down recently because there was a rat in the kitchen," Thelma informed them.

"I don't want any weird ethnic food. Let's go to the Rotisserie on Williston Road," George said. He had been raised eating meat and potatoes every night and it wasn't until he entered the army in WWII that he began expanding his palate. Army fare had not done much to open his mind about food. He had never even tried spaghetti and meatballs until the Army, and it was the one "ethnic" meal he requested often from Thelma. She was an amazing cook throughout their marriage, but catered to his fussy ways just as his mother had. He refused to eat pasta, except for spaghetti, rice or anything of a soupy nature.

"Oh yes, I love the Rotisserie," Thelma said as Ken rolled his eyes. "It's always so good there and they have the best French onion soup and we haven't been there in awhile." Ken hated the Rotisserie, in part because he was tired of eating there every visit to Vermont. They made it through dinner with two rounds of cocktails, French onion soup and roast beef sandwiches large enough to feed a family of four. It was a relief to walk out into the sunshine after being cooped up in the dark. Thelma recounted the story of how the Rotisserie used to be a post office. Ken listened patiently.

As they arrived back at Champlain Waters, Ken pulled up front under the covered entrance to deliver George and Thelma. It required him to get out, open both doors and physically unbuckle both parents. He then needed to steady his father while handing him his cane. George immediately took his cane and poked Thelma in the backside.

"Jesus George, I'll hit you if you do that again," Thelma growled. George just smiled and Ken ignored them.

"OK you two, I'm going to park the Explorer. Just wait for me inside and I'll be right back."

George and Thelma were greeted by several friends congregating in the lobby. By the time Ken arrived at the lobby and saw the group, he knew it would be ten minutes of his life he would never get back. They group yammered about nothing and would not remember the conversation five minutes later. Ken sat down waiting, remembering his mantra for the weekend. They eventually strolled down the corridor at an agonizingly slow pace.

Opening the apartment door, Ken was overtaken by the rank odor of rancid kitty litter and the bouncing energy of a little kitten. He was no bigger than a large fist covered with orange fur and green eyes. The kitten darted between Ken and Thelma, successfully escaping into the hallway.

"Ooh, ooh, ooh. Catch him Ken!" Thelma hollered. "He always tries to get away."

"What the hell was that?" Ken asked. He managed to retrieve the fur ball and cuddled him close to his chest.

"That's Ortiz," George answered. "The kitten your mother was given a couple weeks ago by another resident. I named him, good name, huh? Named after David Ortiz on the Red Sox. We named our other cat Oscar after Oscar Gamble of the Yankees, so this was only fair."

"Yeah, great name, but geez it stinks in here." Ken continued, "Do you guys ever change the kitty litter?" Ken inspected the litter box and Ortiz's empty food dishes. Ken wondered what the hell they were doing getting a pet when they couldn't even take care of themselves.

"Oh, he's so cute," Thelma said. "But he has too much energy for me. And he's always jumping on me and I'm afraid he'll scratch me. You know how easily I bleed."

Ken was busy filling the water bowl and food dish while Ortiz nudged his hands trying to get at the kibble. Ken turned his attention to the litter box, where mounds of cat excrement sat piled like the pyramids of Egypt. With Ortiz's immediate needs attended to and the apartment aired out, Ken sat down to relax and inspect the homestead. Ken watched the kitten spin around the room jumping from one piece of furniture to the next, stopping only for a quick caress before bounding off again. Thelma made surprised noises every time Ortiz jumped as if she were afraid of him. Ken knew how this was going to end.

Ken awoke early the next morning to tiny claws kneading his chest while sending sharp pains through his body. He grabbed Ortiz with one hand and pried him off his chest before placing him gently on the floor. Ken knew his priority for the day was to find a new home for Ortiz. The kitten was too much for them and certainly not being properly cared for.

"Morning Ken, you sleep ok?" asked George walking into the living room in his underwear, white briefs and a wrinkled white t-shirt and tousled silver hair.

"Just great aside from the couch being two feet too short and Ortiz using my body as a pin cushion," replied Ken. "Geez Dad, can you please put on some clothes."

George grinned and continued, "scrambled eggs would taste great for breakfast. The breakfasts here are lousy; all they have are platters of stale pastries and fruit. There should be eggs and Cabot cheese in the fridge."

George was hopeful Ken caught the not so subtle hint. Rummaging through the refrigerator Ken discovered at least a half dozen Styrofoam containers with questionable leftovers inside. He pitched everything and checked the past due dates on other items, adding to the garbage heap. He unearthed a dozen eggs, orange juice not past its prime, and a block of Cabot Seriously Sharp cheddar still in its original wrapper but not sealed well. The ends were dried out but Ken was able to salvage a large chunk.

"Hey Dad, you should wrap up the cheese better."

"I've told you kids, cheese stays fresher in its original wrapper. Your mother and sister are always trying to seal it up with plastic wrap." Ken busied himself preparing cheesy eggs and coffee while George shaved and Ortiz bounced off the walls. The breakfast aromas stirred Thelma who appeared in the kitchen wearing the same clothes she had worn the day before. Interesting, thought Ken.

"Oohh, it smells good in here. Oooo, oooo," she yelled and jumped as Ortiz darted past her. "I had to put him out of the bedroom last night because he was attacking me and now I'm covered with scratches and I'm bleeding."

"Yeah, thanks Mom. He attacked me instead! And about the kitten Mom, I think maybe we should try to find a new home for him because it's clearly too much for you guys." He was unsure what to expect for a reaction. Surprisingly, they both agreed on the wisdom of the idea, but wanted Ortiz to go to a good home. It would be the first item on Ken's to-do list. After numerous inquiries and phone calls, he found a home for Ortiz in the woman who came to help his parents a few days a week. She had fallen in love with Ortiz and promised him a loving home. Ken considered this a win-win. He continued chipping away at the list, and high on the list was a trip back out to Monkton to visit the orchard and check on the vacant house.

Ken drove the Explorer with no argument from either parent. Thelma sat in the back seat where she spilled the beans that George had been driving out to the house about once a week just to walk around. Ken wondered about the accuracy of the statement but tended to believe it. Both George and Thelma were quiet for the remainder of the ride. They made the turn down Church Road, past the small white church with green shutters sitting quietly among a cow pasture. Its paint was peeling and its ancient foundation was covered with ivy. Ken and Marie had been married at the church years earlier.

Just as the house and orchard came into view, George said, "I need to prune the trees soon and the lawn hasn't been mowed lately."

"I thought Ed was mowing the lawn once a week? And how do you think you're going to prune the trees with an arm that doesn't work?" Ken was hoping to get a reaction.

"Oh Ken, your father has been working really hard with the physical therapist, it's hard for him, you know. You just don't know what it's been like for us."

"I'm just saying it's going to be hard to take care of the orchard if you're unsteady on your feet and your left arm doesn't work." Ken knew he was going to have to broach the subject of selling the property, but was at a loss on how to begin. He decided to jump right in. "Have you two given any thought to selling the property?"

"Why would we do that?" asked George.

"Because it costs a lot to live at Champlain Waters and the longer the house stays empty, the more work it will require, and the less it's going to be worth." Ken waited for the response.

"I thought we were moving back here soon," Thelma remarked. George remained quiet and Ken knew this was the beginning of an ongoing discussion. His siblings would need to join forces. They spent the next hour wandering the property and inspecting all the belongings left behind. Ken watched the faraway look in his father's eyes with great sadness. Thelma walked from room to room touching everything, picking up items and placing them in new spots. Nothing was accomplished, aside from transporting George back to the only place he wanted to be. Neither parent grasped the fact that life in Monkton was over. The drive back to Champlain Waters was silent.

Over the next few months Ken spoke to his siblings regarding the sale of the orchard and the future of their parents. All four agreed selling the house was the right thing to do because none of them could afford to buy the house in order to keep it in the family. And none of them really wanted an apple orchard in Vermont, they all lived too far away. The key was getting George to agree; he loved Monkton. He often repeated his one wish; to die in Monkton out on his orchard.

"Hi Dad," Ken spoke slowly. "You said you needed the weekend to think about putting the house on the market. It's Monday night and spring is approaching, the best time to sell the house. I've spoken with the real estate agent and he wants to look at the house, talk with you guys and come up with a reasonable selling price. I'll fly up next weekend to walk you through the process and make sure this guy isn't taking advantage of you." Ken held his breath unsure what type of response he was about to receive.

"I spoke with your mother and we'll talk with the real estate agent but we have to agree with the price," countered George. He needed an out. "What do you think the property is worth?"

"I'm really not sure Dad, that's why we're hiring an agent who does this for a living."

After an exhaustive search, Ken located a real estate agent named Bradley Paulson who came with stellar recommendations from a friend in a similar situation. Bradley had a reputation for possessing an impressive amount of patience when dealing with elderly clients. Elderly clients were known for their wishy-washy decision-making abilities and their inability to deal with change. The selling of a family home can be quite emotional, and a catalyst for family drama. Bradley had a knack for calmly navigating these rough waters.

Ken, Thelma and George met Bradley at the orchard in Monkton on an overcast early spring day. The temperature had lost its bite from the previous month. The gray sky gave an aura of doom as Ken tried to ignore the feeling. Bradley was in his early forties with short neatly trimmed black hair, stylish glasses and a trim build. His best feature was his easy smile and calm demeanor, which immediately put the trio at ease. They sat on mismatched chairs in the middle of the empty living room in the middle of a mostly deserted house. Bradley spent over an hour chatting with the group trying to get a feel for the mindset and tolerance level for change. He now had a pretty good idea of what he was dealing with.

"George and Thelma," Bradley spoke slowly in anticipation of a reaction. "You have a beautiful property here. It's clear you've put your heart and soul into the orchard and we'll have to market it to someone who can appreciate the fruit trees. I've looked at the comps in the area to calculate an asking price." Bradley paused. "I think you should list the house at $425,000."

"Bradley," George said. "That's below what I want for the house. We were hoping to get over $600,000 because the orchard is worth a lot and I've invested a great deal of money into it." George was adamant about the price and was not known for his business acumen.

"George, I completely understand where you're coming from but to most people, the orchard carries little value. The land, the ten acres, and the house are what most buyers are looking for. You folks have a lovely house and the new hardwood floors are a beautiful upgrade, but the kitchen and bathrooms are dated. This tends to be a selling point these days."

After two hours of discussion and smooth talking on Bradley's part, George agreed to list the house at $495,000, well below what he was hoping for. They parted ways with assurances to be in touch soon with any updates or activity on the house.

Two weeks later Ken received a call from Bradley. "Ken, I just spoke with your father and he's taken the house off the market. He said he's uncomfortable with the price we set because the orchard and trees are worth much more than I'm giving them credit for. He feels insulted by the asking price. I thought I would check with you to see what you think, and what will ultimately be best for your parents. This is a hard thing they're doing." Bradley waited and Ken sighed.

"Why am I not surprised," Ken said. "Okay, I'll call him tomorrow to find out what he's thinking and give you a call back. Thanks Bradley." Ken hung up and headed out to his weekly basketball game with Stu.

Ken and George had the conversation the next day, a very predictable conversation. George felt he was being robbed and the orchard meant too much to him to let it go. Ken tried to convince him selling was the prudent thing to do, in part because the housing market was hot and spring was the best time to sell. George was not hearing it. Ken dropped it but knew the subject would be revisited in the near future. George still had a death grip on the idea that he and Thelma were going to be back in Monkton to live out their dying days.

Within a few weeks Stu took his turn visiting Champlain Waters. He flew into the Burlington airport and was greeted with hugs and kisses from his parents. "Who drove here?" Stu asked.

"I had your mother drive today, but I think I'll drive home because she doesn't stay in the lines very well. I try to tell her how to drive but she doesn't take it very well." Stu was horrified.

"I will be driving this weekend." And Stu confiscated the keys. "You guys know Champlain Waters has their own bus service and will take you shopping, to your doctor appointments or on outings."

"Oh, I'm not riding that bus," piped Thelma. "There are crazy people on that bus and I am just fine to drive. Your father just gives me too many directions, and then I get all confused. I wish he would just shut up while I'm driving. And did you know a lady in Florida went on one of these buses to Walmart, and a man came up to her and tried to molest her? It is just too dangerous and I'm not riding the bus."

On the trek back to Champlain Waters they made a stop at the Rotisserie for dinner. George wanted a nostalgic drive down Davis Parkway to see the house where Stu and Sue were born. Stu was happy to oblige. Thelma was thrilled to share the story of walking Karen in the stroller to the old post office.

Back at the assisted living facility, George hit the automatic handicap door opener with his cane, a simple activity never ceasing to put a smile on his face. Thelma was happy not to be poked with the cane. Thelma quickly spotted several friends milling about in the lobby, but could not remember their names to introduce them to Stu. He made polite conversation for a few minutes, a few minutes being the saturation point, before heading down to the apartment with George. Thelma remained behind to chat for a while.

Thelma had always had a knack for chatting. During many of their dinner parties, Thelma would stand at the door as guests were leaving to chat for another twenty or thirty minutes. It drove George nuts because often it was during the winter and with the door open, he was heating the outside. George always referred to this as "thresholding".

Stu sat his parents down, each with their favorite libation; a sweet Manhattan with a cherry for George, a highball made with Crown Royal for his mother, and a Grey Goose and tonic with an orange slice for himself. It was time to have a serious discussion. "Listen, I want to talk to you both about selling the property in Monkton. As it stands right now, the house is sitting empty and we're approaching one year of a vacant property. Already the house is looking tired, the orchard is not being properly tended to and we run the risk of losing potential profit on the house the longer it sits empty. I understand you don't agree with Bradley's figure on the house, but maybe we can negotiate something in the middle. You can then invest the money because there is no mortgage on the house. The reality of the situation is that you will not be living there again." Stu finished, knowing this last part was brutally honest.

"I don't know Stu, it's a big decision. I put a lot of work into those trees and I don't want them sold to someone who doesn't appreciate them." George hesitated before continuing. "I want the property listed at $500,000 and I won't go any lower."

"Mom, what do you think?"

"I know your father can't take care of the orchard anymore, but this place is the pits. The food is horrible and there are some really nutty people here. I hate this place. If we sell the house, maybe we can move to Florida and buy a small place down there."

"Florida is nothing but God's waiting room," said George.

"You'll have lots of options if you sell the house, besides there's no hurry to make a decision right now about where you want to live. All your friends are here, you go to church every Sunday and you know all your doctors here." Stu pressed on, "not to mention, we have no idea how long it will take to sell the house because it will take a special buyer." George reluctantly agreed to put the orchard on the market under the condition it be listed no lower than $500,000.

The remainder of the weekend Stu carted his parents all over the Burlington area to visit friends. Each stop resulted in reminiscing. In one story they retold their adventure renting a houseboat on the Hudson River and taking it through the locks on the Erie Canal. Stu did not get all the details, but it sounded as though docking the boat met with a minor accident and some damage, a search for food led to some unsavory characters, and clearly there had been some hardcore partying.

They ran numerous errands including the obligatory trip back to Monkton, where signs of vacancy were becoming more apparent. White paint peeled from the unused garage doors, weeds sprouted from every crack in the walkway, and the once pristine croquet court was buried under a sea of crabgrass.

After sleeping on the couch for several nights and suffering a creaky back, Stu looked into the possibility of a two-bedroom. "Dad, I just spoke with the manager and there's a two -bedroom unit available. It'll be a lot more convenient for everyone if you guys have a two-bedroom. You'll be in the same building but will have a lot more room."

"How much more will it cost me?" George asked.

"Actually it's only a couple hundred more a month, but it would give you space for your computer and all the crap you leave lying around." Stu smiled waiting for his reply.

Thelma chimed right in, "Oh God, it's worth it if I don't have to look at his mess. He leaves papers everywhere and I'm afraid he's going to trip and fall. You know, I ask him to pick up and he doesn't." A couple hours later Stu, Thelma and a friendly young staffer showed them the two-bedroom apartment. It was bright and sunny with an exit directly to the center courtyard. The apartment was in the middle of being repainted and recarpeted.

"Oh, I love it," exclaimed Thelma.

"When will it be available?" Stu asked..

"It should be ready to move in by next weekend." And so it was decided they would move down the corridor. Later that afternoon Stu wanted a second look at the new apartment to get measurements for furniture placement.

"Where are we going?" asked Thelma. Stu was taken aback.

"Where are we going? We're going to look at the new apartment again."

"What new apartment?"

"Remember this morning we looked at a new two bedroom unit and you guys decided to take it?" reminded Stu.

"Ahh shit, I don't remember. I don't know what's wrong with me," Thelma said. Stu realized it was the first time Thelma actually admitted trouble remembering. Usually she tried to cover her tracks by pretending. The two-bedroom looked just as good to Thelma the second time around, but she was confused about turning down the hallway in the opposite direction. Hopefully the large plastic insect would help identify their new door.

Anderson's Movers were called again, hopefully for the last time. Although this move was only down the hallway, it required belongings to be packed, moved and rearranged. Anderson's would be paid well. Kathy, their housekeeper and friend, was also hired to help organize the apartment, because on such short notice none of the kids were able to make the trek to Vermont. If left up to George and Thelma, it would never happen.

Thelma was becoming more confused about the upcoming move down the hall. She began telling other residents at Champlain Waters they were moving to Florida at the end of the month. One morning Ken received a call from the facility.

"Hello," Ken answered with trepidation when he noticed Champlain Waters in the caller ID. Calls from the assisted living facility were never a good thing, it usually meant Thelma had been found wandering around lost or one of them had fallen.

"Is this Ken MacCollom?

"Yes."

"This is Angie from Champlain Waters, and I am just confirming your parents, George and Thelma, are moving to Florida and won't be changing apartments at the end of the week?"

"What?" Ken responded. "Who told you they were moving to Florida?"

"Your mother came to the office yesterday and explained that you and your brother were coming to move them next week. We've already filled both apartments." Angie's tone tapered off, realizing a mistake might have been made.

"Call me crazy, but why would you listen to my mother who has Alzheimer's? The only place they're moving is down the hall to their new two-bedroom unit, which by the way, we put a deposit on. We expect the unit to be available when the movers arrive in two days." Exasperated, Ken continued, "Listen, we are paying thousands of dollars every month, we pay the bills on time and we always speak with you first about any issues. Why hasn't the same courtesy been extended to us? And just where do you think my parents are going to go if not into their new apartment?"

"I am terribly sorry," Angie replied, embarrassed and in a hurry to get off the phone. "We will resolve this immediately, Mr. MacCollom."

Thankfully the move happened, on time and with great ease, thanks to the expertise of Anderson's Movers and their past experience with George and Thelma. Change was not easy for Thelma. For over a year she had exited the elevator and turned left, now she had to turn right. And two doors down from their new unit was the locked entrance to *The Garden*, her worst nightmare, the memory unit.

"Oh, I don't like being so close to that place," said Thelma. "People who end up there have lost their minds, say anything that pops into their head and they don't even know where they are. I do not want to end up there." Her future was scary, especially when she had glimpses of it every day. For the time being, they settled into their new apartment but confusion was gaining on Thelma. On more than one occasion she was found wandering the halls in search of her new apartment. One day she broke down in uncontrollable sobs because she understood she was losing the battle. Other days she happily cruised the hallways chatting with everyone in her path, until she found her way home. George remained parked in his recliner, oblivious to Thelma's dilemma or perhaps just unconcerned, due to his own issues with left side neglect.

Left side neglect is a phenomenon occurring after a brain injury to the right side of the brain. The patient has impaired awareness of stimuli on the left side of the body. They are unaware of movement or sound on the left, despite not having any sensory loss on the left side. As a result, the table next to his recliner was set up on his left side in order to force him to attend to that side. The family tried to always sit on his left, forcing him to focus to his left. It did little to improve his condition.

Thelma befriended the hairdresser, Carol, who had a small beauty shop on the ground floor of Champlain Waters. She was a rather stout woman with bleached blonde hair lacking the style one wants to see in their stylist. Carol loved to gossip with the ladies about her hard-knock life, her loser husband and her weekend adventures camping in her prized RV. The ladies of Champlain Waters enjoyed sitting around Carol's shop because she listened, making them feel important. They told her everything, sometimes too much. During one of Sue's visits, Thelma had an appointment scheduled with Carol. Sue decided to venture down with Thelma to check out the salon and keep her mother company.

"Thelma darling," Carol sang. "You look lovely today. What are we doing today? Come on in and have a seat while I finish up with Priscilla." Thelma made introductions and despite her mental decline, she always knew who everyone was, even if their name escaped her.

Priscilla was a petite lady with fluffy gray hair, beautifully wrinkled skin and crazy eyes. Her nails were recently manicured in blood red polish, which contradicted her baby blue velour pantsuit. "Priscilla, your nails are gorgeous and now you have hair to match," Carol cooed as she teased the back curls.

"Ooooo, oh yes, you know I have to look good. I'm getting married this afternoon," said Priscilla. Carol winked at Sue and Thelma.

Thelma leaned into Sue, "She's crazy."

"Well that's wonderful, Priscilla. Are you marrying Howard again?" asked Carol.

"What do you mean again?" Priscilla said. "We are in love, and Mother and Father have planned a big wedding for us at the Methodist church. I think I need to start getting ready and I have to pack for the honeymoon. Mother will be worried if I don't return soon." Priscilla fumbled in her purse for money to pay Carol. "Oh dear me, I can't find any dollar bills but I do have a checkbook."

"A check is fine darling," Carol responded, keeping a close eye on the purse. Priscilla played with her checkbook for several minutes before Carol offered to help.

"How much tip do you want to give?" asked Carol. Sue had an uneasy feeling, but said nothing as she didn't know the normal protocol.

Thelma and Carol gossiped or rather Carol yammered on the entire time she was washing and setting Thelma's baby-fine hair. She told them stories of taking Champlain Waters residents on weekend trips in the RV. Sue thought it was odd. Sue continued to half-listen while flipping through old copies of People and Better Homes and Gardens.

"Thelma darling, you are gorgeous. George won't be able to keep his hands off you." Thelma fumbled in her purse with Priscilla watching closely. Sue was now on high alert.

"Oh, Carol, how much do I owe you again?" Thelma asked.

"Twenty one dollars, sweetie." Carol answered.

"Oh my, I only have two twenty dollar bills," Thelma said as she continued to rummage through her purse.

"That's ok darling. I'll get you change the next time you come in." Carol was very nonchalant as she took Thelma's money.

"Carol," Sue said. "You don't have any money to give back to my mom?"

"No Sue, but we do this all the time. No worries, right Thelma?" Carol was ready to dismiss them.

Sue gathered up her mother and began walking back to the apartment. "How often does Carol owe you money?" Thelma could not remember but went on and on about how nice Carol was and how she had offered to take Thelma on a weekend camping trip. Once Thelma was safely back in the apartment, Sue found the manager. She made a complaint about Carol taking advantage of women with memory issues. The manager was not surprised as they had received other complaints. Sue suggested immediate action.

The next morning, Sue quietly entered the apartment following an early morning run. Her parents were still asleep and she took a moment to take in the apartment. She noticed how disorganized everything was despite the weekly housekeeping visit. Newspapers were scattered on every surface, mail both opened and unopened lay in piles, and dishes sat unwashed in the sink. Her parents had never been neat freaks but this was different, more chaotic.

"Oh, good morning Sue. Oh, you've been out for a run already?" Thelma asked.

"I sure have. I ran down to Laurel Hill past our old house and through the old neighborhood. Geez, I've got to say the old house looks like shit. The front is moldy, the lawn is half missing and the wrought-iron rails on the front steps are broken. And, the birch trees are gone. The entire neighborhood looks tired."

"Oh, I loved that house," Thelma commented. "You know I was able to pick out everything in the house when we built it in 1964. We had a lot of happy memories there." *If the walls could talk,* thought Sue.

"Do you want some breakfast, Mom?" Sue asked. " I can make whatever you want and the coffee is ready."

"Oh, I need to take my pills first."

"Well, let's get going then." Sue pulled the wicker basket filled with an assortment of pills and pill boxes. "Wow Mom, you've got a regular pharmacy here!"

"Oh God, it's so confusing. I think they've given me the wrong pills again. It takes me so long to figure out what's what," complained Thelma.

"Hey Mom, let me help you get it all sorted. I'll fill your pill boxes for two weeks and all you have to do is remember to take them each morning. I can even fill Dad's too, but he has nightly pills he'll have to remember." She did not wait for an answer.

Sue placed Thelma's morning pills in a pile on top of a napkin with a glass of water on the table. Thelma stared at the pills, rolling them in her hands as she inspected them. The daily ritual of swallowing pills by allowing them to dissolve into a murky white backwash was still alive and well. None of her pills were bigger than an aspirin but it was so difficult for her mother to swallow them.

Sue spent a couple hours sorting and organizing both sets of pills for the next two weeks. She realized it was a rather difficult task, or at least a time-consuming task requiring attention to detail. After speaking with her siblings, they decided it would be in everyone's best interest to hire someone. The person could come to the apartment everyday to supervise the pills, tidy up the place, make trips to the store or any other odd jobs. The front office recommended a woman named Marion, who worked privately for a number of other residents. Thankfully Marion was willing to take on George and Thelma. Sue left the next morning for Maine, feeling better with a few supports in place.

Later that month Thelma was hungry and in the mood for some leftover lasagna from their dinner out the night before. The cardboard container had been carefully covered with foil by the restaurant. She simply placed the container, foil and all, into the microwave and pushed the button for five minutes. She left to use the bathroom when she was startled by the fire alarm.

"Jesus George! What's going on? Jesus George, do something!" Thelma hollered as she saw the kitchen filling with smoke. George was sitting in his recliner, oblivious to the emergency unfolding in front of him. While George and Thelma were frozen with inaction, an employee rushed into the apartment and ushered them out into the courtyard with dozens of other confused residents. Several firemen quickly descended upon the apartment and killed the arcing fire in the microwave.

"Oh shit, did I do that?" asked Thelma. Luckily there was minimal damage, just an acrid odor that would dissipate with a good airing out. Thelma had to endure a lecture from management about the hazards of putting metal in the microwave. Ken had to endure yet another phone call from Champlain Waters. The event was the talk of the facility for the remainder of the day and then it was promptly forgotten.

Marion knocked and entered the apartment bright and early the next morning to find Thelma wildly searching for something. "Good morning, Thelma. What are you looking for?" Marion asked as she immediately began picking up the kitchen.

"I am so mad," Thelma growled through her teeth. "What have you done with my pills? You all think I can't do anything for myself. Well I have news for you, I am just fine and I want my pills back!"

"Thelma, we've been over this before. I am helping you with your meds because it was getting too confusing for you and you weren't taking the right pills. It can be very dangerous. I am only doing this because we all want you safe and healthy." Marion was calm, but Thelma was not having it.

"This is so insulting, I hate all you people! I hate this place and I want to get out of here." She was shaking now and George sat quietly in his recliner watching TV, not wanting to be involved in the confrontation. Marion was well-versed in dealing with irate clients scared to death of their slipping memories and loss of independence. She knew enough not to engage Thelma in the argument. She would call one of the kids later with an update, and no one would be surprised. Marion turned her attention to George.

"Hey handsome, do you have any new jokes for me today?" Marion kept an eye on Thelma as she continued to sputter about her pills.

"Good morning beautiful," George grinned. "Have you heard the one about the boy who ran through the screen door?"

"No, I haven't George."

"He strained himself!" Marion giggled at the punch line and gently ruffled his white hair. George returned to his newspaper and Marion reviewed the plans for the day. "I'll make you bacon and eggs for breakfast, and then we can go to the grocery store, and you both have a dental appointment."

"Marion, we're fine. We've got this," George said. "I am perfectly fine to drive and Thelma and I can handle this on our own." Marion had reservations about letting them tackle the day's agenda, and she made a mental note to add this to her discussion with the kids.

Later that day Ken made a phone call to his parents with big news; the house had been sold. Their ambivalent reaction was not fooling Ken, as he knew it was a hard day for them. It placed a finality on the fact they would never again live in Monkton, and that phase of their lives was over no matter how hard they wished for it. George's one unwavering wish for the future was never to be placed in a nursing home, while Thelma's was never to be placed in an Alzheimer unit.

No, you can't always get what you want
You can't always get what you want
You can't always get what you want
But if you try sometime you'll find
You get what you need

Keith Richards/Mick Jagger

1969

Plans were quickly thrown together to gather as a family in Burlington for the daunting task of clearing out the house in preparation for the new owners. A dairy farmer from upstate New York purchased the house in order to be closer to his children, who lived in the Monkton area. George was relieved a farmer bought the property, and he held high hopes the new owner would maintain his precious orchard.

Chapter 7 The Garage Sale

When is a door not a door?
When it's ajar.

It proved to be an emotional day. The four siblings bounced down the long dirt drive towards their parents' home. They were all unusually quiet as they prepared for the massive downsizing. Monkton Valley Orchard had not been their childhood home, but it had been home to George and Thelma's retirement years. It was the place where the grandchildren carved memories of their grandparents. Wisely, all spouses were not in attendance but George and Thelma would be there as supervisors and a few family friends had offered to help. It was up to the kids to sell off or donate anything not claimed, clean up the mess in the workshop, and leave the house ready for closing before Sunday afternoon. It was now Friday morning, no pressure. They spent Friday organizing, pricing, making junk piles and putting up signs.

"What are we supposed to do with all of Dad's insecticides?" Stu asked no one in particular.

"Just burn the shit," Ken replied. "It's a hazardous waste site and no one's going to remove it without the proper permits which will take weeks to obtain."

Saturday morning, there were already customers driving slowly down the drive before 7:30 am. The notice clearly stated the sale started at 9:00 am. The early birds stepped out of a 1992 faded blue Ford Taurus sedan in search of bargains. Things were not ready yet.

"We're here to look around a bit and we'd like to go inside too." The heavy-set man pushed his fingers through his combover as it flapped in the breeze. His female companion waddled behind him into the garage.

"You'll have to give us some time to get things set up," Sue explained. She walked away from them not waiting for a response.

"If you see something you want, make an offer because it all has to go," Karen countered as Sue kept walking.

For the next hour and a half piles of Corning ware with little blue flowers, plastic tomatoes which once held ketchup, countless baking pans, a mish mash of croquet sets, snow tubes in various states of disrepair, an old toboggan, ice skates dating back to the 1960's, piles of clothes once thought hip in the 1980's and a hodgepodge of tools were hauled into the garage. All of Thelma's Limoges china, family silver, antiques and personal effects had long since been moved to Champlain Waters or claimed by one of the children. George and Thelma asked the kids numerous times over the last few years to decide what pieces of furniture or items they would like to have. Amazingly, there had been no squabbling between siblings and everyone ended up with the items they wanted.

"Hey guys," Sue sighed, wiping dust from her brow. "Dad has three filing cabinets chock full of papers which I am not moving to Champlain Waters. What should we do with them?"

"Well we can't just dump them," Ken replied. "We have to go through them because I'm sure he has important papers and documents in there." Ken continued moving towards the blazing bonfire carrying a tattered bag of DDT he had found in the shed.

"Fine, I'll make a pile to burn, a pile to look through and a pile to definitely keep," Sue mumbled to herself as everyone was absorbed in their own tasks.

Clouds of ominous smoke billowed behind the house as years of toxic chemicals, DDT, Malathion, Chlordan and Guthion were illegally burned. Bird life had wisely disappeared with the onset of fumes. In the warm June sunshine, yard salers swarmed like mosquitoes hatching after a humid rain. Years of history were being sold off to the highest bidder or to anyone willing to make an offer. The more that sold, the less they would have to trek to the dump.

Thelma wandered around touching her items as she tried to retrieve memories. At times the memory was as clear as yesterday and she would recant tales of bygone parties, bridge games and family vacations. She prattled on with anyone who would listen.

"Mom, put those bags of yarn back out in the garage," Karen instructed. "You don't need them."

"But I might want to knit again. I promised Charlie I would knit him a pair of mittens."

"Mom," Sue said. "You can't take any more stuff to Champlain Waters. We've been over this a hundred times, you have everything you need there and you already decided what to keep." Sue explained patiently for the twentieth time that morning. "Are you honestly going to knit again?" Feeling for her mother, she put together a small bag of yarn and one pair of knitting needles, quietly placing them in the car, knowing her mother would never knit again. She could at least pretend.

George wandered too. He wandered amongst the workshop housing his beloved John Deere tractor. He silently wondered why he couldn't have just suffered a stroke while driving the tractor in the field, with the tractor ending it for him. His left arm barely worked, and he walked with a gimpy left leg which Stu constantly reminded him to lift. He had lived his dream of being a gentleman farmer and now his own children were forcing him off his land. He could still drive, despite arguments from his children, and he could still tend to his orchard, with help. Unfortunately the kids all lived out-of-state and none of them were interested in taking over the orchard.

Karen and Sue decided to tackle the old freezer sitting at the rear of the garage. It was a faded almond-colored stand up freezer, where George and Thelma stored blueberries from their impressive grove of high bush varieties, plus leftovers stored in

Cool Whip containers dated with a black Sharpie that had no hope of ever being consumed–and dozens of packages of meat purchased through a traveling salesman years earlier.

"Can you read any of the dates?" Sue asked her sister.

"Oh my God," Karen said. "This one is marked 4/12/93. Do you realize it's almost fourteen years old?"

"Ugh, check this out, Karen." Sue pulled a vacuum sealed package of what might have been chicken but was now an alien shade of green. "We can't throw this stuff into the trash, it will stink and create another toxic site."

"Let's lug it over to the field and throw it there. Maybe the coyotes will eat it," Karen suggested. No one ever checked, but if they had, they would find that not a morsel was ever touched.

By five o'clock everyone was exhausted and overwhelmed at what still needed to be accomplished by the next day when everyone scattered for home. The garage was still filled with miscellaneous junk never bought or given away, the shed was still full of flammable chemicals and rusted paint cans unfit for burning or the transfer station, and the house still needed to be cleaned up and the remaining items tagged for storage. A call was made to JUNK-R-US who was willing to take everything away, for a price. A self-storage unit was rented, for a price. Ken and Stu climbed into the Explorer with their parents. Karen and Sue hopped into Sue's car.

Two hours later they were all seated at the restaurant freshly showered, a tad more relaxed and ready for their first libation. The waitress made quick work of the drink orders until she reached Thelma. The whole group moaned as they prepared for the detailed description of how to concoct the perfect dry Manhattan.

"She wants a dry…," Stu started to order for his mother but was abruptly cut off.

"I can order myself if you don't mind. I would like a very dry Crown Royal Manhattan, up with a side of ice and a twist," Thelma ordered, copping a bit of an attitude.

"Why don't you just tell them you want a lemon twist and only two drops of dry vermouth because you know it's going to arrive wrong," Ken suggested, from experience.

"Any bartender worth their salt will know how to make a dry Manhattan. I shouldn't have to educate them when I'm paying for the drink," she said. They all waited for the arrival of their drinks and Thelma's disappointment with the bartender's lack of knowledge. He got it right on the second try.

Thelma had first encountered the perfect dry Manhattan when she and George made a weekend visit to Montreal and stayed at the Bonaventure Hotel. The hotel restaurant, Le Castillion Room, was five star dining where Thelma was in her glory. They made countless trips to the Bonaventure over the years and all four kids knew the story well.

Fried oysters, crab-stuffed mushrooms and bruschetta were being passed around as a first course. George was busy telling jokes, many of which had been heard at least a dozen times before. Thelma was quiet; conversations in large groups overpowered her these days. She scanned her menu for several minutes before Sue leaned in.

"Mom, can I help you? What do you feel like eating tonight?

"Oh, I left my reading glasses at home and I can't see the menu very well," Thelma replied.

"OK, let me read you what they have. Or is there something you're in the mood for like fish or pasta or steak?" Sue asked.

"I don't like fish, I'm afraid I'll choke on a bone," Thelma said. "Maybe pasta."

"I want a rare ribeye steak with garlic mashed potatoes," George informed the crowd. "I don't like anything of a soupy nature or anything with rice in it." There may have been a few eye rolls in the group.

They ordered, Thelma settled on spaghetti and meatballs, drank a few rounds and laughed a lot. It was a rare night when George and Thelma were alone with just their four children and the moment did not escape them.

"So what are you going to do with all your money?" Stu joked.

"Maybe I'll buy a new vehicle for the drive to Florida," George said, leaving his kids wondering if he was serious. "The Explorer has close to 100,000 miles on it now." No one commented on the horror of them driving to Florida. Dinner lasted several hours and the waitress was compensated well for her patience with the group and the restaurant's leniency on the noise level from the table.

Karen and Sue left in the morning for their drive back to Maine, where Karen would spend a few days before flying back to Florida. Ken and Stu made a final trek to Monkton. The goal was to leave everything in organized piles for JUNK-R-US to pick up on Monday. Their task took much longer than anticipated, leaving only minutes to spare for a shower prior to arriving at the airport via taxi. George and Thelma were now permanent residents of assisted living with no hope of ever living in Monkton again.

Chapter 8 A Change is Coming
Embryonic Cranial Nephrosis

The next few months passed with a new normalcy. Phone calls were now more often than not initiated by the kids and consisted of thirty seconds of small talk from George and thirty minutes of complaining from Thelma. *The food is inedible, the girl at the front desk is rude, the toilet keeps plugging up, everyone is crazy, everyone needs a walker and people tell her what to do all the time.*

They still had their circle of friends in Burlington, but they too were beginning to show their age. Hugh, George's friend, gave them rides to church on Sunday or took them to the Ethan Allen Club every once in a while for the prime rib dinner. Barb, a close friend who had been married to George's best friend Peter before a tragic fall took his life, still did her best to keep in touch. She contacted Sue every few months to get the real scoop on how things were going. It was hard for their friends to see Thelma slipping away mentally and George slipping away physically, because it served as a brutal reminder of what was in store for them. Almost as if aging were a contagious disease.

Marion, the helper, was making more frequent calls to the kids. Thelma was now continuing to get irate over the control of her pills. George sat quietly in his recliner, seemingly oblivious to the chaos.

"Where are my pills?" Thelma screamed at Marion as she entered the apartment right on schedule. "I really resent the fact that you people don't think I'm able to take care of my own pills." Thelma had a deranged look in her eyes which came to be called *"crazy eye."* I hate you people!" And then as soon as it started, it was over. Thelma would suddenly be pleasant and have little memory of her outburst. She knew at all times she hated Champlain Waters, but was losing her way back to their apartment with increasing frequency. She wandered the hallways until she was so confused she broke down in tears. These were the moments she understood she was losing her mind.

The reality that George and Thelma needed even more support was becoming more apparent with each phone call. The kids conferred and agreed it was time to think about a move to Florida. Ken and Stu began looking at assisted living facilities near the St Pete area where they lived, to get a feel for what was available. They figured the St Pete area was the best choice as two of the kids lived there and Karen was only a couple hours away. The ALFs (assisted living facilities) ran the gamut from exclusive resorts with high-end facilities, gourmet food and a high ratio of staff-to-resident all the way to what resembled bad public housing with institutional food and patients slumped in wheelchairs parked in the hallway for hours on end. Luckily there were facilities in between the two.

"Hello," George answered his cell phone while glancing at the caller ID. "Hey Stu, how is everybody down there?"

"Good, Dad, Keith and Cameron are playing basketball and Allie's still in school up in Orlando. Elaine is working on her paperwork right now before she heads out for a walk. What are you and Mom up to?"

"Nothing much, it's pretty quiet here. Your mother is napping on the couch right now. I'll wake her up so you can talk with her."

"No! Don't wake her up, let her sleep," Stu said, really not wanting to listen to the litany of complaints. "I was calling to say hi and to let you know that Ken and I found a really nice place near us that you and Mom might want to take a look at. It's called Whispering Oaks and you would have your own two-bed, two-bath apartment with a balcony. There's a dining room with three meals a day, you can even order eggs and bacon every day for breakfast if you want. It's about twenty minutes for both Ken and I, so we'd be able to stop by often and take you out to dinner and get you to appointments. You'd also be able to see a lot more of your grandchildren, except for Henry and Charlie."

"Sounds good, Stu." George sounded unimpressed. "You should tell your mother about it." George had always viewed Florida simply as the final destination before expiring. Despite instructions to leave Thelma to her nap, George hollered over to her. She groggily took over the phone, where Stu proceeded to sell the high-end accommodations and benefits of being in close proximity to family.

"Oh Stu, that sounds nice. So much better than this dump, where the food is disgusting and the girl at the front desk is very rude to me. I am so sick of the people here telling me what to do." Thelma could have continued with her list of complaints but Stu cut her off.

"You and Dad should fly down and have a look. You can stay at our house in the guest room for as long as you'd like." Thelma seemed to like this idea, so Stu knew they needed to address the issue of George and Thelma flying to Florida unchaperoned. Their ability to navigate anything out of the ordinary was becoming a real concern. Stu would brainstorm with Elaine and Ken about a possible escort, knowing full well it would not be him. One concern was if Thelma wandered into the bathroom at the airport, would she know where she was when she exited? Would George have the patience or stamina to walk the long gateways while keeping Thelma in tow? If flights were canceled or gates changed, could they navigate the change? Stu realized it was quite similar to planning a trip for an unaccompanied minor—except these were his parents. It was all turned around.

Stu and Elaine convinced their sons Cameron and Keith to fly up to Burlington and escort George and Thelma down to Florida for a mini-vacation. Once in Florida they could make the hard sell for Whispering Oaks. Cameron was a sophomore at the University of Central Florida and Keith was a junior in high school. The boys figured it would be an all-expenses-paid vacation to Vermont. Little did they know it would be no vacation.

Cameron had the natural gift of charisma, and could talk anyone into anything with his smile. Keith was thinner and blonder with a passion for eating and sleeping just about anywhere— and what he lacked in his brother's gift of gab, he made up for in academics. Both boys were gifted basketball players.

Elaine dragged the boys out of bed the morning of their flight to Vermont. If all went according to plan, their flight would leave on time with an arrival in Burlington before noon, giving them time to take George and Thelma out to lunch. That left them all afternoon to pack and time for a drive out to Monkton before leaving the next day. Their flight north went off without a hitch and both boys were able to grab a few more hours of sleep on the plane. George and Thelma met the boys at the airport despite a full conversation about taking a taxi to Champlain Waters.

"Hey Grandpa! Hey Grandma! I see you haven't gotten any prettier, Gramps," Cameron said as he hugged both his grandparents. Keith followed his brother's lead with hugs and small talk. They quickly made their way out to the parking lot.

"So Gramp, where did you park?" Cameron asked.

"I know it's somewhere right around here. Do you remember where we parked the Explorer, Thel?" George asked.

"Jesus George, how can you not remember?" Thelma remarked, also with no clue where they had parked.

"You know you can hit the panic button on your keys," Keith suggested. "And the car will start beeping so we can find it." He took the keys from George and activated the panic button with an immediate commotion one row over from where they were standing.

"Oooo, Ooooo, okay, okay that's enough," Thelma said. "Oh, shut that off!" She appeared to be embarrassed, almost as if she were afraid everyone was staring at them. This only encouraged all three boys to keep it up. George was grinning from ear to ear thrilled to have his grandsons and partners in crime with him. Thelma also adored being with her grandsons, but at the moment was preoccupied with the sounding alarm. They climbed into the Explorer, with Cameron as driver. George was copilot. It took Keith and Cam several minutes to realize both their grandparents were struggling with the seatbelts and required assistance. The familiar discussion of where to stop for lunch ensued.

"How about the Rotisserie, it's just down the road, and they have the best lunches," came a suggestion from Thelma in the backseat. But Cam and Keith already knew exactly what they wanted for lunch, in fact they had been salivating over it the entire flight up.

"Gramps, you know where we both want to go, don't you?" Keith piped up from the rear.

"They have the best fries, best greasy burgers and they even know you personally, don't they Gramps?" added Cameron.

"Al's French Fries!" George answered, and Thelma remained quiet, knowing her grandsons loved Al's as much as George. She preferred a restaurant with linen tablecloths, proper utensils and table service. She had to admit though, Al's French Fries were rather tasty. She ended up ordering a hot dog, French fries and root beer while the other three ordered double cheeseburgers, fries and large milkshakes. Tucked into a sunny corner booth, they drenched their fries in malt vinegar and ketchup. A happy silence descended while they all ate.

Cam and Keith pushed, punched and wrestled each other in the parking lot of Al's while they waited for George and Thelma to finish chatting with friends they bumped into while exiting the restaurant. They hopped into the Explorer, and again it took Keith and Cameron a minute to realize their grandparents needed assistance with the seatbelts.

"Cam, the big pedal on the left is the brake and the pedal on the right is the gas!" quipped George with a grin on his face.

"Thanks Gramp, that's helpful."

They made their way back to Champlain Waters with a pit stop at Hannaford for more Pepsi, Cabot Seriously Sharp cheddar and White Owl Miniature cigars, which George still had a fondness for chewing which left a trail of soggy dottle. The end table adjacent to his leather recliner was littered with brown crusty bits of chewed-up cigar and his shirts were frequently speckled with stray remnants he had failed to capture with his fingers. The family questioned if this was better than actually smoking the nasty things.

A silver Cadillac pulling out of the Champlain Waters parking lot nearly hit the Explorer just as Cameron was about to make a left turn. A small gray-haired man who barely rose above the steering wheel was completely oblivious to Cameron's hand gestures and horn blowing.

"There's a guy with embryonic cranial nephrosis," George said.

"What's that Gramp?" wondered Keith.

"The scientific definition is the guy has urine on the brain, but it really means he's a piss head." Keith and Cam howled with laughter, Thelma just rolled her eyes, because even she remembered hearing that joke at least a hundred times in her life. They settled into the apartment and gabbed for a while before the boys discovered a collection of DVDs and popped *The Italian Job* into the DVD player.

Cam and Keith had a brief argument about who was going to help their grandmother pack. Cameron won the dispute on the grounds he was older and would kick his brother's ass if he didn't help his grandmother. George was a notoriously light packer. He loved to tell the story about a time he was on a business trip passing through the airport when they asked him to open his briefcase. This was years before 9/11 when traveling by air was simple, even enjoyable. George was traveling with only a briefcase and to the surprise of the security guard, they discovered a folder containing lecture notes, a half finished bottle of VO, a toothbrush and a pair of dirty tighty whitey underwear. The guard quickly waved him through.

"OK Gram," Keith said. "Why don't you pull out what you'll need for Florida." He watched as she pulled a mass of tangled necklaces from her jewelry box with very little success at untangling them. "Gram, I think you should start with pants and shirts. Why don't you pick out a few outfits you like to wear, and maybe a couple of skirts." Keith was trying hard but clearly not comfortable with the assigned task.

After forty-five minutes Keith felt confident Thelma had enough packed to get her through a week in Florida. Keith exited the room while she packed her underwear, knowing his mother would buy more if need be. Cam and George had finished their packing job within seven minutes and had been telling jokes in the other room when Keith made his appearance. George expressed an interest in taking a drive out to Monkton and the boys were game for anything to get them out of the apartment. Like their cousins, Henry and Charlie, they had spent countless summer hours in Monkton racing go-karts, driving the pick-up truck well before the legal age and shooting guns. This trek back out to Monkton was a walk down memory lane for all of them, but the new owners had taken possession of the house so the nostalgia tour would be experienced from a distance.

"Keith buddy, can you get my cane from the bedroom?" George asked. Keith quickly jumped up and made his way down the hallway. Upon entering the bedroom, he stopped in his tracks. Thelma's suitcase was completely empty and there were piles of clothes all over the bureau.

"Gram!" he hollered, confused. Thelma popped her head into the bedroom. "What happened here Gram?"

"What do you mean?"

"Why did you take everything out of your suitcase that we just finished packing for the trip tomorrow?"

"I was getting ready for the trip. I was having trouble deciding what to pack," Thelma answered.

"But Gram, we just spent an hour getting everything ready. You didn't like what we packed?" Keith was confused, but Thelma seemed fine with her answer. "Let's put your clothes back in the suitcase before we head to Monkton." He carefully placed the piles of clothes back in the suitcase while Thelma watched. He closed the suitcase and encouraged his grandmother to go check on George and Cam. As soon as she left the room, he took the suitcase and hid it in the other bedroom by sliding it under the bed. It was a trick his mother had suggested, but at the time he thought she was nuts. His mother had been right.

Following the sightseeing tour of Monkton, they made their way to a popular family restaurant in Hinesburg not too far from the orchard. They all ordered hot turkey sandwiches drowning in brown gravy served with French fries and coleslaw. George and Thelma frequented the restaurant back when dining out with friends was a common occurrence. The boys noticed how relaxed their grandparents seemed just being in old familiar places. The boys silently wondered how the trip to Florida would pan out.

At precisely 6:00 am three separate alarms were ringing next to the boys' sleeping heads, two cell phones and one actual alarm clock. Neither boy was known as an early riser, but with a flight to catch and no parent to rouse them from bed, they took no chances. Cam insisted Keith get up first to shower, but he realized he also better get up to wake George and Thelma, who no longer were quick to do anything. Cam had been given strict instructions from his mother to pack all the medications including all pill boxes and prescription bottles as soon as the morning pills had been doled out.

By 7:00 am they were piling into the Explorer for the initial leg of their trip. The boys decided to check all bags as it would be impossible for George and Thelma to negotiate their rollerboards, escalators, and long walks, not to mention having to load bags to the overhead compartment. Keith and Cam had their hands full just trying to keep their grandparents walking in a straight line. They settled into their seats sitting two-by-two with the boys sitting directly behind George and Thelma, where they could keep an eye on things. Miraculously, it turned out to be an uneventful flight except for George's midflight visit to the bathroom. Cameron escorted George to the rear of the plane, making sure he was able to get into the bathroom without falling.

Cameron patiently waited outside the folding bathroom door by chatting with the two attractive flight attendants. George emerged with his fly unzipped and water stains down the front of his pants. At least Cameron hoped they were water stains.

"Cam, those stewardesses have nice posture!" George remarked as Cam smiled.

At the Tampa airport, Stu and Elaine awaited anxiously to see the mental and physical condition of the expedition party. Cameron and Keith had never been so excited to see their parents.

"Tag, you're it!" Cam joked. "These guys are a lot of work." The boys survived their first experience tending to the elderly and it shook them to their core. "Mom, Dad, you guys better have a plan before you get to this point."

"Oh don't worry, we won't do this to you guys," Elaine said. The group made their way to baggage claim, the parking garage and finally the forty-five minute drive back to the house. Cam and Keith quickly disappeared into the night with friends, ready for some relief from their weekend of adult responsibilities. Stu and Elaine assumed the role of caretakers, not realizing just how involved it was going to be.

Elaine settled them into the first-floor bedroom, knowing the staircase up to the guest room would be trouble for George. In the past, they had always used the guest suite overlooking the water with a private bath, but things were changing. By 7:00 am the next morning, Stu and Elaine prepared for work. Cam was heading back up to Orlando for school, Keith was needed at high school and George and Thelma were slowly waking up. Elaine ventured down the hallway towards her office, when she stepped on soggy carpet in front of the bathroom.

"What the hell?" She stopped in her tracks to figure out where the water was coming from. Clearly it had seeped from the bathroom. Lifting her drenched stocking feet with an air of disgust, she followed the trail of water deep into the bathroom until she found the source. Someone had overstuffed the toilet with what looked to be an excessive amount of toilet paper, consequently creating an overflow of dirty water. "Oh my God! I can't believe I have to deal with this first thing on a Monday morning. Stu? Stu! Stu get over here and help clean this up." He came running at the sound of her desperation.

"Jesus, this is disgusting. What happened?" he asked.

"Your parents."

George and Thelma were slowly waking up in the bedroom next door to all the commotion. They popped their heads out of the door just in time to be bombarded with questions formed in frustration.

"What on earth happened in the bathroom?" Elaine asked as calmly as possible. "There's water all the way down the bathroom floor into the hallway. Didn't you notice the toilet wasn't flushing well?"

"Oh, Elaine, I'm sorry. I think I tried to flush one of my Depends." Thelma did not appear to be overly concerned or embarrassed. Elaine was at a loss for words. What could she say? Stu and Elaine promptly cleaned up the water, disinfected the floor and strategically placed a couple of fans to dry the carpet. They both finally left for work, but not before leaving strict instructions on how to flush a toilet and to please use a different bathroom. George and Thelma were officially on their own for the day.

Without a vehicle at their disposal, trips to the store were out of the question, and without the physical ability to walk far, venturing across the bridge to stroll the beach was also a no go. Elaine had left a quiche Lorraine, Thelma's recipe, in the refrigerator along with a freshly brewed pot of coffee. George did not eat quiche; he loved the joke from the 70's, *real men don't eat quiche*. This left him on his own as far as food went. Thelma assembled a breakfast of quiche, black coffee and an assortment of pills. The process took nearly an hour to complete with another hour for getting dressed and making the bed. George rummaged through the kitchen until he found a box of cereal and poured himself a cup of coffee, heavy on the cream and sugar. He quickly settled in for a day of TV. Thelma wandered out to the screened porch and settled herself into a wicker chair. From this position she was content to sit and watch the activity on the intracoastal.

Boats filled with tanned people laughing and drinking as music wafted over the water was a common sight. There were yachts motoring at a crawl due to the *No Wake* zone, steered by gray-haired men with brightly colored shirts and big bellies. Thelma watched as dolphins occasionally swam near the dock, and listened as seagulls created a cacophony. George remained parked in the chair in front of the television. Late in the afternoon Stu arrived home after a long day of working to find his parents quietly still sitting in their respective spots.

"Hey guys, how was your day?" Stu asked. "What did you do all day?"

"Oh, not too much Stu," his mother said. "I sat on the porch and watched all the excitement. Your father watched you know what all day." Thelma rose from her spot on the porch and moved toward the kitchen. Stu wondered if they had indeed just sat there all day doing nothing.

"Elaine and I thought it would be nice to go out to dinner with Keith, and Ken said he'd meet us. I think Marie and the boys might also join us. What do you feel like having for dinner?" Stu looked through a pile of mail. "Hey look, here's another American Express bill addressed to George B. MacCollom. What surprises did you purchase this month?"

"I don't remember buying anything," George responded, while twirling a half-chewed cigar in his mouth with his right hand. A few bits of dottle stuck to his lower lip. He was unconcerned. Stu slowly tore open the Amex bill for increased dramatic effect.

"$587.16! What the hell did you buy for $587?" Stu scanned the bill to find his answer. "You actually bought a Bose Stereo? Why? You guys have trouble playing a DVD. And when was the last time you guys listened to music other than Johnny Cash in the car? Did you order it over the phone, like all the other stuff you've bought?"

"Your mother mentioned she wants to listen to music, and I always like to make her happy," George grinned. "I ordered it over the phone after I saw the ad on TV. I thought it was a good idea."

"OK," Stu said. "Tell me who is going to hook it up for you? Who is going to put the CDs in for you, and who is going to teach you how to use it? Also, if the television is on 24/7, when will Mom ever be able to listen to music?"

"She can listen to it in the bedroom," George answered quickly, not having thought through his purchase. Stu dropped it for the time being but worried about future purchases. Ken was still fighting with Oreck over the air filter George had purchased where the company was claiming he still owed hundreds of dollars on a payment plan, which included an extended warranty. No one even knew where the air filter was at this point. Stu had taken over the finances when they first entered assisted living, and it was proving to be a bigger job than anticipated.

They ventured to a local seafood restaurant, where the group assembled around the table with a few of them jockeying for the position at the end of the table. Drinks were ordered with the usual drama over Thelma's Manhattan. When the waitress arrived with drinks, she placed two drinks in front of everyone, informing the group it was a two-for-one happy hour. Ken and Elaine were seated on either side of Thelma and quickly made eye contact. They both had the same thought; Thelma could not handle two Manhattans. She would be loopy after only one drink, carrying on about how awful life was at Champlain Waters in a voice loud enough to carry across the entire restaurant. It was also when her anger made an appearance. This was all new behavior with the onset of dementia.

As soon as Thelma was looking the other way, Ken stealthily slid the second cocktail just behind a vase of flowers, out of sight from Thelma. She never missed it. Thelma held the menu upside down as Elaine explained her options for dinner, limiting it to two choices. She decided on veal marsala with a bowl of the house soup; roasted garlic. George ordered a steak, medium-rare with a salad drenched with blue cheese dressing and a mound of garlic mashed potatoes. He never failed to order an entree which required an additional set of hands to cut, crack open or break apart. Stu had the honor of cutting George's meat tonight. The evening ended with a round of chocolate desserts for everyone. Thelma had barely eaten five bites of her veal, but devoured the chocolate mousse cake. The entire family was a tribe of chocoholics.

When the kids were young, Thelma cooked homemade meals every night which always included dessert. More often than not, chocolate was involved. A few favorites among the kids were chocolate pudding with Cool Whip, chocolate cake with chocolate frosting and whoopie pies. With four kids and a chocolate addiction, these desserts never lasted more than a day.

Ken and Marie said their goodbyes in the parking lot as Stu and Elaine ushered George and Thelma to the car, buckled them in and closed the doors before hopping in. Keith had taken a separate car for a quick getaway. Back home, Stu parked the Tahoe in the driveway to allow more space to maneuver his parents out of the vehicle. The driveway was at an incline, making it awkward for George to easily step out. Both Stu and Elaine hurried over to his side, where they instructed him how to carefully place his feet while they positioned themselves to catch him in the event of a fall. He was a little unsteady after having two cocktails. With their attention on George, they did not notice Thelma struggling to get out of the backseat. As she stepped down from the Tahoe, a combination of the driveway being at an odd angle, and her being unsteady after one cocktail, she lost her balance and fell flat onto the driveway. The sudden thud caught Stu and Elaine's attention, who had their hands full holding up George. Elaine quickly moved over to Thelma where she lay on the pavement, awake but struggling to get to her feet.

"Thelma, just sit here for a minute. Are you OK? Does anything hurt?" Elaine squatted next to her as she checked out her mother-in-law, praying to God the hip wasn't broken.

"Oh, I didn't know the step down was so far and I just lost my balance. I think I hit my head when I fell." Thelma rubbed the side of her skull. Elaine carefully felt her scalp and detected the beginning of a nice egg. Stu guided George into the house as quickly as he could but it was the speed of a sloth on Xanax. Elaine gently wrapped her arms around Thelma and lifted her to a standing position. By this time Stu had returned to help escort his mother inside.

"Once we're inside let's get some ice on your head and get you settled in the chair." Elaine noticed Thelma starting to shake as they eased her up the walkway towards the house. Stu and Elaine glanced at each other with silent head shakes. George was already relaxing with his feet up. His concern for his wife was underwhelming, but this also was new behavior since the stroke. The bump on Thelma's head proved to be minor, but the fall in the driveway could have been serious. It was now crystal clear to Stu and Elaine, as well as everyone else, that living on their own away from family was not a viable option.

The following morning the crew, including Ken, made an excursion to Whispering Oaks to have a look and lunch in the dining room to sample the cuisine. The Tahoe drove down the palm-lined entrance to the lushly landscaped complex of five buildings. Each building was assigned a name designed to trigger calming peaceful images: *Whispering Oaks, Bay Breeze, Palm Oasis, Sunshine Village and Gulf Waters.* The five-story buildings had pale gray stucco, ample widows, screened balconies and people in varying states of mobility. Each building offered a different level of care, from independent living to skilled nursing. Whispering Oaks offered assisted living. Stu parked in the far corner of the parking lot under the shade of an oak tree after dropping the group at the front entrance. The entrance to Whispering Oaks welcomed visitors with floral cushioned chairs, sofas and tables in the outdoor seating area. It made for a nice first impression.

"So Mom," Ken asked. "What do you think so far? Better than Champlain Waters, the prison we sent you to?" Ken was trying to get a reaction from his mother.

"Oh, I hate it there. You just don't understand what we have to put up with there, you just don't get it. I hope you never have to go through what we're going through. These aren't the Golden Years Ken, they're the tarnished years. That's what my brother Richard always says, and he is so right." Thelma continued her diatribe but it fell upon deaf ears. They had all heard it a hundred times before.

George was excited to see the large blue handicapped button outside the entrance. He lifted his cane and pushed it, watching the double front doors open on cue, releasing a burst of air-conditioned breeze. They all entered the two-story foyer and made their way to the front desk. Just like all other assisted living facilities, they had to sign in. They were greeted by the manager, a woman in her 50's who appeared to have lost interest in exercise but was dressed nicely, and quickly put the group at ease. They toured Whispering Oaks, viewing several apartments, both one-bedroom and two-bedrooms equipped with two bathrooms and a screened balcony. They also toured *The 4th Floor,* known as the Alzheimer's unit. Thelma was not pleased to be touring this floor.

"I don't know why we're looking at this floor. These people are all crazy and they're mumbling to themselves, they're hunched over and they look like zombies," Thelma announced, not caring who overheard. "I certainly hope you're not thinking of putting us here. I know this is the floor where all the crazies go!"

"We're just getting a tour of the whole facility Mom," assured Ken. They found themselves seated at a large round table in the dining room on the main floor. Several waitresses dressed in black pants and white collared shirts scurried about taking orders and delivering meals. If one didn't know better, it resembled a restaurant. The daily lunch special was a Greek pita with chicken, feta, tomatoes and tzatziki. George opted for the trifecta of tuna, egg and chicken salad, each mounded separately on a bed of lettuce. Thelma ordered a tuna sandwich and bowl of tomato soup while the others ordered the special. Beverage options were limited to water, iced tea or juice. Everyone at the table decided to live dangerously and ordered cranberry juice.

Following lunch they gathered back in the manager's office to discuss questions and availability. George's main concern was access to his vehicle, but he was reassured the Explorer would be available. Thelma questioned whether or not she could dispense her own medications. The manager diplomatically explained that would be determined by staff and family, leaving Thelma less than satisfied. Availability was not a problem as a two-bedroom apartment in the assisted living building, Whispering Oaks, would be available in one month. The price tag for the monthly rent and partial assistance was steep, but George and Thelma had a nice pension and had taken out long-term care insurance years earlier. They left Whispering Oaks for Stu's house for the debrief, and to feel out George and Thelma.

Stu grilled a heaping bowl of gulf shrimp doused in butter and garlic while everyone was enjoying a cocktail. "So what did you think about Whispering Oaks? Can you see yourselves living down here in the warm sunshine with your family nearby?" Stu prodded.

"It's not Monkton," remarked George. Stu understood his father would never be excited about living anywhere but his precious orchard. George was not one to complain or be negative; instead he would remain silent. He took to heart the advice his grandmother had dispensed: *If you don't have anything nice to say, don't say anything.* Thelma was cut from a different cloth. Although she had always been a kind and loving mother and wife, she did not hold back her opinion on things. She initially liked the idea of living in warm sunny Florida, she liked the idea of the spacious light-filled apartment, she liked the idea of being close to her sons and grandkids, and she liked the idea of their friends coming down to visit Florida. After all, there was an extra bedroom. Ken pointed out that being so close by, only twenty minutes to either his or Stu's house, they could easily dine out once or twice a week. Thelma loved to dine out, especially if linen napkins and knowledgeable bartenders were part of the mix. Amazingly, her comments were all positive.

It took no real convincing to hear George and Thelma agree to move to Florida. It was proposed as a trial move, but everyone knew there would be no other moves except perhaps to a facility with increased care. Since the night of the stroke, they had moved home to Monkton from rehab, a miserable two-month stay in Maine they still viewed as a kidnapping, a temporary failed move back to Monkton, a move to Champlain Waters, a second move within Champlain Waters and now a move to Florida. This had all been in less than two years. Everyone was tired and the changes were becoming increasingly difficult for Thelma.

The next few days passed without incident while George and Thelma enjoyed the comfort of Stu and Elaine's home and the therapeutic sunshine. They were able to spend time watching Keith play basketball, they were able to watch Connor and Duncan, Ken's two boys, perform in a school play and they enjoyed numerous meals out with Stu, Elaine and Ken. Karen had not been able to join them as she had just started a new job in Gainesville. Cam and Keith begged their parents not to send them back to Vermont for the return trip. Stu figured he could recruit Ken or Karen to escort the dynamic duo down to Florida. They realized just how lucky they were not to be only children.

Chapter 9 God's Waiting Room

I went to look for my camouflaged duck boat but I couldn't find it.

"How are we getting to Florida?" Thelma asked Sue for the third time since arriving the night before.

"Remember I told you Karen is flying up here and will fly with you back down to Florida." Sue had driven over from Maine to help ready her parents for the move. "Karen will be here Wednesday afternoon, and she'll fly with you down to Tampa. Remember you're moving into a beautiful place called Whispering Oaks near Stu and Ken. It's going to be warm and sunny, and you'll be close to family, except me! But I'll come down as often as I can."

"Oh, I get so nervous lately. I tell you though, it will be good to be out of this hell hole," Thelma ranted. "The people who work here are horrible; they just walk into our apartment and think they can tell me what to do. I am so sick of everyone telling me what to do, and they won't even let me take my own medicine. They let George take his own medicine, and he had a stroke."

"I know Mom, but it's for your own good because you were mixing up your meds and getting confused. This way you don't have to worry about it." Sue tried to reason with her mother but gave up. "Let's go to your room and go through all your jewelry to separate it into the good stuff and the not-so-special stuff. When you fly down to Florida, Karen will carry your good jewelry so it doesn't get lost or stolen."

"I think the people here have been stealing my jewelry," Thelma announced.

"Why do you say that Mom?" Sue asked as she dumped out a massive tangle of beads, earrings and bracelets onto the bed.

"Well, I haven't seen my mother's gold beads in a long time. I think they stole them."

"OK, then let's go through all your jewelry before you start accusing people. I bet they're just stuck somewhere or hidden in one of your jewelry boxes. What do you have, like fifteen of them?" Sue handed her mother a pile of tangled necklaces to work on while she gathered the menagerie of jewelry boxes. They worked for nearly two hours before the tangled mess had some semblance of order. They discovered the treasured gold beads carefully wrapped in a purple Crown Royal bag, and Thelma felt no remorse for her earlier accusations. They placed the pile of jewels to be hand-transported into a cloth satchel Karen could easily fit in her suitcase or carry-on bag. In the collection were special pieces George had given her over the years, a few sentimental pieces from her mother and several items bestowed from a cranky old neighbor. The old neighbor had adored Thelma because she had always been kind to her.

Thelma had always taken great pride in her appearance. For the times, she was stylish and had a petite figure, allowing her to wear almost anything. One time during the early 70's she managed to find enough money in their limited budget to purchase a brand new powder- blue polyester pantsuit from the high-end local department store, Abernathys. At the time, she thought she was the cat's meow. George had not been nearly as excited as Thelma about the pantsuit, because he felt women belonged in heels and skirts, not pants but Thelma often just ignored George. Coordinating the accessories was of the utmost importance. The earrings would have been clip-ons because Thelma was terrified of getting her ears pierced. The girls had tried to convince their mother to allow them to get their ears pierced, but Thelma regarded piercings on the same level as tattoos.

Sue carefully placed the satchel of jewels on top of the refrigerator to prevent Thelma from unpacking them. Sue also compiled a list for Karen on what needed to be carried with them and where to find it in the apartment.

The whole packing process became a game of cat and mouse, hiding things from her mother when she wasn't looking. When Thelma had moments of clarity and inquired about certain items, Sue simply changed the subject. They went out to dinner one last time before Sue headed back to Maine and Karen arrived.

Sue felt a chapter of her own life was ending. Her parents would no longer be living in Burlington, so there would be no reason to make the trek from Maine to Vermont on a regular basis. There was no other family in Vermont as all their extended family were spread across the country. George's family was from Massachusetts and Thelma's was from Ithaca, New York. All of Sue's siblings were in Florida.

Karen arrived late the following afternoon on a choppy flight from Charlotte, NC. She breathed a sigh of relief as soon as the wheels touched down, but quickly remembered George had insisted on picking her up. Descending the escalator into the airport lobby, she noticed an old couple. It gave her pause because it was her parents, they looked so old and frail. Intellectually she knew her parents were aging, but to witness it after not seeing them for a few months was shocking.

Smiling, Karen approached them with her arms outstretched and hugged them. "Hi honey," Thelma said. "It's so good to see you."

"Give me your bags," George chirped.

"I'm good Dad, but thanks." She knew there was no way he could manage his cane, walking and toting luggage, but he liked to think he could still do it. Karen quickly volunteered for driving duty back to Champlain Waters.

"So are you all packed?" Karen inquired. "Sue said everything you need for the initial part of the trip is packed. Our flight tomorrow is early, 7:30 am, so we'll need to be out of here by 6:00 am."

"What about all our things?" Thelma asked.

"Cameron is supposed to fly up here with friends in a couple weeks and drive the Explorer down. We'll have movers move all the big furniture." Karen entered the apartment and saw no visible signs of an impending move. She wondered what her sister had accomplished because clearly nothing was ready to go. Taped to the refrigerator was a note indicating where the bag of jewels was hidden, where the two packed suitcases were hidden and where to find the new wheeled carry-on bag. Karen verified the jewels were in the wicker basket on top of the fridge but the suitcases remained open, heaped with a jumble of clothes in the spare bedroom.

"I thought Sue already helped you pack?" Karen was in disbelief. "I thought you guys were all set to go?" She now knew it was not going to be a relaxing night.

"Oh, I thought she asked me to pack." Thelma said. " I found the suitcases under the bed and I don't know why Sue put them there because I had a hard time getting them out. My back really hurts now."

"Where are my guns?" George asked abruptly. "Does Norm still have them? I want them back and I want them in Florida."

"Dad, your guns are here in this apartment right where they've been for months. Cameron will drive them down to Florida when he brings the Explorer, because the movers are not allowed to transport firearms," explained Karen. "And by the way, Norm never stole your guns. He was safeguarding them for you, and you really owe him an apology for the way you've accused him." George had no response.

Karen gave Sue a quick call. "Hey Sis, I thought you said you had them all packed ready to go, it sure as hell doesn't look like it." Sue heard the frustration in her sister's voice.

"Just a little advice Karen, pace yourself. Mom has a tendency to unpack, move and rearrange things."

It was easy to believe Thelma had unpacked the suitcases, but it was a little surprising she had the strength to pull out the loaded suitcases from under the bed. Sue thought it was rather impressive. She explained to Karen everything else in the apartment did not need to be packed as the nice people from Anderson's Movers would once again come to the rescue.

Karen quickly repacked both suitcases for her parents while they watched the news in the other room. She gave strict orders not to touch either suitcase, and placed their traveling outfits on the bureau. Karen had a hankering for Bove's spaghetti and meatballs, a Burlington institution carrying fond memories from childhood. Often when the family had returned from a weekend road trip, George would make a run to Bove's for dinner. The usual take-out dinner was cardboard containers of spaghetti and meatballs with a side of bread and butter. Karen placed a call to Bove's and took Thelma with her to pick up the dinner while George held down the fort.

Karen slept, but not well. Like most people before an early morning flight, she worried about oversleeping or missing the plane with her parents in tow. When the obnoxious buzzing started at 5:00 am, she was already awake. She arose without thought, jumped in the shower and packed before rousing her parents. They were both out cold and it took several minutes of prodding and coaxing to get them moving. She busied herself in the kitchen brewing a pot of coffee and readying the array of pills for her mother.

"Good Morning Mom. Are you all ready for our adventure today?" She handed a mug of black coffee to her mother. "Oh my God Mom, what do you have on your feet?"

"I have shoes on, what do you think I have on my feet?" Thelma answered indignantly. On her right foot was a white lace-up shoe Karen had laid out and on her left foot was a large black dress shoe clearly belonging to George. Karen felt her stress level rise and almost decided to just let it be, but understood Thelma could not travel with a shoe five sizes too big on her left foot. It would be inconvenient and embarrassing for all of them.

"Well, say goodbye to Champlain Waters. You probably won't ever be back here," Karen announced.

"Good riddance, but I'd rather be moving back to Monkton," George said.

"Well I won't miss this dump. I am so thrilled to be leaving and to be going somewhere warm." Thelma fumbled with the seatbelt in the backseat of the taxi.

"Jet Blue," Karen directed when they approached the airport departure lane. It really didn't matter what airline, as the airport was small and all entrances led to the same counter. Karen had to extricate herself first before helping her mother out of the cab. Once Thelma was safely on the curb with instructions to stay put, she went back to the passenger's door to help her father. He required someone to have his belt in a death grip to prevent falling as he stepped up over the curb. It was 5:45 am and Karen was already exhausted.

Karen's heart sank when she saw the security line winding its way through a maze of adjustable poles at this early hour. Glancing at her watch she realized they would have just enough time if the line continued to move. She prayed her parents could endure the long wait. Luckily they moved slowly but steadily until they reached the TSA officer standing at the podium directing the already weary travelers to the appropriate scanning line. Karen handed over their three boarding passes and licenses waiting for the okay. They were directed to the x-ray line while Karen juggled her purse, the carry-on and her parents.

"Mom, you have to take off your shoes and place them in the basket. Dad, you're supposed to take off your shoes too, but there is no way we can manage that here. Just stick with me." Karen bent to untie her mother's shoes, and watched the queue grow longer behind them. Luckily people were aware she had her hands full.

"Why do we have to do this? The floor is dirty, I think this is disgusting!" Thelma remarked but followed orders. Karen placed the clear bag of toiletries in the bins along with their shoes, sweater and belt. She gently guided her mother towards the x-ray machine and breathed easier once she had made it through. George went next with his shoes and belt still on when the alarm sounded, startling Thelma.

"What did you find inside me? You know I have a few bionic parts holding me together," joked George, but the humor was lost on TSA.

"Step aside sir."

Karen quickly passed through her x-ray exam but was now faced with a dilemma; stay near George or follow Thelma. She glanced at George, who was being instructed to remove his shoes and raise his arms while Thelma looked confused. Karen made a quick decision.

"Can you please hold my mother's hand while I attend to my father?" Karen did not wait for the TSA agent to respond and moved next to George.

George was amused with the whole process, "you know I might be going commando today!"

"Sir, raise your arms," directed the TSA agent who was wearing a dark blue polyester uniform at least one size too small for his doughy body. George grinned as he raised his right arm, but the left arm only moved about an inch.

"Excuse me," snipped Karen. "My father had a stroke and cannot raise his arm. Can't you just wand him?"

"Ma'am, please step back while I do my job." Karen glanced over at her mother who was holding hands with an impatient looking TSA agent. George was wanded, but his artificial knee set off alarms before he was free to proceed.

"Ma'am, can you please take your mother now, I have a job to do." After ten minutes of tying shoes and fastening belts, they made their way to the gate with nine minutes to spare.

"I have to use the bathroom," George announced. Karen looked skyward as she nodded her okay.

"You know," Thelma whispered. "I should really try to go before I get on the plane. You know those bathrooms on the plane are gross." Karen waited for George to exit the bathroom where she could keep an eye on the gate. Missing the plane was not an option. George exited with his fly zipped and shirt tucked in. Karen sat him directly across from the women's restroom and left him to guard the carry-ons while she escorted Thelma to the bathroom. They emerged just as their zone was being called to board. They followed a young mother with a five-year-old and a screaming toddler on her hip. Karen prayed they were not sitting near this family. George was placed in the window seat, Thelma the middle seat and Karen in the aisle seat to help corral her parents. The young family continued to the back of the plane.

Had it been an hour later, Karen would have ordered a drink, but she figured 6:30 am was a tad early to start drinking. She pulled out her new Jodi Picoult book and kept her fingers crossed that her parents would sleep. She had a fleeting thought of drugging them.

The remainder of the flight went as smoothly as anyone could have hoped: no delays, no meltdowns and no lost parents. Stu and Elaine met them at the airport with hugs.

"Oh my God! I am NEVER doing that again," Karen ranted. " I am so exhausted right now, I feel like I was in charge of a preschool class for a week. These guys are not moving again or if they do, I am not helping."

"You are coming to our house for the night, right?" Elaine asked.

"I am so overwhelmed and tired, I think I'm just going to drive home now, but thanks," Karen said.

"That's crazy Karen, just stay with us tonight and you can leave early tomorrow. You really shouldn't be driving if you're that tired," Stu chimed in. Karen made up her mind and said her goodbyes after handing over the satchel of jewels and folder of paperwork. "At least stop for some coffee and be careful." Stu and Elaine gave her a weary hug.

Elaine settled the duo into the first-floor bedroom once again. They would be staying with Stu and Elaine for about three weeks until their apartment was ready at Whispering Oaks. Stu and Elaine both worked in the morning, but Keith had the day off due to a teacher workshop day so he would be in charge.

"Morning Gramps! Morning Gram! Sorry I missed you last night but I had a basketball tournament and I got home late." He hugged his grandparents, "so you guys are officially Floridians now, huh?"

"Oh, we're just checking it out, Keith. The warm weather will be good for your grandmother, but we'll be back in Vermont at some point." Keith didn't say anything.

"What do you guys want to do today? I can take you out on the boat." Keith forgot just how little mobility his grandparents now had.

"Oh, no thanks," Thelma said." I'm not going on the boat and I don't think George is very steady on his feet."

"What are you talking about Thel? I'm a regular Fred Astaire, I'm so light on my feet."

"Who's Fred Astaire?" asked Keith. He finally understood entertaining his grandparents required staying close to home, watching movies, eating and perhaps a game of cards later. He fried up a pound of bacon, a half dozen eggs and did his best to brew a pot of coffee. George and Thelma were tickled by his efforts. They spent the day watching a trio of movies: *The Dark Knight*, *Taken* and *Quantum of Solace*. George was enthralled, while Thelma napped and Keith played on his phone.

Stu arrived back home by 4 pm with several pounds of gulf shrimp destined for the grill. He had invited Ken and family to join them for dinner and a game of Hearts later on. George had trouble holding his cards due to the stroke, but managed to place his cards in the crack of the dining room table. Thelma was dealt into the game, although her ability to follow along was greatly diminished. There was a long family tradition of competitive Hearts. An outsider might view it as a family feud where arguments and questions of integrity were frequent.

"Who has the two of clubs?" Keith asked, trying to keep the game moving. Thelma fumbled with her cards and placed the two in the center. Keith was seated next to his grandmother and resorted to leaning in to assist her. She insisted she was quite capable of dealing the next hand. It took long enough that everyone had time to use the bathroom and refresh their drinks.

"OK, remember we're passing two cards to the right," Ken said, having to repeat this each hand. They played through the hand until there were only two cards left in each player's hand, everyone except Thelma. She had three cards left and Ken was set up to take zero points.

"Mom, why do you have three cards left?" Stu asked.

"I don't know, someone dealt them to me."

"Well, it's a misdeal and by the way, you dealt them!"

"What!" Ken said. "That's the third time tonight and I had a great hand. This is bullshit! Mom, you've got to pay attention," Ken half joked. Thelma was unconcerned by her lack of ability to play the game properly.

In her younger days, Thelma was an accomplished card player, especially bridge. She belonged to several bridge clubs where women met at each other's homes once a month. They were free to gossip, chat and socialize without their husbands or children. She and George also belonged to a bridge club for couples. When she hosted the bridge groups, she would pull out her wooden snack bowls shaped like a club, a heart, a diamond and a spade. The typical treats were nuts, non-pareils or some sort of chocolate covered nuts. The kids always tried to sneak a few tidbits without getting caught.

The game ended with Keith as champion. He proudly placed the scoresheet on the front of the refrigerator with a magnet. There were cries of questionable plays and misdeals. Keith smiled and savored his victory.

George and Thelma fell into a routine of hanging around the house, watching television or sitting on the porch for the next few weeks. Stu and Elaine both had to work, Keith had school and Ken dropped by when his schedule allowed. Elaine had two girls working for her who were in and out of the house and were able to keep an eye on the duo.

Elaine arrived home one afternoon with a mountain of paperwork requiring immediate attention. She headed towards the office and as she passed the bathroom entrance, her feet made an unmistakable squishing sound.

"Ahhh, Shit! Not again!" Elaine placed her plastic tote loaded with paperwork on the office floor and returned to the crime scene. Upon inspection of the toilet, she noticed a large amount of toilet paper balled up and engorged with water. A steady stream of water flowed into the hallway once again soaking the carpet. She placed an armful of towels onto the carpet and decided to leave the rest for Stu.

"As soon as your parents move into Whispering Oaks, we're putting in wood floors," announced Elaine. "I think they've overflowed the toilet three times since they arrived two weeks ago. Today there was a surprise floating in the mess!"

"Fine, we'll get them moved in this weekend and then we'll deal with flooring. I can't even think about it until we move them," Stu said.

Moving day arrived, again, with torrential downpours and moments of brilliant sunshine. Stu decided to have Keith stay home with George and Thelma while Elaine, Ken and he met the movers to set up the apartment. It was just easier that way. With all their recent moving experience, the process was completed in less than three hours. They figured George and Thelma would want a few things rearranged, but for now it was move-in ready. Stu loved his parents and felt a twinge of guilt over his relief that they were moving out..

"OK Mom, here we are at Whispering Oaks," Ken said. "You can sit out here with your new friends and people-watch. Dad, you can sit out here watching for women with good posture." They had been quiet on the drive over, and Ken understood all this moving was taking a toll.

"All I see are old women on scooters wearing Depends, and old men with swollen legs and white socks," commented George.

"How do you know they're wearing Depends?" asked Stu.

"Their bottoms are puffy."

"What, you're suddenly a bottom expert?" Ken asked.

"I've been known to check out a few asses in my time," George replied.

Thelma was quiet as they were greeted by the manager whom they had met on an earlier visit. She rode the elevator up to the fifth floor with the group, chatting about all the perks of living in such a fine facility. She rattled off numerous activities: singalongs, games, jigsaw puzzles, arts & crafts and discussion groups, among numerous other options. Something for everyone. Thelma tried to look excited, but this was their third assisted living facility and she knew the drill.

The elevator stopped at The 4th Floor, letting off an attendant. Thelma immediately became interested in The 4th Floor, knowing full well this was the memory unit, the place of her nightmares. She was becoming more aware of her mental decline, which triggered panic attacks. She had them under control with medication, but there were times her future simply overwhelmed her. Her own mother had suffered from dementia towards the end, and Thelma clearly remembered being yelled at, sworn at and even having a glass of Coke thrown at her. This was not what her mother had been prior to dementia.

They paraded down the long corridor, passing doors adorned with plastic wreaths or kitschy plaques offering a glimmer of the person residing inside. They arrived at apartment 523 with a name plate already in place, and a wreath of dried purple flowers hanging from the door. Sadly, the plastic insect had been lost in the move. Entering the apartment they were greeted with a wall of windows allowing sunlight to drench the room. The kitchen had a stove, dishwasher and full refrigerator, while the living area was arranged with a sofa and George's nasty recliner facing the large TV. There were bedrooms on either side of the living room, both equipped with a full bathroom and a screened balcony off the guest room.

"What do you think, Mom?" Stu said. "There's more room than you had at Champlain Waters and you've got a nice view from up here."

"Oh, it's very nice. It's hard getting used to all these changes you know."

"The cable's all hooked up so you won't miss your news, Dad." They moved a few things around to suit George and Thelma before settling in for happy hour.

"Dinner is from 4:30-6:30 downstairs in the dining room, so I thought we could eat there tonight," Ken suggested. "We'll join you so we can all check it out. It's 4:45 now so when we finish our drinks we can head down."

"4:30?" Thelma was not sounding pleased. "Who eats at 4:30? We used to eat at 7 or 8 when we lived in Monkton. We used to joke about the old people who wanted to catch the early-bird specials."

"Just think, you won't have to cook or clean up. You can just enjoy the meal," Elaine said.

"Oh please, we've been through this at that other place, the food was horrible and the servers were rude," Thelma said.

They made the trek from apartment 523 to the dining room. While waiting for the elevator, Thelma looked out over the white roof.

"Oh, look at the beautiful snow out there." The others all looked at each other.

"Hey, Mom," Ken said. "We're in Florida, that's just the white roof of the building." Thelma ignored him as the elevator doors opened. They waited while a small elderly woman in a scooter made a nine-point turn to get off the elevator. Stu held the door with his hand to prevent the doors from closing prematurely and squashing the determined lady. Descending to the dining room, the elevator made a stop at the third floor to pick up three residents; two with walkers and one with a cane. The elevator trip took thirteen and a half minutes.

Chapter 10 Tragedy
I don't like anything of a soupy nature.

George and Thelma slowly settled into their new normal at Whispering Oaks adjusting to their new surroundings. Unlike Champlain Waters, Whispering Oaks included assistance in the form of attendants stopping into the apartment at all hours. A cleaning crew of two stopped in daily to empty trash, clean the bathrooms, make the bed and remove dirty laundry. Nurses stopped in to check on the two of them, a counselor popped in to chat, the manager, activities director and others popped in for a myriad of reasons. Thelma found it unnerving to have different people in and out of her apartment and tried her best to be pleasant; something that was once her innate personality was becoming increasingly difficult for her.

"Hey Thelma, how's my sweetheart today?" Cookie was a petite black woman with a gentle soul, perfect for dealing with Thelma's new prickly personality. "You need to go down to the nurses' station for your morning meds," Cookie reminded her as she gave Thelma a warm embrace.

"Oh Cookie, why can't I take my own pills? George is allowed to take his own pills. You people all treat me like I'm incapable of doing anything. I really resent this, you know! I'm so sick of everyone telling me what to do."

"Thelma honey, hold my hand and I'll walk down with you, because I've got to visit Ethel on the second floor. Besides sweetie, you don't need the trouble figuring out all those pills. Let someone else do it for you." Cookie had a knack for soothing Thelma.

"I'll miss you Thel!" George called out. Thelma ignored him.

The nurses station was a large counter situated in front of a bank of generic tan metal filing cabinets chock full of medical charts and ever-changing medical directions for the residents. Residents had the option of visiting the nurse's station for their pills, blood pressure and blood sugar checks if families deemed it necessary. Several upholstered chairs arranged in a haphazard manner sat near the counter for the residents while they waited on their vast quantities of pharmaceuticals.

Cookie delivered Thelma to the pill station seating her next to Gil, a feisty woman in a wheelchair who smoked, drank and swore. Thelma's face was pinched, ready for a fight.

"Hey, you take any good drugs this morning?" Gil asked Thelma, trying to break the ice and stir things up.

"Oh, I don't know what they're giving me. I don't know why I can't just take my own pills."

"I haven't seen you around before, are you new?" Gil asked. "I've been here for over a year when my son dumped me in this prison because he didn't want me living in his house any longer. Can you imagine, throwing out your own mother? I live on the third floor by myself and I'm always looking for a drinking buddy or a partner in crime."

"Now you're talking," replied Thelma. "George and I love to have a drink before dinner, you should come up later today."

"I'd love to! What's your apartment number?" asked Gil.

"Ahh shit, I don't remember. I think it's on the fifth floor and our name is on the door, *George and Thelma MacCollom*." They continued to chat while waiting for the nurse to attend to them. Fifteen minutes had passed before a male nurse, lacking any sign of a personality, approached both of them with paper cups filled with water and miniature paper cups filled with a variety of medications. Thelma was handed her inhaler; she inspected it before she placed it in her mouth. She was confused about her next step. The male nurse grabbed the inhaler from her and wound the dial before roughly handing it back to her without a word.

"What a bastard he is," said Thelma. "I bet he's not even a real nurse."

"You can bet your sweet ass he's not going to wipe my ass," Gil added. Thelma laughed, and returned to apartment 523 in a much improved mood having met a new friend.

Cameron had recently delivered the Explorer to Florida after the excursion to Vermont with friends that took them skiing at Killington for a week. The Explorer carried the collection of the alleged stolen guns and odd items the movers considered illegal or too questionable to transport. It was decided to leave the Explorer at Whispering Oaks even though it was a widely- held view George should not be driving. No one had put their foot down yet.

Ken arrived one day with the keys to the Explorer and a trunk full of weapons. Although guns were forbidden at assisted living facilities for good reason, no one in Florida wanted the responsibility of the guns or George's scorn. Ken placed the guns in an old ratty wool blanket, wrapping them like a baby in a papoose and nonchalantly strolled through the lobby towards apartment 523.

"Look what I've got Dad!" Ken said as he ceremoniously revealed the guns. "Fresh off the boat from Vermont."

"How'd you get the guns away from Norm?" George asked.

"They've been in your apartment at Champlain Waters for months." Ken decided not to beat a dead horse and placed the guns under the bed. He carefully positioned them to prevent either parent from easily reaching them. He suddenly remembered it wasn't a problem because the second something was out of sight, it was out of mind. Not to mention, neither one of them was capable of bending or squatting that far down. There was no ammunition, so no accidental shootings. Ken ducked out at the first available moment.

"Hey Gramps, hey Gram! Love you guys," Keith pronounced as he entered the apartment. He occasionally stopped by on afternoons free of basketball practice and other school commitments. He especially loved stopping at the popcorn and ice cream machines in the lobby on his way up to the apartment. The refreshments were free to all visitors and residents, and Keith took full advantage. He hung out with his grandparents for an hour. George and Thelma were thrilled to have him there.

Stu and Ken found a rhythm for taking turns at Whispering Oaks during their lunch hour. Typical takeout fare was KFC, Firehouse Subs or pizza. They coordinated their visits a few days apart but also scheduled a weekly dinner out, and any interested family members were more than welcome to join. Thelma loved nothing better than dining out with family.

One Sunday afternoon in early April, Stu and Elaine were exhausted from the flooring remodel and decided to take a boating excursion to the American Legion. They did not ask George and Thelma, they simply picked them up and explained they were heading out on the boat. George required careful supervision boarding the boat as his confidence was far greater than his ability. No one wanted to fish him out of the intracoastal. Thelma was usually a little nervous on the boat, but Stu promised to motor at a leisurely pace where conversations could be had and hats did not fly off. Ken joined the group with nothing better to do on a lazy afternoon. They slowly motored, sipping from their to-go cups, until they reached the American Legion docks. The Legion had a sprawling deck perched over the water lined with tables, umbrellas and an older generation dancing to a live band. After nearly losing George off the dock, they made their way to the deck and snagged a table in the shade. Stu took drink orders and headed to the bar, as only members of the Legion were allowed to order drinks. The others perused the menu.

George watched the crowd, relaxed and happy to be out with his sons and in the company of fellow veterans. A group of spry but older women strutted by their table.

"You know," George announced. "I don't like gray haired women with red lipstick."

"Yeah, well I bet they don't like men with urine stains on their pants," Ken retorted. They all laughed.

Drinks and jokes flowed for the next several hours but Thelma was quiet. Elaine noticed since arriving in Florida, Thelma was quiet and withdrawn when out in a crowd. It was too overwhelming for her to process all the conversations and contribute, so she sat quietly but content. They tried to pull her into the conversations with limited success.

Stu and Elaine decided with Easter fast approaching and beautiful new floors installed, they would host the holiday dinner. Ken, Marie and the boys, George & Thelma plus Elaine's extended family would all be invited. The Friday evening before Easter, Stu and Elaine were enjoying a rare weekend evening home. Stu was watching basketball, Elaine was untangling Thelma's jewelry and Keith was hanging with his friends upstairs in his bedroom.

Around 10:30 pm, Keith's friend needed to return his car home because Florida law required teen drivers to be off the road by 11pm. The five boys departed Keith's bedroom littered with pizza boxes, soda bottles and paused the video game. They planned to walk back to Keith's through the neighborhood. A half hour later, Elaine received a phone call from one of Keith's classmates.

"Mrs. MacCollom, you need to come over here, there's been an accident."

"Why do I want to go see an accident?" Elaine asked.

"You just need to get over here."

Elaine did not understand but agreed to go over and asked Stu to join her. They drove the five blocks past quiet suburban homes to the scene. As she rounded the corner, she did not hear any sirens or see any strobing emergency lights, but saw a gathering of people. She saw the devastating remains of a smashed vehicle still smoldering, the angry destruction of a tree and then she saw the bodies sprawled on the road. One of the bodies was undeniably Keith. People were screaming and others were trying desperately to reach 911. Elaine stood alone feeling separate from her body, and in the distance she began to hear the cry of sirens. One of Keith's Nike basketball sneakers lay on its side about five feet from his body, still laced up and warm. She picked it up and watched as some woman attended to Keith. The paramedics arrived and placed Keith in the back of the ambulance. Stu felt vomit rise as the acrid smell from the burning car wafted through the crowd. Social media had informed the town of the accident well before the police arrived. Stu found Elaine and they held each other. No words were spoken as darkness engulfed them, paralyzed them and changed them forever.

Ken had missed about fifteen calls during the night, and with a feeling of dread he returned the call to receive the devastating news. Four of the five boys in the car were killed, and the fifth boy was in critical condition. It was only 6 am and Ken knew he could not allow his parents to learn about Keith via the morning news. He and Marie drove to Whispering Oaks, where they found George and Thelma still sleeping among twisted sheets. George and Thelma were confused by the early morning visit.

"Mom, Dad, we have some horrible news to tell you. Keith was killed in a car accident last night in Seminole." Ken waited for a reaction that never came. They stared at Ken and he repeated the news. Still they remained quiet but Thelma's mouth quivered.

"Oh my God," Thelma whispered, trying to make sense of it. George sat mute with a deep sadness in his eyes, never one to be over emotional. Ken and Marie sat encased in an awkward silence, so they moved in closer with a firm embrace as words were woefully inadequate. Ken waited for the questions that never came and looking at his parents he realized they were not the same people they had been just a couple years earlier. They did not fully comprehend the situation because they now lived in their own world. Ken and Marie made every effort to inform them and comfort them before leaving to deal with the unthinkable.

It was a parent's worst nightmare, a car full of teens and four out of five of them killed only five blocks from home. Over the next week arrangements were made for four different wakes, four different funerals and a memorial service at the high school. The town rallied around the grief-stricken families and friends. Stu and Elaine's vast network of friends engulfed them like a warm blanket.

With each passing hour, the weight of the truth became almost too much to bear. They expected Keith to come bounding through the front door and the next moment they were wracked with grief.

George and Thelma never talked about it. Stu and Elaine, somehow, continued their weekly visits but struggled with their emotions because George and Thelma could not or would not talk about it. Stu and Elaine craved and encouraged open dialogue about Keith, his friends and his life.

Chapter 11 The Boyfriend

You're as safe with me as if you were in the arms of Jesus!

Ken doubled his efforts visiting George and Thelma and dealing with Whispering Oaks, as Stu and Elaine were already dealing with a lot.

"Hello?" answered Thelma, holding the phone upside down to her ear.

"Hey Mom, it's Ken. MOM, turn the phone around so you can hear me." Ken was well practiced in this routine. "I'm just down the road and thought I'd bring you lunch, so do not go down to the dining room for lunch. OK? I'll be there in twenty minutes." Ken had stopped at Firehouse Subs stocking up on a variety of warm "fully engaged" subs, chips and Pepsi. With his arms loaded and only an hour for lunch, he hurried down the corridor towards apartment 523. He knocked and entered, only to discover an empty apartment.

"Mom? Dad?" He knew there was no one home. He took a deep breath, set the sandwiches on the counter and headed down to the dining room. As he entered the dining room he scanned the tables in search of his parents through a sea of gray-haired folks sitting amongst a wide assortment of scooters and walkers. He spotted them sitting with another couple, looking happy and engaged.

"Hey, I thought I told you I was heading up to your apartment with lunch," Ken said, amused that nothing ever went as planned.

"Oh, you meant today? I guess we forgot," Thelma said, unfazed by her lapse in memory.

"These are our new friends Norman and Edith, they live on the first floor."

"Hi, I'm Ken, their youngest son who they have a hard time listening to!" Ken gave up and joined them at the table. The waitress promptly took his order for a BLT and glass of cranberry juice, figuring he could bring the subs home for dinner. Ken noticed his parents were in an especially cheerful mood joking with Norman and Edith, telling stories and actually making plans to leave Whispering Oaks on an outing. They agreed that following dinner, Norman would take the foursome to Panera for coffee and dessert. Ken remembered a time, not that long ago, when his parents were out almost every evening with friends, and now a trip to Panera was an adventure. Observing his present company, he realized it just might be an adventure.

Later the next week Ken made his weekly parental check during the day when his legal work had him in the vicinity. He had not bothered to call ahead this time because he was only bringing a box of Frida's jelly donuts. These were the best jelly donuts this side of The Bakery Lane in Middlebury Vermont. During summers when Ken had worked for George in his lab at UVM, George and Ken split a half dozen jelly donuts and a quart of milk on more than one occasion.

Quietly knocking on the door he entered the apartment to find his father sitting in his recliner watching the History Channel for a change, when Thelma emerged from the bedroom. She was wearing only a thin black lacy slip accessorized with nylons and pumps.

"Wow Mom, that's an interesting outfit."

"What? What's wrong with what I'm wearing?" she asked.

"Well, you're only wearing a slip, and it's time to head downstairs for lunch."

"Why are you looking at me like that?" Thelma replied, taking Ken aback. He had no words. He glanced around the apartment, noticing numerous empty cocktail glasses and a bottle of Crown Royal half empty. Ken decided to keep quiet but it was evident they had been entertaining in the apartment the night before. Ken figured if they weren't driving anywhere and they were making friends, that was a big deal these days. He quickly tidied up the kitchen by placing glasses in the dishwasher and returning the Crown Royal to the cupboard.

"Hey Ken? Have you seen the clicker?" George asked. He appeared to be making a move to get out of his recliner. He fumbled around the littered end table to his left covered with dried up bits of dottle, nose hair clippers, a glass half-filled with flat Pepsi and numerous pieces of forgotten mail. No clicker. Ken began searching all the familiar places: on the counter, in the drawer of the end table and on the floor under his recliner. No clicker. Once George made it to a standing position, Ken tentatively reached into the crevices of the recliner dreading what he might find. Too grossed out to continue after touching something soft and gooey, he placed a baggie over his hand and continued the search.

"Aha! Here it is buried in the recliner again and covered with melted chocolate. At least I hope it's melted chocolate." Ken removed the baggie with the finesse of a surgeon following a delicate surgery. It took Ken another fifteen minutes to get his mother into appropriate dining apparel and his father upright and moving before they headed to lunch. So much for an hour lunch.

Entering the dining room Thelma was unusually alert and excited. "Ooooh, Ooooh, there they are!" Her entire being brightened as she smiled and quickened her step towards Norman and Edith, who were saving seats for them. George perked up a bit too, and from Ken's perspective, Norman seemed like a regular guy and relatively healthy. He was able to carry an intelligent conversation, joked with George and was even okay to drive. Edith was a petite woman and soft-spoken; she needed the assistance of a wheelchair to get around.

Ken did his best to engage the group in conversation and gather background on Norman and Edith. He learned they moved down to Florida from Ohio upon the insistence of their daughter who lived in the area. Edith required some extra support while Norman was completely independent, making Whispering Oaks a good choice for them. Ken was happy his parents had made friends and actually had someone to socialize with other than Stu or himself. Ken realized he felt the exact same way when his boys started kindergarten and had made new friends.

The next day Stu and Elaine made their weekly visit to Whispering Oaks, hoping to get them out for a meal, organize their closet again and collect important mail before it was thrown away. Entering the double doors at the front of the facility, Stu and Elaine were greeted with lively music and a crowd. Curious, Stu and Elaine inched closer and saw a couple dancing with great enthusiasm.

"Oh My God! Stu, that's your mother dancing and that is NOT your father dancing with her!" Elaine was shocked at the sight before them. She glanced around but did not see George anywhere. As the music faded, Thelma continued to cling to Norman. Stu and Elaine stood stunned before greeting Thelma.

"Oh hi. I want you to meet my new friend. Oh, I haven't had this much fun in a long time!" Thelma cooed. "I feel like I'm sixteen again."

Stu and Elaine introduced themselves to Norman, feeling amused that Thelma was so happy but somewhat uncomfortable with her fawning all over Norman. They were then introduced to Edith, who was sitting quietly in her wheelchair watching the spectacle.

"You remember we're here to take you out to dinner, right? We're heading up to your apartment to see Dad, are you coming with us?"

"Oh, I think I'd like to dance a few more times with Norman," Thelma said, rubbing Norman's arm. Stu and Elaine rolled their eyes at each other.

"Stu and Elaine, if you don't mind, I'll dance with your mother a few more times and make sure she gets safely to the apartment."

Stu and Elaine reluctantly agreed before shaking Norman's hand. They walked to the elevator in silence, not sure how to process what they just witnessed. They found George parked in his recliner holding a newspaper, with the television running a repeating news feed on the spread of the Swine Flu epidemic.

"Hey Dad, did you know Mom is downstairs dancing up a storm with Norman?" Stu asked, curious if George was aware of the shenanigans in the lobby.

"She wanted me to dance, but I've got shrapnel in my knee and I don't dance. Norman loves to dance and it makes the apartment really quiet." George grinned.

"Norman is supposed to have Mom back here soon, so why don't you change your shirt?" said Stu. "You seem to be wearing your breakfast, and I know you have a drawer full of clean shirts." Elaine was busy cleaning up the apartment when Thelma waltzed in, happier than they'd seen her in a long time. She talked about dancing and Norman through the entire dinner, causing Stu and Elaine to worry about George. He did not seem bothered but he did not show much emotion these days.

"Dad, what do you think of Norman?" Stu asked.

"He seems like a good guy and it's somebody to talk with at meals and have a drink with at night. Your mother seems to like him."

"What does his wife Edith think about all the dancing?" asked Elaine.

"Oh Elaine," Thelma chirped. "She can't dance, she's in a wheelchair because there's something wrong with her legs. She just loves to watch us dance, you know. I feel so young!"

Exiting the restaurant after their weekly meal out, Stu was curious.

"Did you enjoy your dinner?"

"Yeah, it was great." replied George.

"OK, what did you have?"

"Uh, I had a steak," George guessed, clearly not remembering his meal.

"Hey Mom, how was your dinner?" asked Stu.

"Oh, it was fine."

"And what did you have Mom?"

"I had chicken, I think." Thelma had zero recollection of the grilled shrimp and rice.

Stu suggested including Norman and Edith the next time they all went out to dinner. George and Thelma thought it was a fabulous idea.

The following Thursday evening Stu and Elaine met the others at a local steakhouse. Norman drove himself, as Edith required extra assistance with her wheelchair and Ken had George and Thelma duty. The group was seated at a large rectangular table in the center of the restaurant. Edith was parked at one end of the table in her wheelchair while Thelma managed to seat herself right next to Norman. The drink order was placed and only the Manhattan order was botched. Ken was thrilled to see his parents out socializing, but wondered if it was possible sans chaperones. With the second round of drinks the conversation became more animated. Stu and Elaine were having a lively disagreement about something trivial, and Edith was seated next to them and became very quiet. Ken was at the other end of the table facing her, when he noticed she wasn't responding to stimuli at the table. He was just about to say something when her eyes rolled back in her head. Ken's stomach twisted before he managed to speak.

"Stu, Edith!" he nodded his head in Edith's direction.

"Oh my God. Call 911 Ken," Elaine ordered jumping into action. She positioned herself to administer the Heimlich maneuver when Edith slumped over in the wheelchair. Elaine quickly changed tack by carefully dragging her from the wheelchair to the carpet next to the table. Ken called 911 with the phone shaking in his hand; medical emergencies were not his forte. Elaine straddled Edith, feeling for a pulse and signs of breathing, but found nothing. She placed her hands together pressing in the center of Edith's chest and instantly heard the cracking of frail ribs. The snap reverberated through her body but she continued with the chest compressions as Norman administered mouth-to-mouth. George and Thelma were confused, but Ken corralled them at the other end of the table.

"Excuse me, can you please do this somewhere else?" the hostess inquired, clearly perturbed by the disturbance. "People are trying to eat their dinner."

"And you expect her to get up and walk somewhere else while we perform CPR?" Ken snapped. "I am so sorry we've interrupted your dining hour, next time we'll ask her to wait until she's in the privacy of her own home to pass out. And thank you for your support through this emergency, it's enough to warm my heart." The hostess slunk away.

The paramedics arrived, creating high drama for the fellow diners. A young EMT relieved Elaine of her duties and nodded his thanks to her. Elaine suddenly felt weak but incredibly thankful she had known what to do. Ironically, she had just completed a CPR class the prior week. Ken followed the ambulance to the hospital with Norman, while his daughter planned to meet them there. Stu and Elaine took George and Thelma back to Whispering Oaks.

It turned out Edith had choked on a piece of meat but passed out before Elaine was able to perform the Heimlich. The hospital extracted the meat and explained she had suffered several broken ribs, but it was a small price to pay for her life. Elaine quietly wished she had had the power to save Keith. The chaos of the situation put stress on Edith's heart condition, which required an extended rehab stay. Ken sat with Norman's daughter at the hospital, and left feeling something was off with the relationship between father and daughter. He couldn't put his finger on it.

Later that week Sue called her parents to check in. Her mother was no longer capable of using the phone well enough to make an outgoing call.

"Hi Mom, how are you guys doing? I'm just calling to see if you're behaving yourselves."

"Oh Sue, I've never been better. I've met a new friend you know, and we go dancing every day. Oh I feel like I'm sixteen again!" her mother said. "You know, when I used to be married to your father, we never went dancing, even though I begged him."

"Wait a minute. Back up the bus," Sue demanded. "What do you mean when you used to be married to Dad? Are guys divorced? You were married last week as far as I know. And who is this new friend of yours?"

"His name is Norman and we are having a ball."

"Norman??? The same name as my husband, your son-in-law? Oh my God Mom, what does Dad think about all this?"

"Oh, he doesn't care. He just sits in his chair all day watching the boob tube, and you know he doesn't like to dance. I've asked him if he wants to come watch, but he just says no."

"Well, I guess it's good you're having fun and I can honestly say I haven't heard you this happy or excited in a very long time. Is Norman married?" Sue had heard the stories of dancing and the restaurant from her brothers, but had no idea the friendship was moving in this direction.

"Well, yes. Edith used to love to watch us dance, but she's in rehab so it's actually a lot easier for Norman now. You know she has some problems with her legs and can't walk, and then there was something that happened at the restaurant, but I can't remember what it was."

Sue was listening, trying desperately to make sense of the absurdity. It would not be the last interesting phone call.

A week later George felt a hankering for Pepsi and his stash was depleted, and the dining room did not serve soda. No vending machines were available in the ALF. He decided it was time for a little adventure. Thelma was off somewhere with Norman, sparing him a lecture about driving. He recalled a convenience store about a half mile down the road, and felt confident he could handle the short drive. His kids had been harping at him not to drive, and he agreed Thelma should not be driving but he would show them he was capable.

The keys were hanging on the hook along with the apartment keys just begging to be used. George grabbed his cane, keys and Lake Mansfield Trout Club cap before heading out of 523. At the last second he remembered to grab his cell phone. In the lobby he passed the front desk without signing out, a task his kids normally performed. He was a grown man after all, and did not need to be treated like a child. He exited Whispering Oaks into the sweltering summer heat and humidity, the kind that takes your breath away. The Explorer was parked a few spaces away in a handicapped zone. Slowly he made his way to the car using the fob to unlock the doors and suddenly felt a combination of excitement and anxiety. It briefly flashed in his mind how drastically things had changed if he was nervous about driving to buy Pepsi.

George backed out slowly just as the seatbelt alarm started dinging, sending a jolt of adrenaline. He stopped and actually fastened the seatbelt himself, a task that suddenly boosted his self-assurance. This task took five minutes to complete. Pulling out of Whispering Oaks he looked around and felt confident of his surroundings, despite not driving since arriving in Florida. He knew he needed to turn left and go to the traffic light. At the light, a horn honked behind him, bringing George out of his reverie. Excitement surged as he pulled out onto the main road, staying to the far right lane. He traveled a good fifteen miles an hour below the speed limit.

One block up he recognized the convenience store sign and pulled in, forgetting to use his blinker. This generated another round of honking from an impatient Florida driver. The parking spot was evidently too small for the Explorer because it sat askew between three sets of lines. George did not notice.

Entering the store he found his Pepsi, never Coke. When the kids were growing up he was adamant about Pepsi but when the kids began polishing off his six-pack of glass Pepsi bottles before he made it home from work at night, he switched to Moxie. He had hoped the kids would detest the medicinal taste, but they grew to love Moxie. George also preferred Hydrox cookies over Oreos, a peculiarity the kids never overcame.

George spoke with the young girl behind the register who required a crate to reach the White Owl Miniatures. Upon returning to the Explorer, he took a moment to observe his whereabouts and made a mental plan for his return to Whispering Oaks. With no left turn out of the parking lot due to the four lane road and median, George headed for the next intersection to make a U-turn. This maneuver required George to cut across two lanes of traffic into the far left lane, but by the time he managed to accomplish this, he was rattled. The light turned green and George simply followed the car in front. He was unaware he made a left turn and not a u-turn. After traveling several minutes it occurred to George that perhaps he had missed his turn, because nothing seemed familiar. He continued driving down the busy six-lane road, air conditioning blasting and Johnny Cash crooning.

Twenty minutes later George found himself crossing the Howard Frankland Bridge during five o'clock traffic that was barrelling along at 70 mph. Naturally, the exhausted drivers had little patience for a slow vehicle in the fast lane. This elicited several annoyed honks. Others weaved in and around George, but he felt empowered by chucking them the bird. Then he saw the sign: *Welcome to Tampa.* He now knew he had gone too far with no idea how to get back.

Ken's phone rang, he glanced at the Caller ID. "Hello? Dad? Is everything alright?"

"Hey Ken, I need some help."

"You do? What do you need help finding your remote again?" asked Ken.

"No, I seem to be lost."

"What are you wandering around Whispering Oaks, are you getting like Mom now?" Ken tried to joke, not understanding the problem.

"No, I'm driving and I'm in Tampa. I don't know where I am, I guess I took a wrong turn."

"Jesus Dad, why are you in Tampa? Where are you exactly? Is Mom with you?"

"I don't know. I know I just went over the bridge and I'm looking for signs now. Let's see, I think I see a sign for the airport and there's a Hilton on my right. And your mother is not with me."

"OK, listen Dad. You can make a u-turn and go back over the bridge and it will be a straight shot to Whispering Oaks. Make a u-turn at the next light, you'll see signs for the bridge and St Pete. Just follow the signs and call me as soon as it's safe." Ken knew the solution was not this easy. He alerted his siblings to inform them of a possible silver alert. Ken suggested they wait to see if George made it back safely before calling the police. As a former prosecutor, Ken knew involving the police should be their last resort. His phone rang again.

"Hey Dad, where are you now?"

"I must have missed my turn again because I'm near Salmon Expressway. I don't see any bridge." He was sounding less nonchalant.

"Listen Dad, It's Selmon not Salmon, but I'm driving right now, forty-five minutes away from Tampa. Stu and Elaine are tied up with patients, so you need to pull over and wait for me. DO NOT keep driving. Tell me exactly what you see out the car window." Ken became worried as George rattled off a few street names.

"You need to pull into the Hyatt parking lot, which should be coming up on your right. Pull into the lot, keep the Explorer running with the AC on, because it's 96 degrees outside. Crack your window and sit tight. Do NOT get out of the car, do NOT keep driving and I will be there as soon as I can."

Ken developed a quick plan where he would head home to pick up Marie, who could drive him to George and he could drive the Explorer back to Whispering Oaks. Ken would just have to keep the Explorer for a few days, not a bad thing.

Close to an hour later, Ken arrived at the Hyatt parking lot. Ken and Marie spotted the Explorer with the same sense of relief a parent feels when a lost child has been found. They parked and ambled over to George, who was sitting in the Explorer with the windows open and the vehicle off. Perspiration dripped down George's face, dotting his polo shirt. Marie headed home to pick up Connor and Duncan from play practice.

"Hey Dad, out for a joyride this afternoon?" Ken asked opening the driver's door to let in what little breeze was blowing. "Where the hell were you going, and how did you end up in Tampa? Do you have any water?"

"No, but I have Pepsi."

"Get out! I'm driving now and let's get you back to Whispering Oaks. Have you called Mom to let her know you're alright?" Ken helped George navigate over to the passenger's side. Ken was about to comment on George's attire of stained khaki shorts, black socks and dress shoes, but opted to focus on the crisis at hand.

"No, I didn't tell her I was leaving." Ken immediately called her, but no one answered.

"So Dad, tell me how did you manage to cross the bridge at rush hour without having an accident? There are some crazy drivers out there."

"Oh, there were a couple drivers who tried to cut me off, but I gave them the finger," George said grinning with pride.

"And how the hell did you give them the finger when you only have one working arm?"

"I let go of the wheel, and chucked them the bird!" Ken was horrified and decided he really did not want to know any more. Thirty minutes later they pulled into Whispering Oaks, realizing the dinner hour was over. Ken settled George in the apartment, where there was no sign of Thelma. With strict instructions to stay put, Ken set out to find his mother. He poked his head into the dining room, hoping to spot her, when he saw her sitting with Norman and another couple.

"Hey Mom. Where's Dad?" he asked, curious what answer he might receive.

"Oh, I don't know. He's probably in the apartment watching his boob tube," she answered, unconcerned.

"When was the last time you saw him?"

"Oh Ken, I don't remember. Are you hungry, would you like to join us?" she asked. All the tables had been cleared and the residents were making the nightly exodus back to their apartments.

"Mom, I just returned Dad home after he took the Explorer on a joy ride through Tampa in rush hour traffic. You didn't even know he was missing!"

"Oh boy, I'm sure glad I didn't go with him. You know his driving scares me and I told him I would not be his passenger anymore." Ken shook his head and wondered if George had been driving recently. He decided the time had come to hide the keys, and if asked where the keys were, Ken would feign ignorance. He was confident his siblings would be on board. And so, after several years of strategizing unsuccessfully how to end his driving career, it died a natural death. George never asked again to drive.

A few weeks later Stu and Elaine found a letter from the auto insurance company, while scouring the apartment hoping to find the Medicare checks before Thelma threw them away. Stu opened the letter to find a threatening tone of cancellation due to non-payment for the last six months. He went directly to the Explorer's glove compartment to find paperwork, and was surprised to find the Explorer not only uninsured but also unregistered. George had dodged a bullet.

George and Thelma continued to socialize with Norman, who took them to Panera several times a week following their 4:30 pm dinner. Edith was still recovering in rehab, allowing Thelma and Norman to dance away the afternoons with the freedom of young lovers.

Every afternoon at 2:00 pm the music commenced, the crowds of scooter bound residents formed, and Thelma and Norman danced. A crowd of several dozen gray-haired residents, some with attached oxygen tanks and others hunched so far over they were staring at their knees, watched and clapped as the two dancing fools sashayed across the lobby floor.

As Thelma walked past a group of women, she overheard them talking about her.

"I think it's awful what she's doing, you know with Edith in rehab and all," one lady commented.

"I don't know what she's thinking, and really she's not a very good dancer. You know she's just making a fool of herself," commented another resident.

"Oh hell, shut up you fools," Gil said. "Norman is a rat! I trust the asshole as far as I can throw him." Gil wanted to set the record straight. "I've seen him operate in this place before, and poor Thelma isn't thinking clearly these days." Gil headed upstairs to visit George, knowing he was generous with his jokes and his whiskey. He was also much better company than the meddling biddies in the lobby.

Gil rolled her wheelchair at a good clip down the 5th floor corridor, stopping only long enough to tap on the door before entering without permission. She found George happily parked in his recliner, chewing on a cigar, with a mess of newspapers by his feet.

"Hey Georgie!" Gil hollered. "Your drinking buddy is here. I couldn't take anymore of those fat bitches downstairs who apparently have nothing better to do than find fault in everyone else. I wonder when they last got laid? And my God, that Robin, the activities director, is a pain in my ass always asking me to join the idiotic craft group. What the hell do I want with making decoupage shit when I could be drinking and smoking?" Gil made herself at home. "So Georgie, you're not down there dancing? You know, I think Norman has the hots for your wife."

"I've got a bum knee and with Thel dancing, it's peaceful around here."

"Well tell me Georgie, what do you think of Norman?"

"He's a nice enough guy. It's nice to have someone to chat with at dinner who doesn't drool." George seldom said anything negative about anybody. George poured a couple bourbons on ice while the two of them swapped jokes and stories.

Thelma pranced into the apartment about an hour later, feeling the high of dancing with Norman. The look Gil shot George escaped Thelma. Gil decided to make it her mission to convince George of the truth regarding Norman. She knew things were headed down a rutted path and wanted to warn her friend.

"Ooooo, Ooooo, do you see those people on the grass?" Thelma announced as she stared out the window. "They're having sex!" Gil quickly moved to the window in hopes of catching a glimpse of the entertainment.

"Awww Sweetie, I am not seeing any hanky panky happening down there. Where are you looking?" asked Gil, a bit disappointed.

"Right there, right there on the grass. Don't you see the man and the woman having sex?" insisted Thelma. Gil did not see them, nor did she see anyone at all. Gil shot George another look and slid over to whisper in his ear.

"Is she seeing things or am I going crazy?"

"Gil, I don't know what's happening but she's been seeing some crazy stuff out that window lately. We just try to get her away from the window and distract her." George had a sadness about him as they convinced Thelma to sit down and chat. Within ten minutes she was quietly snoring.

Chapter 12   Seeing Things
Your mother can hear a mouse fart from 50 yards away.
And smell it 10 seconds later.

"God I hate this place!" growled Thelma. "They're not even real nurses in the nurses station." She returned aggravated from the pill station. George ignored her as she suddenly decided to empty the trash despite daily housekeeping.

"I'm taking the trash down the hall to the chute, George," declared Thelma.

"I'll miss you Thel."

Ten minutes later Thelma returned empty-handed. "Where's the trash can, Thel?" George asked.

"Oh, when I was dumping it down the chute, the waste basket just disappeared, I don't know what happened."

"I should have tied a string around your neck." mumbled George.

Gil knocked on the door at that moment and rolled herself into the apartment emitting a strong odor of cigarettes. It was only 10 am, too early for cocktails, but Gil was in need of company.

"Well you two, I have some big news that might just knock your knickers off," Gil announced. "Have you seen the new guy in the dining room, Edgar is his name, he's always eating with Ethel and Phyllis? Well guess what folks? He has asked me out. He's on oxygen and can't drive, so the date will be an event here at Whispering Oaks, but it's the best offer I've had in a while."

"Be careful, Gil," said George.

"Oh Gil, George is right, because there are a lot of weirdos around here," offered Thelma.

"Honey, the guy's on oxygen and if he tries any hanky panky with me, I'll just squeeze his oxygen tube for a few minutes and leave," Gil said quite seriously. "And Thelma, you're not one to lecture me on weirdos with that asshole you've been hanging around with."

"Who are you talking about?" asked Thelma.

"Geez Thelma, that asshole Norman who's always hanging all over you when his poor wife is in rehab."

"He happens to be a very nice man who enjoys dancing with me. George won't even get out of his chair, so what am I supposed to do? His wife doesn't care if we dance, she can't even walk."

"Well Thelma sweetie, just promise me you'll be careful with him. I don't trust him." Gil looked from George to Thelma. The phone rang, abruptly ending the Norman discussion. Stu and Elaine were stopping over for a visit within the hour, and wondered if they would be around.

Stu and Elaine gave a quick knock and entered the apartment without waiting for permission. Thelma would have regarded this behavior as uncouth and rude a few years ago, but had come to accept it as normal behavior now. After hugs and kisses, Elaine set out like the Tasmanian devil cleaning, organizing and purging piles of unwanted papers while Stu sat on the couch chatting with his parents. Chatting these days meant asking questions and waiting for one or two-word answers, unless Thelma decided to go on a tirade about Whispering Oaks.

Elaine found her way to the closet, where she matched tops with pants on the same hanger in an effort to make dressing easier for Thelma. No matter how many times Elaine reorganized the clothes, Thelma continued to wear the same unmatched clothes. Frustration engulfed Elaine with every visit, because the staff had been informed to dress Thelma in coordinated outfits but it never happened. Elaine often found Thelma in dirty inside-out clothes, a situation Thelma never would have tolerated before her mind was ravaged with disease.

"Oh I hate it when she comes here and acts like I'm an idiot," Thelma told Stu through clenched teeth. "She even has her own mother come up here to move my clothes around and pick up the apartment. I really resent it, you know!"

"Mom, she's just trying to make things easier for you by organizing your outfits and keeping the clutter under control. She's doing it out of love," Stu explained.

"Well, I don't like it. God, I hate this place."

"On that note, I have some news you two might like to hear. How would you guys like to take a trip back to Vermont with Allie and Matt as your chaperones? They'll fly up with you, drive you around to visit your friends, take you to the Trout Club and you'll stay at the Hilton on the Lake in downtown Burlington.. How does that sound?" Stu waited for a positive reaction, but all he received was silence and blank stares.

Finally George said, "That's nice." Stu was stunned by his lack of enthusiasm.

"Geez, you two have been complaining about Whispering Oaks and how badly you want to be back in Vermont, and now you act like I asked you to go for a walk. I expected a little more enthusiasm."

"Oh Stu, that's wonderful, but you just don't understand what it's been like for us here. Can we stay at…at that place? You know the place, umm, where we were before?" asked Thelma.

"You mean Champlain Waters? No, but Allie and Matt will take you to visit friends there. In fact they'll take you wherever you want to go in Vermont."

"Well, I guess that sounds OK. When are we going?" asked Thelma.

"Allie has some time off at the beginning of September; do you have plans that might interfere with this?" Stu asked.

"Sounds good Stu, but I want to visit Monkton," George said. Stu explained they could visit anywhere they wanted, knowing it would be their last visit to Vermont. He wanted them to make the trip sooner rather than later. Thelma was sitting sideways on the sofa peering out the window, fascinated by something.

"Do you see him?" Thelma announced. "He's in the tree!" Stu and Elaine moved to the window to see who was in the tree but didn't see anyone. "Right there, he's naked in the tree. Oh, isn't he handsome? He's so athletic."

"Mom, who are you talking about?" Stu asked.

"Norman, that's who. Don't you see him? Look, he's jumping from tree to tree."

Elaine closed the blinds before leading Thelma into the kitchen on the pretense of finding snacks for everyone. Stu and Elaine were shocked by the hallucinations. They had heard stories from others, but had not witnessed the actual event. A new level of heartbreak. Elaine planned on calling the doctor to discuss meds and the possible cause. Ken also had an upcoming appointment for Thelma with the memory doctor in Tampa, where they would discuss this new development.

A few days later Ken decided to take George and Thelma out for lunch and a movie. He wanted to catch the new movie *The Hangover* and being midweek, his schedule was slow. He knew George would enjoy the movie and Thelma would likely just fall asleep. He called Whispering Oaks to warn George and Thelma not to eat lunch and to be ready, a request he suspected would fall on deaf ears. Arriving at Whispering Oaks he entered through the double front doors and was greeted with an arctic blast of air and a public display of affection by his mother and Norman. Ken's face expressed horror as he approached the couple.

"Hey Mom, are you ready for our lunch date?" Ken was getting a smarmy feeling from Norman. He knew his mother was happy, but there was something just not right about the situation and he couldn't put his finger on it, other than his mother being publicly involved with another man.

"She's welcome to stay here with me this afternoon, Ken," Norman said with an air of arrogance, knowing her son was there to take her out.

"Thanks anyway Norman, but I'm taking both my parents out for lunch. Mom, I'm heading up to the apartment, so why don't you walk up with me?" Thelma gave Norman a sad puppy dog look but acquiesced and went along with Ken.

"You know Ken, I've never been happier in my whole life!"

"Wow, gee thanks Mom. That makes me feel all warm and fuzzy inside knowing that the years you spent raising me were not the happiest of your life," Ken said, teasing.

"Oh Ken, I loved raising you kids but I feel like a schoolgirl again with Norman. You know he's my special friend," she said, nudging Ken with her elbow. Ken shivered but said nothing. "You know we do things together." Ken placed his fingers in his ears while making noise to block out anything else she might say. Thelma looked at Ken and smiled.

Ken was pleasantly surprised to find George in a clean polo shirt, shoes on and hair combed, looking ready to go. "Hey Dad, what's up today? You look raring to go for a change."

"Just feeling like I need to get out of this place. Everyone here is gimping around on those absurd scooters or stuck in a wheelchair. I'd like to find some girls with good posture!"

"Okay you two, do either of you need to use the bathroom before we go?" George decided to take heed of the suggestion delaying the adventure by ten minutes. Thelma stood near George as they were leaving the apartment, partially blocking his way.

"Thel, just keep moving."

"Jesus George, I'm just making sure you don't fall." George took his cane and poked Thelma in the rear end, making her turn around, shooting him the evil eye. Ken smiled to himself and kept on walking.

"How does Chili's sound to you guys for lunch?" Ken asked.

"I don't eat Mexican food, it's full of rice and beans," George said.

"Dad, how many times have we been over this? Chili's has a huge menu and you can order yourself a cheeseburger, fries and a chocolate shake."

"Really? All right then." They made their way to Chili's with ample time to spare before the movie. Ken knew lunch conceivably might take close to two hours, counting the transition times to and from the car, trips to the bathroom and the process of eating. Ken ordered a margarita as soon as the waitress approached the table.

"I'll have what he's having," George said. Thelma ordered a Pepsi, no longer enjoying alcohol as she used to. They talked while waiting for their food, which was actually Ken creating conversation and Ken keeping the conversation going. Not so many years earlier George commanded any audience with amusing stories, jokes and a world of knowledge. And Thelma could talk on the phone for hours on end with her friends.

George consumed his cheeseburger and every last french fry, and he even managed a second margarita, much to Ken's dismay. Thelma ate only two bites of her soup before declaring she was full, but managed to suck her Pepsi dry, a beverage she once shunned and ridiculed. George became a tad unsteady after drinking, and now Ken had to get them out of the restaurant and into the theater. Ken felt fortunate when George managed not to fall on the way to the car. It took all of Ken's strength to help him into the front seat of the Explorer with reminders to scoot his butt over and lift his left leg. Thelma struggled with opening the rear door, but never seemed frustrated. She just toiled away until Ken offered assistance with the seatbelt and shut the door. Ken hopped into the driver's seat and blew out a long slow breath that neither parent heard. They were off to see *The Hangover*.

They had the theater to themselves as it was a Wednesday afternoon and the choice of new releases was limited to teenage vampire sagas and remakes of superhero movies. Ken settled George and Thelma just as the previews were starting. Thelma's head began bobbing even before the opening scene, but maintained her death grip on a movie-sized bag of M&Ms. Ken was thankful she would enjoy a nice two-hour nap, but forty minutes into the movie, the bag of M&Ms slipped from her grip, spilling down the sticky theater floor while making a racket. She never woke. George stayed awake for the entire movie and Ken enjoyed his midweek break. They left the theater with a confused Thelma still groggy from her nap, and George unable to recall anything about the movie.

Ken decided to make a pit stop at the grocery store before returning his parents to Whispering Oaks. They needed to replenish their supply of Cabot cheese, water, chocolate, Poise pads and Pepsi.

"Do you want to wait in the car or come in with me?" Ken asked, hoping they would opt for the car.

"I'll go in," George said. "There are a few things I want to pick up." Thelma followed his lead. Ken glanced at his cell phone to check the time, knowing this trip would not be quick. Ken dropped them off at the front entrance before parking the Explorer. When he entered the double doors, he was surprised George and Thelma weren't right there waiting. And then he spotted George in an electric scooter.

"Hey Dad, what's up with the scooter? You're always talking trash about scooters and how only geriatric idiots ride them."

"I thought it might be fun," George said and zoomed off at a speed Ken thought was a tad excessive. Thelma did her best to keep up. George was smiling and had a twinkle back in his eye as he accelerated down the aisle.

"Dad, you're driving a little fast. You need to pay attention to the other people shopping, this isn't your personal race track." Ken realized he was talking to his parents in the exact manner he spoke to his boys. George narrowly missed an elderly woman lost in thought at the spice section and continued down the aisle until he spied the cheese case at the far end. Ken found himself half jogging to keep up and Thelma was left to wander at her own pace. After collecting all items on the list, Ken herded his parents to the check out where he hoped they were safe.

"Listen, I'm going to get the Explorer and I'll pull up right out front. Use your Amex Card to pay, and they can place the bags back in your scooter, okay? Meet me right out front," instructed Ken and he left. Ken hopped in the Explorer and pulled up front, it was amazing how much quicker things were when he wasn't corralling his parents. He waited patiently with the engine idling, but after ten minutes he began to wonder where they were. It certainly shouldn't be taking this long. Just as Ken was about to climb out of the Explorer the doors parted open. George emerged on his scooter traveling at full speed with the wire rack that holds plastic grocery bags dragging behind him. Ken stared in amazement, he didn't know how to respond. George was grinning, Thelma was following him on foot, yelling at him to slow down, and a young male employee followed them both. The racket generated by the metal on the pavement rivaled a marriage vehicle driving off with tin cans attached. Everyone in the parking lot was suddenly curious.

"Jesus Dad, what the hell are you doing? You tore the rack right off the checkout? Don't you hear it dragging behind you?" George slowed the scooter to an abrupt stop and turned his head to check out the damage.

"I've still got it. Pretty impressive driving move, huh Ken?" Thelma was confused by the chaos and stood watching, not sure what to do. Ken spoke with the young man who was clearly at a loss how to handle the situation. Ken apologized for his father's behavior and explained about his father's stroke and mother's Alzheimer's, hoping to find forgiveness rather than a lawsuit. The store manager appeared to the relief of the young man who quickly disappeared back into the store while Ken smoothed things over with the manager. Sometimes Ken's law degree came in handy. Thirty-five minutes later Ken had his parents safely buckled and heading home.

"I think that's enough excitement for one day folks. I'm getting you two back upstairs and I'm going home, I'm exhausted."

"Why don't you stay and have dinner with us in the dining room tonight, you're already here," George suggested.

"Well, I'm not hungry," Thelma said. "The food here is horrid and I'm not eating there tonight." Ken quickly said his goodbyes before he got sucked into another drama, and drove straight home where he poured himself a vodka, tonic and cranberry with a wedge of orange. He would only have one, since there was a basketball game scheduled with the guys later that evening.

George and Thelma promptly found their respective places on the sofa and recliner; both were snoring within minutes. They slept for several hours before hearing a knock on the door, followed by Gil rolling in for a cocktail.

"Hello folks, I'm here for my evening libation. Do you know what those dirty bastards did to me today?" she asked without waiting for an answer. "They caught me smoking in the apartment and threatened to kick me out if they catch me again, something about being a repeat offender." Just then there was another knock on the door and in waltzed Norman. Thelma's entire demeanor brightened as she jumped to her feet to welcome him. George and Gil exchanged a look of disgust.

"Hello George, Gil, how is everything treating you tonight?" he asked.

Gil glared at him before speaking, "so you here for your booty call?" Norman ignored her, Thelma didn't understand the comment and George wore an amused grin. Norman went on to recap the day at Whispering Oaks, with gossip relating to residents and staff. Norman seated himself on the couch right next to Thelma, where he was rubbing her back and she was clearly enjoying it.

"Gil," Norman said. "I hear you went on a date with Edgar from the 3rd floor the other night. How did things go?"

"He died, something with his breathing," Gil said but did not elaborate. The others wondered what happened to poor Edgar, but no one asked. Gil turned her attention to George, where they swapped dirty jokes and laughed while Norman and Thelma giggled on the couch. Finally Norman suggested they go dancing.

"How the hell do you think I'm going to dance in my wheelchair Norman?" Gil said. "I can spin around and take out a few of those bitches, but I'd rather drink up here with my buddy George."

"I've got a bum knee from WWII. Still have shrapnel lodged in there and the doc tells me dancing is forbidden, so I guess I'll have to pass," George said. Norman and Thelma left the apartment on the premise of dancing downstairs.

"George, buddy, you do know there's no dancing going on at this hour, at least not the ballroom kind. They only have dancing in the afternoon, I think our lover boy is taking your wife somewhere else and he's a lowlife."

"What do you want me to do Gil? You know Thelma is much happier when she's with him and she's not here complaining to me." George avoided confrontation at all cost.

"Well, George, I've told you before, the guy's a creep—and I worry about Thelma because she's so naive about things." The two talked and joked over a cocktail for a few hours, before Gil rolled down to the pill station for her nightly fix. Thelma returned to the apartment with her clothes in disarray a short time after Gil left, and her mood was giddy.

Sue arrived in Florida for a visit before the end of summer to see George and Thelma as well as her brothers. Ken picked her up at the airport and delivered her directly to Whispering Oaks before he headed out to his last appointment of the day. The Explorer was still parked at Whispering Oaks, but no longer driven by George.

She knocked softly on the apartment door, but hearing silence, she entered. Sue was greeted by a faint smell of urine and two snoring parents in a dark living room. The noise startled Thelma, who took a few seconds to comprehend who was in the apartment.

"Ooooh Susie, I'm so glad to see you. You have no idea what it's like here, I hate it here. We can't wait to go back to the other place. It's so nice to see you, honey." Thelma and Sue hugged.

George awoke at the sound of talking, but made no effort to get out of his recliner. Sue bent over to hug him, turned on some lights and sat down. She tried her best to carry on a conversation. After about thirty minutes, she convinced her mother to take a walk around the property for some fresh air.

"Oh, I don't know Sue, my back really hurts."

"Well, I hear you go dancing almost every day, does your back hurt when you dance?"

"Oh no, I feel wonderful and I'm with my special friend." Sue wanted to vomit.

"Well, there you have it, we're going for a walk with no complaining, because today is a no complaint day," Sue said. "I'll help you get your shoes on and we'll walk slowly. You want to join us, Dad?"

"I think I'll stay here and hold down the fort. I'm afraid you girls would just slow me down!" They headed down towards the elevator, an experience in patience as three people entered the elevator on the fifth floor, but one forgot where she was going. The second stop was *The 4th Floor* where the doors opened and a staff member entered the elevator. Several residents were trying to make their escape by hanging near the elevator hoping to enter. The staff member pleasantly told the residents of *The 4th Floor* the elevator was going up and the doors closed. The residents calmly waited for the next elevator; this continued for hours. On the second floor, several scooter-bound residents tried to enter the elevator, despite being told they really wanted to go up. They got on anyway. The elevator doors slid open on the first floor with seven people crammed into the elevator, three of them in scooters.

"What floor is this?" asked a dour-looking woman parked in one of the scooters.

"I think it's the third floor," answered her friend who had entered with her.

"Ladies, this is the first floor and y'all need to stay on the elevator to get back upstairs where you were headed," explained the kind staff member.

"How in the world are we supposed to know where we are when nothing is marked? It's no wonder everyone is lost around here," snapped the dour lady. The doors closed on the scooter brigade, leaving them to fend for themselves as they headed back up.

"See, I told you, Sue, everyone here is crazy. I can't wait to get out of here. I hate it here. And some of these women are real bitches, they whisper about me and my special friend while we dance and they just sit on their fat asses."

"Wow, Mom, sounds like they're just jealous and you just need to ignore them," Sue said, surprised at her mother's attitude. They checked in at the front desk, adhering to protocol, to let them know they were walking the property. Just as they stepped outside into the oppressive humidity, they saw Norman sitting right by the front door. He burst into a smile and Thelma quickened her pace to greet him with a hug. Sue made a silent groan. Thelma introduced them.

"Hello, Sue, I was hoping I would see your mother this afternoon because I want to make sure she knows I'm having a celebration Saturday night in the dining room with my family. You are invited too, of course."

"Oh, Norman, that sounds wonderful," gushed Thelma.

"Well, Norman, unfortunately we won't be able to make it because the family is taking Mom out for her 80th birthday on Saturday evening. My sister is coming down from Gainesville and I have a cousin joining us, too. It's just not going to work." He pulled his hand away from Thelma's arm, his smile faded and his muscles went rigid. Sue sensed this was a red flag.

"Norman, nice to meet you." Sue led her mother away from the awkward moment.

"Oh, it's too bad we can't have dinner with Norman, he was looking forward to us meeting his family."

"Well, Mom, I flew down here from Maine to celebrate your 80th birthday, which is far more important than eating dinner with Norman. What's his problem anyway? He just got angry when I said we were busy Saturday night and besides, you are married to Dad." Sue waited.

"We have such a nice time together." Sue shook her head and directed her mother to the sidewalk, where they walked at a pace approaching one mile per hour. At least her mother was outside and moving. Every minute or so Thelma complained about her shortness of breath, so they stopped and took a break. They were about halfway around the building when Thelma stopped short and pointed up at a telephone pole.

"Look, do you see him?"

"See who?" Sue looked up at the pole but saw nothing.

"Norman, don't you see him up on the telephone pole with the scantily clad mannequin?" Sue made a face, but Thelma was busy staring up at the pole. Sue debated whether or not to say something or just go along with it.

"Mom, there is nothing up there you know. Norman is not up on the pole, there is no mannequin, and remember we just left Norman at the front door a few minutes ago. There's no way he could have climbed the pole that quickly, plus he's 80 years old."

"Ah, shit, I don't know, Sue. It's so real to me, you really can't see him up there? I don't know why none of you can see them when it's real. It's really them." Sue didn't know how to proceed with the conversation, so she kept walking, hoping a change of scenery would diminish the hallucination. It did.

The following day Sue returned to Whispering Oaks for a visit and to take her mother out for lunch and a shopping trip to TJ Maxx. George was happily watching TV and pretending to read the newspaper. He asked the same questions from yesterday.

"How's Henry enjoying the Ranger?" George had given his old beat-up Ford Ranger to Henry, who viewed it as a lifesaver on his college student budget. "How's Charlie liking UMass?" George was thrilled Charlie was attending his alma mater. The answers had not changed since yesterday.

Thelma was not in the apartment, so Sue decided to go search for her since she couldn't be far. On the second floor near the pill station, there was a sing-along event with residents parked in scooters and wheelchairs. A few residents were fast asleep with heads tilting, while others were enthusiastically clapping and singing along to Perry Como and Judy Garland songs. Sue hesitated before entering, thinking she'd rather have a root canal than join in, but reminded herself she was there to visit her mother. Spotting her mother, she quietly slipped in next to her and noticed tears running down her face.

"Mom, what's wrong?"

"Oh, Sue, he's so upset with me. He was looking forward to having us join him for his family dinner here tomorrow." Thelma wiped her tears with a tissue.

"Are you talking about Norman?" Sue's lip curled in disgust. "Why are you crying? Did he give you a hard time? What did he say that has made you so upset?" Sue was getting upset.

"Oh, he is so angry with me that I'm choosing my family over his celebration that he said he doesn't want to see me anymore." Thelma began to sob.

"Okay, first of all it's ridiculous that he's pissed off at you because your family is taking you out for your 80th birthday, and second of all, he has no right to bully you." Sue was agitated now. "Gil is right, he is an asshole."

"Oh, Sue, I'm so hurt. I was so happy with him here, and now I just want to leave. I don't think I can stay here anymore." Thelma continued to weep with gasping breaths. Just then a staff member approached them, asking to speak to Sue in private.

"I'm glad you arrived when you did because your mother is very upset and so are we. Norman became agitated with your mother during the sing-along and physically grabbed your mother's arm in anger. We asked him to leave, but your mom has been inconsolable. We're very concerned about the situation."

"I appreciate you telling me," Sue said. "I knew she was upset, but didn't realize he had put his hands on her. God what an ass. Where is he now?"

"We asked him to leave the event and I assume he returned to his apartment. We'll keep an eye out for him whenever your mother is around," explained the nurse.

"I'm not sure that's going to be enough. I do appreciate what you've done, but I'll be talking with my brothers and management." Sue was trying to process what was happening. "Have you witnessed this before with them or with anyone else?"

"No, this was the first time I'm aware of and it is very disturbing." Sue returned to the now-empty function room, where Thelma sat looking like a lost bird. She attempted to talk with her mother about the incident, but Thelma was not in the mood to talk. Details were already fading from Thelma's memory.

They sat in the apartment with George for a while, but after thirty minutes of Thelma's sobbing, Sue was completely drained and decided to return to Stu's house for a dose of sanity.

"I knew there was something off with the guy," Ken said after listening to the afternoon saga at Whispering Oaks. "How are we going to deal with this, because it's the only time Mom has been happy lately, but we can't have an abusive jerk around her. At this point, we can have Mom declared incompetent."

"We could take him out back and teach him a lesson, or sic George on him," suggested Stu.

"The problem with George taking care of it," Elaine said, "is he doesn't care. George is not the same person since the stroke and I think he enjoys having Norman around to take Thelma away from him. George is not the caregiver type and he is not up for a confrontation with anyone. When Norman is not in his manic moods, he's very doting on Thelma and this is new for her. We can't reason with Thelma so we'll have to deal with Norman."

Dinner reservations were set for 6:00 pm at a nice upscale Italian restaurant with reservations for thirteen. All four kids were in attendance along with some of the spouses, the grandkids who lived locally and one of Thelma's nephews. Thelma sat at the head of the table and was dressed in a periwinkle dress that brought out the beautiful blue in her eyes. She was surrounded by her family, which made her happy. Everyone over the legal drinking age ordered a cocktail to kick off the evening and toast Thelma's 80th birthday.

Sue was seated next to her mother and took over the ordering by reading the menu and offering only a few options. Thelma settled on spaghetti and meatballs with a Pepsi, but by the time dinner arrived, she was full. Full on what, no one knew because she barely took a bite of bread and had maybe three bites of her salad. Thelma glowed in the midst of her family and never once mentioned Norman. As the bill was being paid, Thelma nudged Sue.

"Oh, Sue, I need to use the ladies room."

"No problem Mom, I'll take you." Sue gently guided her mother through the restaurant towards the bathroom in the rear. Thankfully all the stalls were available.

"Do you need any help, Mom?" Sue could hear her mother fumbling with her dress and could see through the unlatched door Thelma was clueless on how to proceed.

"Oh, these darn clothes. I don't know how to do this." Sue stepped into the stall only to find Thelma all twisted up in her dress, unable to find the waistband on her pantyhose. Sue helped her mother onto the toilet and backed out of the stall.

"Mom, just let me know when you're done and I'll come back to help you get dressed." Sue waited for the trickle of pee to stop as her cue. "Mom, how are you doing in there?"

"Okay, I'm having trouble with these darn stockings." Sue went back to help her mother by guiding the panty hose into position, straightening the dress and instructing Thelma through hand washing. The bathroom visit took fifteen minutes.

"Oh, Sue, I have terrible heartburn." Thelma rubbed her chest.

"Do you want a sip of Pepsi or a glass of milk?" Sue asked. Back at the table the group looked at Sue smiling, knowing she had drawn the short straw for bathroom duty.

"Mom has heartburn and needs a glass of milk." The waitress brought her a glass of milk and Thelma took a small sip, clearly not feeling any better. She refused any further suggestions and the group headed outside to congregate in the parking lot for the production of a lengthy family goodbye. Karen had Thelma by the Explorer while Sue was saying goodbye to her cousin and Ken. Stu and Elaine were helping George into the Explorer, while the younger cousins were horsing around in the parking lot.

"I need help here!" Karen hollered. "Somebody help me!" Everyone turned their attention to Karen who was bent over a slumped periwinkle body on the ground.

Karen scooped her arms underneath her mother in an effort to stand her up. Stu and Ken rushed over to lend a hand and move her to the back seat.

"I have a pulse," Karen said. "A faint pulse and there's shallow breathing." The others hoisted Thelma up onto the rear seat of the Explorer just as her eyes flew open.

"Oh, I don't feel good," and vomit poured all over her and the back of the vehicle. She promptly passed out again and slumped over in the seat. The group took a minute to process the situation before someone said, "I guess we should take her to the ER." They all agreed and were thankful she had waited until they were outside, not in the restaurant. A caravan of vehicles proceeded to the hospital where Ken, Stu and Karen wheeled her into the ER. Sue and Elaine escorted George back to Whispering Oaks, and after consuming three cocktails, he could barely stand.

Through a flurry of texts, Sue and Elaine learned Thelma's blood pressure was 80/30; she had a weak pulse and was dehydrated. Thelma was hooked up to an IV and surrounded by three of her children. After a mere five minutes of fluids being pumped into her, she perked right up.

Meanwhile Sue and Elaine struggled to get George into the apartment. Upon entering they were assaulted with the odor of urine.

Elaine looked at Sue, "I say we get a staff member to get him ready for bed, it's what we're paying for." There was no argument from Sue, who immediately went in search of help and returned with Nate, a young male attendant who liked George.

Elaine took charge. "Nate, you have to make sure George is wearing a Depends before he gets into bed, because there have been too many accidents on the way to the bathroom." Nate was unfazed. He grinned and whispered loud enough for George to overhear.

"He's always taking them off. We always put them on and tell him, but he's not the best listener."

"I don't need to wear diapers!" George said.

"Dad, we've been over this," Sue said. "If you continue to have accidents you cannot stay here, you'll have to go to a nursing home. It's the rule at this facility. When a resident is incontinent, they have to be moved to a nursing home, due to all the extra work involved. All you have to do is wear a Depends and there's no problem, but if you don't, then it's a huge problem for everyone. Nate will help you get ready for bed so Elaine and I can head up to the hospital to check on Mom. We'll come back here after." They waited until George was changed and in bed before they kissed him goodnight. They turned on Fox News and ventured off to the ER.

The process of finding Thelma in the ER felt like breaking into a maximum security prison with ID checks, security stops and limited visitors. Elaine and Sue finally found the small examining room tucked in the corner of a hallway. Faded blue curtains gave partial privacy to the three siblings sitting in plastic chairs. Karen, Stu and Ken were all texting away on their phones, but looked up and filled them in on Thelma's progress. Her blood pressure was back to normal, her pulse was better and with an IV for hydration, she was feeling much improved. She had suffered a severe case of dehydration despite having a Pepsi with dinner. The doctor made a hurried visit to Thelma's room, as if another elderly patient wasn't worth his time. He offered the group the option of keeping her overnight, but they all answered in unison that she needed to be released. If Thelma stayed overnight in the hospital, she would become confused, likely worsening her condition. Within the hour she was dressed in several layers of hospital gowns and wrapped in a blanket for her exit, due to the vomit-soaked periwinkle dress.

Stu situated her in the BMW figuring it was easier to climb into, being lower to the ground than the Explorer. Everyone else piled into the Explorer, careful to avoid the recently cleaned backseat. Ken drove Elaine, Karen and Sue back to Whispering Oaks so they could all help settle Thelma and check on George before heading home.

"I'm just going to say this out loud," Ken said. "Maybe we made a mistake. Maybe we should have just kept driving around for a couple hours rather than taking her to the ER. What would have happened?" Ken waited for a response, but it was silent for a few minutes.

"I think," Sue started. "We all had the same thought, but were too chicken to vocalize it. In theory it makes sense, but could we live with ourselves afterward?"

"No," Karen said. "We did the right thing, but it is an interesting thought because no one would ever know and her suffering would be over."

"We would all know," said Elaine.

"That starts getting into the realm of playing God, and I don't think we're quite there yet," Sue said.

"Yeah, but we had to think about it." Ken said. "At least we're able to talk about it; you know how many families would be horrified at even admitting to thinking about it?"

"Most families are in denial," Karen added. "We live in reality." They drove the rest of the way in silence.

Stu pulled the BMW up to the front entrance of Whispering Oaks. The sidewalk was desolate and dotted with puddles from a recent downpour. The others caught up to

Stu and took over the task of unfolding the wheelchair they kept stored in the trunk for George. Thelma was shaky as she settled into the wheelchair.

"Mom, why are you hanging on for dear life?" Ken asked. "I can make this thing do wheelies if you want more excitement!" No reaction. With all the residents securely tucked away in their apartments for the night, catching the elevator was simple. They quietly entered the apartment expecting to find George asleep, but the bed was empty.

"Dad? Dad, are you here?" called Sue concerned when she heard a grunt from the bathroom. Sue gave Ken a nod to go check on him.

"Wow, Dad," Ken said. "I didn't need to see that after everything tonight!" Ken yelled out to the other room. "He's standing butt naked in the middle of the bathroom with a wet Depends on the floor. He claims he doesn't need them."

"George," Elaine said in frustration. "We had you all settled." Ken and Stu opted to help George themselves rather than track down poor Nate again. They repeated the same message about the nursing home and threw in the fact that the apartment reeked of urine. George was unfazed, but ultimately complied. They made quick work of getting George and Thelma tucked into bed before departing.

By the next morning, Karen, Sue and Stu were sitting around the kitchen island, drinking coffee while rehashing the events from the evening before. Stu decided to call over to Whispering Oaks to check on things.

"Hi, Mom, it's Stu. It's your favorite son. How are you feeling this morning?"

"Oh, I'm a little weak right now so I think I'll stay up here this morning rather than go down for breakfast."

"So, Mom, you had some excitement last night, huh?" Stu asked.

"What are you talking about?"

"Do you remember going to the hospital?" Stu asked. "Remember after your birthday dinner you passed out in the parking lot and we took you to the hospital?"

"Oh, I don't remember any of that." Thelma clearly did not remember. Stu made faces at the listening crowd in the kitchen as he went over the events with her, to no avail. She accepted Stu's version of events and with no memory, there was no trauma or anxiety from the night before.

Chapter 13 Vermont Revisited
Is the water wet?

While George sat idle in his recliner, activity in the bedroom escalated. One of the nurses, Desiree, knocked softly before entering the apartment to check on George and Thelma.

"Hey, handsome. How are you doing today?" Desiree asked.

"I can't complain," was all George said. The nurse was busy checking her list and assessing the apartment when she heard noise in the bedroom.

"Is that Thelma in the bedroom?"

"Oh, I don't know," answered George, unconcerned. Desiree was concerned so she walked over and pushed the door open. Her jaw dropped and she needed a moment before she could respond. Thelma was sitting on the bed half dressed, and Norman was walking out of the closet completely naked. Desiree glanced back at George in his recliner and then back to the bedroom. George seemed oblivious to the shenanigans in the bedroom.

"Norman," Desiree ordered. "I suggest you put your clothes on immediately and get out of here now!" She turned to face Thelma. "And you, Thelma, you need to get dressed." Desiree again glanced towards George to make sure he was all right, but he seemed blank... or maybe he was protecting his pride with his yankee stoicism. Or maybe he really was unaware of the activity in the other room. She kept shaking her head and was about to say something, when she just clamped her mouth shut. What could she say? She ushered Norman out of the apartment and then took a moment to speak with Thelma in the privacy of the bedroom.

"Thelma, sweetie, what are you doing? Do you know George is sitting right in the very next room and he's your husband? Are you okay, Thelma? Did Norman hurt you?" Desiree asked as gently as she could.

"Ohh, we were just talking. You know he's my special friend, and we have so much fun together." Thelma was not the least bit embarrassed or ashamed at being caught. "He makes me feel like a young teenager again." Before the disease invaded her brain, Thelma was the queen of manners and proper etiquette, making the current situation even more incredible.

Desiree directed Thelma to the shower and helped her dress in a matching purple velour pant suit before going down to the dining room.

Desiree carefully watched George out of the corner of her eye, but he really seemed unaffected. Either he deserved an Academy award, or he honestly didn't care Thelma was fooling around with another man in the other room. Desiree left to report the incident to the manager who would, in turn, call Stu and Elaine.

Word spread quickly among the family who were shocked, but not really surprised after the last couple of years. They faced a dilemma. Their mother was honestly happier than she had been in several years and their father, by all appearances, didn't care about the affair. It was wrong, but they struggled with whether or not they had the right to interfere. Everyone involved was an adult, but one of the adults had limited brain function at this point. The other piece was that Norman was giving off creep-factor vibes. The children had now officially become adults.

A flurry of phone calls resulted in a wait and see attitude. Ken, being an attorney, did a bit of research on sex in assisted living facilities and learned it was very common. In fact, he discovered the incidence of contracting an STD as a senior had doubled in recent years. Residents of assisted living facilities were still human with needs and desires, but the tricky part arises when one or both partners have dementia. *Are they involved in a consensual relationship? Is anyone being hurt? Who has the right to dictate whether an adult can or cannot have sex with another person?* Ken found numerous articles on the subject, and more specifically how facilities need to educate seniors on safe sex. Ken found all this hilarious. How the hell are dementia patients going to remember to use a condom when they can't even find the bathroom in their own apartment?

The four kids, now adult children, discussed the situation frequently trying to navigate the tricky new world of seniors, sex and dementia. No real conclusions were reached other than their mother was happy and their father was not upset. Life continued.

"OK, Gram and Gramp," Allie said. "Are you ready for our big adventure back up to Vermont?" Her fiance, Matt, unloaded suitcases from the back of Elaine's Tahoe in front of their gate at the Tampa airport. Cars were squeezing into tight spots to drop off departing family members, security personnel were shooing people to move along and other cars honked for no apparent reason. The smell of exhaust wafted through the humid air.

"Oh, yes," said Thelma. "It will be good to get out of this hell hole." The others just looked at each other.

"Hang on, George," Matt ordered. "I'll grab you a wheelchair because it's a long walk to the trolley."

"I don't need a wheelchair, I'll do it myself."

"Are you sure, George?" Matt asked. "It'll be a lot faster and easier if you use a wheelchair."

"I'm good."

And so they meandered through the airport, up the escalator, onto the tram and to their gate without incident, but the process took nearly one hour without the wheelchair. Allie and Matt quickly realized the trip would be a test of their engagement and their patience.

Once in Burlington, George sat up front in the rental car as Matt's co-pilot. Matt facilitated George's nostalgic tour of UVM, where he had spent his entire career. He was talkative as he gave a play-by-play of all the buildings and memorable events that had happened there. Thelma sat silent in the backseat, but was comforted by the familiarity. It was impossible to know how much she remembered.

They arrived at the new Hilton on Lake Champlain and Allie got the two couples checked into separate rooms. The reservation was for adjoining rooms but due to a mix up, they were placed on the same floor but down the hall and around the corner from each other. Allie and Matt were secretly relieved. George and Thelma were in a handicapped-accessible room equipped with a large walk-in shower.

"Hey, Gram and Gramps," Allie said. "It's been a really long day and it's dinner time, so how about we find a restaurant close by? My Dad says Bove's is excellent and you guys used to eat there all the time when he was a kid. We can order spaghetti and meatballs."

"Oh, that sounds wonderful, Allie," Thelma responded.

"I really wanted a burger," said George.

"Gee, George," said Thelma. "I had my heart set on Bove's spaghetti and meatballs. It will be like old times." Allie and Matt looked at each other and smiled.

"Well, Gramps," said Allie. "Gram wins tonight so you can come with us and have a fabulous Italian meal, or you can stay in the hotel." Allie looked to Matt, who shrugged his shoulders as if to say 'it's your grandfather.'

"I'll just stay at the hotel."

Allie, Matt and Thelma ventured off to Bove's in the north end of Burlington, where they enjoyed mounds of traditional spaghetti and lacrosse ball-sized meatballs sprinkled with parmesan cheese, and soft white Italian bread accompanied by individual butters with foil tops. No one finished their meal, but they all opted to take doggie bags. When the check arrived, Matt placed the Amex card in the plastic folder, but was promptly informed they only accepted cash. The waitress kindly pointed them in the direction of a conveniently placed ATM next door. Matt hopped up and ran over to retrieve cash. They settled their tab and returned to the hotel with their doggie bags.

"Hey, Gramps," Allie said. "Do you want some spaghetti and meatballs? We have a ton leftover."

"No thanks, Allie. I'm really not hungry." Allie and Matt settled George and Thelma before heading down to their room.

Allie awoke with a start, realizing she had not formally set out a plan for the morning, and checked the time on her phone. It was 8:20 am. She jumped out of bed, waking Matt with all the commotion.

"What are you doing, Allie?" Matt asked, rubbing his eyes and checking his phone for the time.

"Oh my God, Matt," Allie yelled. "Do you see the time? I've got to check on Gram and Gramp because who knows what they're doing." Allie threw on a pair of sweatpants and a sweatshirt, grabbed the room key and hurried down the hall, leaving Matt lying in bed.

As she approached their room she noticed the door was ajar, escalating her anxiety. Pushing open the door, and called out, "Gram, Gramp, you guys okay?"

The first thing Allie saw was George sprawled, uncovered on the bed, wearing only tighty whitie underwear. Apparently he was still asleep. Allie moved to the bathroom where she heard water running.

"Gram? Gram, are you doing okay in there?" Allie entered the steam soaked bathroom and stepped in a pool of water from the flood flowing from the shower. "Gram, you've got to shut the curtain, because all the water's going on the floor." Allie peeked into the shower to make sure her grandmother was all right. Thelma stood mesmerized by the warm water, but there was no sign of soap, shampoo or any attempt to wash. Allie helped her wash up and dry off with the only dry towel remaining after mopping the floor. Matt poked his head in to see if everything was under control.

"Matt, go to our room and grab more towels, and then can you help George get cleaned up." Matt smiled a disingenuous smile.

Allie and Thelma laughed while Matt struggled to get George in the shower, a short but necessary shower.

"I don't need deodorant, Matt," George insisted. Allie was not in sight of Matt so he forged ahead remembering that yesterday George had emitted a distinct body odor by the end of the day. Matt persevered and George departed the bathroom smelling like Old Spice. Thelma's pill routine was anything but quick, it took nearly an hour while she inspected each pill before swallowing the mush. Allie kept a running dialogue in her head to be patient with her grandmother.

Breakfast was George's favorite meal, and he was quite hungry after skipping dinner the night before. They all headed down to the hotel dining room to discuss the day's plans over a proper breakfast. Two hours later, they exited the dining room full of bacon, eggs, toast, coffee and orange juice.

"All right you two," Allie said. "The plan today is a visit with your friends, Jane and Burr, who live down by the lake. I remember going there in the summer with my mom and dad and we swam in the lake. Matt and I will drop you off for the afternoon while we check out Burlington." George and Thelma assured her their friends were very capable of supervising them.

A cold September rain blew off the lake, making it feel like winter to the Floridians. The drive to Jane and Burr's house was only a few miles, but the last quarter mile was a dirt road and currently a sea of mud. Matt parked as close to the house as possible, worried about George's footing on the slippery ground. After knocking several times, they finally heard the faint *tap tap tap* of feet moving through the house. An old man hunched over a walker opened the door and broke into a wide smile when he saw George and Thelma.

"Hello, folks," Burr greeted. "George, buddy, how are you? Thelma, it's sure great to see you both. Come in, come in. Jane's in the other room." They followed him through the old lake house with panoramic views of Lake Champlain. Matt and Allie watched Burr struggle as he navigated through the house into the living room, wondering how the hell he was supposed to supervise George and Thelma.

"I'm recuperating from my second hip replacement," Burr explained. "Jane's had a few health issues herself, but we're both still kicking."

After a few minutes of gushing, hugging and hand holding, they all settled down on chairs strategically placed to capture the view of the Adirondack Mountains across the lake in New York state. Jane offered drinks and everyone accepted, everyone except Allie and Matt who quickly made their escape to a day in Burlington.

"So, Thelma," asked Jane. "How are things in Florida?"

"Oh, Jane, you just don't know how awful things are down there. It's a prison. They have people telling you what to do all the time, the food is disgusting and everyone is either crazy or in a wheelchair." Jane delivered the Manhattans. "George and I are planning on moving back up here to that place we were at before, umm, oh hell, I just can't remember the name."

"Do you mean Champlain Waters?" Jane said.

"Yes, that's it!" Thelma took a sip of her Manhattan, a drink she had not had much of lately. "George and I just need to make some phone calls and then we'll be moving back up here." Jane was beginning to realize Thelma might not be telling the truth, but let Thelma continue.

The foursome spent the next few hours reminiscing about their unsuccessful hunting trips, wild road trips to Montreal, bridge parties often resembling frat parties, and days when their bodies were healthier. Allie and Matt returned late in the afternoon, afraid to leave them alone too long after witnessing the physical condition of their hosts. They also had an inkling there would be drinking involved.

Allie knocked on the door and entered without waiting for an answer, a wise move since the others were deep in conversation and oblivious to outside noises. Allie and Matt found the four old friends parked in the exact same chairs as when they left three hours earlier. There were a few dirty dishes and empty glasses around the room. Thelma's voice was raised as she was still complaining about the ills of living in Florida, while George and Burr were relaxed and telling jokes.

"I'll get George," Matt whispered to Allie. "You can get your grandmother." Allie mouthed *thanks*.

Saying goodbye turned into an hour-long event by the time George used the bathroom and Thelma and Jane finished another story. After consuming a few cocktails, Matt was not sure of the exact number, George was unsteady. Matt gripped the back of his leather belt and walked next to him to help balance him. The sloppy mud between the front steps and the car was very concerning to Matt, so he held George with a death grip. They made it safely to the car. Allie guided Thelma through the mud, but was bombarded with complaints about the cold air, mud and rain. There was no making her happy at this point.

By the time everyone returned to their respective hotel rooms, it was dinner time, but no one was hungry. Allie and Matt were thankful. Matt found George's phone sitting on the floor by the side of the bed and noticed he had missed a call.

"Matt," George said. "Will you listen to the message for me?" Matt handed the phone to Allie as he didn't want to hear anything personal. Allie listened and made a face of disgust.

"Who is it, Allie?" George asked.

"It's that creep Norman checking on Gram."

"Ooh, ooh, can I speak to him?" Thelma asked.

"No, Gram," Allie answered. "He just left a message." Allie closed the phone and returned it to the bedside. Thelma had not mentioned him once since the trip started and Allie wanted to kick herself for telling them who it was. Allie settled her grandparents, turned on the television and bid them goodnight. Allie and Matt headed straight back to their room to crash. They knew tomorrow would be just as exhausting.

"That guy Norman is such a douche bag," Allie said. "You know what he said in the message?" Matt spread his hands waiting for the answer. "He said, *"Oh, Thelma, I miss you so much and I'm counting the days until you return.* He actually left that message on Gramp's phone. I deleted the message because I don't want Gramp to hear that shit on his own phone. This is seriously messed up!"

"I think your parents or Ken are going to have to step in and do something about him when we get back," Matt said. They both crawled into bed and fell asleep with the television running.

"Oh my God Allie," Matt said, glancing at his phone for the time. "What are you doing up at this hour?" It was 7:00 am.

"I'm not cleaning up another flood this morning so I'm going to be proactive before they have a chance to cause trouble."

Matt rolled over, figuring Allie had things under control. It took Allie over an hour to carouse them out of bed and assist Thelma with her morning pill routine, an endeavor was torture to all parties. Matt finally arrived at George and Thelma's room to find Allie manipulating George's hair into a variety of styles; mohawk, greased back, bangs in the face and she even tried pigtails where there was enough hair. George loved the attention but opted to stick with his tried-and-true style of a side part and bangs to the side. He did not sport the hideous comb over as he was blessed with a thick head of silver hair. By the time they finished breakfast downstairs, it was mid-morning.

"Okay, you two," Allie said. "Here's the plan for today. Lunch at Al's French Fries, followed by a drive up to the Trout Club for dinner with Hugh."

"The Trout Club sure is a little slice of heaven," George said as they pulled into the dirt parking lot. Nine miles down a tree-lined dirt road winding through the Nebraska Valley of the Green Mountains sat the Trout Club. The view was spectacular. The lake was surrounded by mountains with crystal clear water, home to several varieties of trout. An old lodge sat perched on the edge of the lake with a wraparound porch adorned with white rocking chairs and boxes of red geraniums. There were rooms, rustic but comfortable, and a dining room that served five-star quality meals. Meals were served family style three times a day. Thirty minutes prior to dinner guests were summoned by the blowing of a conch shell. George had been a member of the club since 1971 and his children spent countless hours there swimming, hiking, playing cards, working on jigsaw puzzles and relaxing.

Matt parked the car and they stopped to soak in the view of the lake and mountains with a hint of the coming foliage. After making their way to the porch, they sat for several hours chatting with Hugh and other members who wandered by. George was content and peaceful. Thelma had always enjoyed the social aspects of the Trout Club, but was not a fan of spending the night due to the high population of mice living in the walls. Thelma did not like mice. By late afternoon it was officially cocktail hour, and those inclined moved to the Fly Room at the back of the lodge. The Fly Room was a large windowed room with gorgeous views, a fireplace and a sink. Guests brought their own liquor and hors d'oeuvres. The one steadfast rule was *No Children Allowed* in the Fly Room. Everyone, including the kids, was fine with this.

Following the social hour in the Fly Room with Hugh, they moved to the dining room and sat at their assigned table when the conch was blown. The night's menu included freshly caught pan-fried trout with sides of Brussels sprouts and rice pilaf. George was in heaven but Thelma struggled to be happy.

"Oh no," Thelma started. "I'm always so worried when I eat fish I'm going to choke on a bone."

"Gram," Allie said. "You'll be fine. I've checked your fish and there aren't any bones."

"Thanks, Allie."

At their table was a honeymooning couple from Rhode Island thrilled to be in Vermont during the fall. Allie and Matt swapped stories with them about weddings, marriage and parents. Thelma and George continued to catch up with Hugh until it was time to pack up and head back to Burlington.

Back in the hotel, the bedtime process went smoothly so Allie and Matt headed straight to their own room.

"Oh my God Allie," Matt said as he rolled over on the bed to look at Allie. "I can't believe we have to go back to the Trout Club again tomorrow with your grandparents."

"Matt, that's why we brought them to Vermont. All their friends are going to be there tomorrow, so we'll be free to go hiking or sneak off by ourselves." Allie kissed Matt. "It's going to be an adventure."

In the morning Matt suggested they just order breakfast from room service to save time, recalling the two hours breakfast took the previous morning. Allie ordered breakfast while Matt showered so he had not heard what she ordered.

"Allie that looks like half a barnyard sitting on the cart!"

"My Gramps likes his breakfast. He claims it's the most important meal of the day, and I don't want them to be hungry." Allie laughed.

"Clearly no chance of that today." Matt rolled the cart over to a small table by the window. Allie herded her grandparents to the table and sat them down to a hearty breakfast. Today breakfast took only one hour to eat.

"This is a little slice of heaven," George said as they pulled into the Trout Club parking lot for the second day in a row. Allie glanced at Matt, knowing they would hear all the same stories again. Patience was the theme for the day.

George and Thelma ambled over to the lodge where they found their friends; Barb, Hugh, Jane and Burr. Thelma perked up as soon as she saw them. This circle of friends had spent countless weekends, hardships and celebrations together and were now witness to the ugly side of old age.

With the early start, they still had an hour before lunch and it was a perfect fall day with crisp cool air, deep blue skies, no humidity and no insects.

"Hey Matt," Allie said. "Let's hike up to Taylor Lodge before lunch. It's an easy climb and Gram and Gramp are fine here with all their friends—and I need a break!"

"Sounds good. Should we bring water or have hiking boots or a backpack with food?" Matt was an EMT and fireman, he knew the importance of being prepared.

"No, it's an easy hike. We can grab the water we have in the car, but I don't think we'll even need that." Allie and Matt took off at 11:30 but somehow detoured off the trail and did not return to the Trout Club until 5:00 pm. Matt referred to the hike as a death march as they hiked for hours without water or food, and very little conversation. A true test of their compatibility. As they approached the Trout Club their concern mounted for George and Thelma, but knew their friends were keeping an eye on them. Matt spotted George and Thelma sitting alone in the Fly Room. Their friends had departed immediately following lunch, leaving George and Thelma alone for the entire afternoon.

"I can't believe their friends just up and left them," Allie said.

"I need food," Matt stated. "I'm going in search of food because I am seriously hangry right now." The kitchen staff was busy preparing dinner and not in the mood to be burdened with finding snacks for the weary hikers. Matt managed to scrape together enough change to buy a couple cans of Coke from the lone vending machine.

"So Gram," Allie started. "How was the visit with your friends today?"

"Oh, it was fine."

"So Gram, what did they serve you guys for lunch?"

"Umm, umm, I don't remember." George was no help.

They both looked exhausted as Allie packed them up and they headed back to Burlington. Neither George nor Thelma wanted any dinner, in fact, they were amenable to the idea of just retiring for the night. Allie was very relieved to not have to take her grandparents out for dinner but she ended up spending close to an hour administering medications and directing the wardrobe change.

Allie noticed George's phone on the floor again, half hidden under the bed. She picked it up and saw there was another message from Norman. She handed the phone to George and watched him as he listened to the message with sadness in his eyes.

"George," Thelma said. "Who is it?"

"It's nothing Thel," he said and clicked off his phone. Allie now realized this drama was in fact affecting her grandfather. By 7:30 pm both George and Thelma were safely tucked in bed with the television on. Both were asleep within five minutes.

Allie and Matt returned to their room in great need of a shower and quick nap before venturing out into Burlington for the night. They found a bar on Church Street that was in the midst of a Sam Adams beer tasting. Exactly what they needed, pub food and beer.

At 7:00 am, the obnoxious alarm woke Allie and Matt. One more day. Their flight was scheduled for 10:45 am so she knew she needed to get moving immediately. Allie headed down to her grandparent's room. She knocked and the door opened with a grinning George standing there in only his tighty whitie underwear, no Depends and no sign of Thelma. Allie made the decision not to check the sheets, because what did it matter at this point?

"AAAAHH." A scream drifted from the bathroom where Thelma was in her pink nightgown stepping into the cold shower. The burst of cold water had scared her.

"Oh my God, Gram," Allie said. "What are you doing?"

"I'm trying to take a shower but this damn thing only sprays cold water. Everything here is so cold. I've never been so cold in my life." Thelma snapped.

"Okay Gram, let me help you. You know it'll feel a lot better if you take off your nightgown before jumping in the shower." Allie bolstered her strength to stay calm and patient.

"Ah, shit!" Thelma said, but Allie wasn't sure who or what it was directed at.

Allie busied herself with organizing Thelma's toilet articles and laying out an outfit for the journey home to Florida. Matt kept his distance from the bathroom, and guided George through the dressing and packing process while exchanging jokes and bad humor. Even with the cushion of extra time Allie had planned, there was no time left for breakfast if they hoped to catch their flight. They completed the room check, double-checked the need for a trip to the bathroom, and waited for Thelma to finish her morning pill ritual. They were buckled in the rental car and headed to the Burlington airport by 9:30 am. Allie felt sadness that this would be the last time her grandparents would be in Vermont, but kept her thoughts to herself.

After an uneventful flight, Elaine was waiting in Tampa with an expectant look. She thought she knew what to expect because Allie had given her daily updates, sometimes twice daily. They all exited the tram looking weary for different reasons.

"So you two," Elaine inquired. "How was the trip?" She hoped to get them talking.

"Oh, it was so cold up there," complained Thelma. "I think I'm finally starting to warm up."

"Well," said Elaine. "You're always complaining how horrible it is down here and how badly you want to move back to Vermont. It must have been nice to be back in Vermont."

"It was good," George said. "It was good to see our friends." Elaine looked at Allie and Matt, who laughed and shrugged their shoulders.

"Okay, come on Gramp," Allie started. "We did more than just see a couple of your friends. Where did we take you two days in a row, a place you love?" Allie waited.

"Ummm, I don't know. Help me out Allie."

"Gramp! Don't you remember going to the Trout Club? We went up and met Hugh one night and the following day we went up and you had lunch with Hugh, Barb, Jane and Burr. Remember?"

"Yeah, maybe."

"Oh my God! I can't believe everything we went through and you guys don't even remember." Allie was getting worked up. "Okay, do you remember going to your all time favorite restaurant in Burlington?"

Thelma and George both looked at each other, clearly not recalling the expedition to Al's French Fries. Allie slapped her hands on the back of the seat and recounted in rapid fire detail their lunch at Al's. For Allie's sake they pretended to remember but they fooled no one.

"Oh, it's good to be back where it's warm," Thelma said. "I was so cold in Vermont." They made their way up to apartment 523 and knew this new-found love of Florida would be short-lived. Just as the elevator doors opened, there standing in front of them, was no other than Norman. He was holding a large bottle of Crown Royal still in its purple bag, and a bag of Hershey Nuggets.

"Hello Norman," Elaine said cooly and walked past him. Thelma gushed and rubbed Norman's arm while Allie shook her head in disgust. Allie hugged George's arm and kissed him on the cheek.

"Thanks for stopping by Norman, but they are tired and they've had a long day," Elaine said, trying to be as kind as possible.

Norman ignored Elaine and made himself at home in the apartment, starting to make cocktails for everyone.

"Norman," Elaine said abruptly. "This really isn't a good time, because as you can see we are just walking in the door. Thelma and George are exhausted and need to rest, and we need to take care of a few things before we leave. Maybe you can come back later."

Norman understood the tone in Elaine's voice but pretended to pout, a very unbecoming look in a grown man.

"Oh Norman, please stay," Thelma begged. Elaine gave Norman a look needing no interpretation. He left with the cocktails still sitting on the counter.

"Oh Elaine, why did you ask him to leave? I really wanted to see him." Elaine explained once again how they needed to unpack and settle in after a very long day. "I resent everyone telling me what to do! Maybe I'll just move back to Vermont."

Elaine, Allie and Matt finished unpacking and double-checked the supply of Depends, Pepsi and snacks—which were all fine for a few days. They made their exit. They did not see Norman as they left the building but felt his presence lurking about somewhere.

Chapter 14 The Break-Up

Have you seen the new band-Ned Nasal and Nine Nasty Nosepickers?
Their hit song is "Dig Me a Boogie".

"Hello?" Ken answered his phone as he was driving to an appointment.

"Ken, how are you?" asked George.

"Hey Dad, what's up?" Ken proceeded through the ritual of the phone call, knowing his father was calling for one of three reasons: he lost the remote, the television was screwed up or he needed more Pepsi and cigars.

"I'm having trouble getting the TV to work. It just says HDMI 2 and I've pushed all the buttons but nothing is working. Can you come over right now and fix it?"

"Gee Dad, I'd love to but I'm about forty-five minutes away from Whispering Oaks and I'm on my way to a meeting with a client. So no, I can't come over right now and fix it. I'll head over your way about three this afternoon when I finish up. You'll just have to read a book or talk to Mom."

"All right, you want to say hi to your mother?"

"No Dad, I'm driving, and I'll see you two later this afternoon." He hung up as soon as his thumb found the *end call* button.

Ken arrived at the apartment after making it through the lobby and cadre of decorators prepping for the New Year's Eve party later that night.

The first order of business was bringing the television back to viewing capability and for Ken it was simply a matter of punching three buttons. This was an impossible task to explain over the phone to his father. Since Ken was currently in charge of the remote, he found an inane show called, *An Idiot Abroad,* thinking it would be a welcome change from Fox News. Neither parent commented. Thelma sat on the couch rubbing and scratching her legs, clearly uncomfortable. Ken plopped down next to her to have a closer look.

"Mom, your legs are really red and swollen." Ken carefully touched her puffy ankle and felt heat radiating out. "Do your legs hurt Mom?"

"Oh, I'm in so much pain Ken, I can barely walk." Ken found a nurse, but she was very dismissive regarding Thelma's condition. Ken made a mental note to talk with Stu and Elaine because her legs looked terrible and she was definitely uncomfortable. Her feet were so swollen she could not get a sneaker on.

Before Ken had a chance to speak with Stu and Elaine, he received a call from Whispering Oaks. Thelma was on her way to the hospital by ambulance. Ken was annoyed that his concerns earlier in the day were ignored, and he kicked himself for not making a scene at the time.

Being New Year's Eve, everyone had plans. Elaine drew the short straw and made her way to the hospital, where she found Thelma propped up in the hospital bed attached to several IVs.

"Thelma, are you planning on partying here at the hospital tonight?" Thelma was not in the mood so Elaine made sure Thelma was settled and checked with the nurses before heading off to her New Year's party. The diagnosis was cellulitis, a bacterial skin infection leading to fever, swollen legs and dehydration. She would most likely be in the hospital a few days.

Ken stopped by the next day.

"Oh Ken, they're awful here. These horrible nurses keep coming in here and telling me what to do. I hate them. I hate it here." She continued to rant as Ken listened to all the familiar complaints.

"I brought you a chocolate milkshake." He handed it to her with the straw in place. She managed to hold it steady enough to wrap her parched lips around the straw. Once she started, it was like a fix of crack and she finished the milkshake in less than five minutes.

Stu stopped by the hospital while Ken was still there. They both realized it would be a busy week between checking on Thelma in the hospital and George at Whispering Oaks.

"Mom is really out of it," Stu said.

"I know," Ken agreed. "She doesn't even know our names or where she is. You know, this might be the end." They were both quiet.

Ken stopped by the hospital again the next afternoon, and as he rounded the corner near Thelma's room he thought he saw a man leaving in the opposite direction. It looked a lot like Norman, but Ken didn't believe he had the nerve to actually visit the hospital.

Ken entered Thelma's room to find brown smears all over her hands, face and sheets. Ken's first thought was she shit herself, but upon closer inspection, he realized it was chocolate. Her advancing disease made it harder and harder for her to properly grasp things in her hands. With her love of chocolate she must have hung onto the chocolate for dear life as it melted. Ken cleaned her up with wipes, but wondered where the chocolate had come from. He knew Norman must have brought it and had snuck out just as Ken was arriving. Ken did a quick scan up and down the corridor but it was empty. Ken decided to just ask.

"So Mom, where did you get the chocolate?"

"Oh, he brought it. He's so thoughtful." Ken's stomach knotted up because he knew the situation was escalating and the time was nearing to deal with Norman. There would be fallout.

With drugs Thelma recovered quickly, and George was barely aware his wife had been gone for seven days. They all survived the ordeal and neither one remembered anything about it.

One weekend Stu and Elaine popped into Whispering Oaks for a visit when they were ambushed by the manager.

"Hello Stu, Elaine. Do you two have a few minutes before you head upstairs?" They felt like they were being called into the principal's office.

"Sure, what's up?" Stu asked.

"Well it seems that your mother has been sneaking out of the building with Norman the last few nights. He goes through the game room so he can avoid the front desk, which is very concerning to us as we have rules. We're concerned for the welfare of your mother."

"Have you spoken to Norman about this?" asked Elaine.

"Yes, we did last night because of what we had witnessed. I must say, we are very concerned for your mother."

"What happened last night?" Stu braced himself.

"Well, the nurses were looking for Thelma to administer her evening pills, but she wasn't in the apartment and your father didn't know where she was. They became alarmed and looked everywhere, when one of the custodians overheard us and mentioned he had seen Thelma and Norman in a car in the parking lot. The windows were steamed up, if you know what I mean."

"Oh my God," Elaine said.

"And that's not all," the manager continued. "A few minutes later your mother comes strolling in the lobby with her skirt tucked into her underwear and her hair was a mess. One of the nurses quickly escorted your mother back upstairs, but she was in a fine mood and just kept saying she felt like a teenager."

"Okay," Stu said. "This thing with Norman has to end. What did he have to say for himself when you spoke with him?"

"Oh, he denied it at first, but then told us some lame story about taking her to Panera, but he had no explanation for not signing her out."

"Our concern," Elaine started, "is that Thelma really isn't competent and if something happens when he's sneaking her out of here, what a mess for everyone."

"We completely agree," the manager said. "We have liability issues regarding the safety of our residents, so we have told Norman that under no circumstances may he leave with Thelma. We spoke with Thelma but honestly, I'm not sure she comprehends the problem."

"We'll speak with my brother Ken and figure something out. Ken's been thinking about drawing up a restraining order but felt funny about it. Maybe it's time."

Ken stopped up for a visit the following morning and in the thirty minutes he was there, Norman called George's phone three times looking for Thelma. Thelma did not have a phone. On the third call, Ken grabbed the phone and answered it himself. Ken was not prepared for the call.

"George…I have called three times looking for Thelma and you refuse to put her on. I really don't like how you're treating me and not letting me speak with her." Norman was short and nasty on the phone, not realizing it was Ken.

"Hello Norman, this is not George, it's his son Ken. I must say I'm shocked at your rudeness and disrespect towards my father. I am informing you not to call this number again and I am informing you to stay away from my mother. If you fail to do so, I will be forced to take legal action. Are we clear?" Ken was calm and Norman hung up without another word.

Ken confiscated George's phone that evening, hoping to save his father from further harassment and to see if Norman had the nerve to call again. Sure enough Norman called again a few hours later.

"Can I speak with Thelma," asked Norman.

"Norman, this is Ken again and I thought I was clear when I told you not to call anymore. Let me state it one more time for you: you are not to call my mother or my father for any reason. You cannot speak to my mother and if you continue to call, I will be forced to call the police. Are we clear?" Ken was stern but polite.

"Yes, Ken. I'm sorry and I won't call anymore." Norman hung up. Ken had his doubts and decided to jot down all the calls that had come through George's phone, especially from Norman.

The next day Ken was back up at Whispering Oaks for his twice weekly check-in, when he was intercepted by the manager as he entered the lobby.

"There's been another development with your mother and Norman."

"What now?" Ken asked knowing nothing surprised him anymore.

"Well, about an hour ago one of the nurses went to your parents' apartment to check on them. When she entered, Norman was standing in the middle of the kitchen. She knew Norman had been told to stay away and ordered Norman to leave. Norman physically pushed her out the door and tried to slam the door shut on her. We had people on it immediately, and he has been told in very clear terms he has two weeks to vacate Whispering Oaks." Ken listened and nodded slightly. "I spoke with his daughter, who is less than happy about what's been going on between him and your mother. Especially because her own mother is very frail. I'm so sorry about all this." The manager waited for Ken's reaction.

"Thanks, and it's certainly not your fault. I've taken Dad's phone and I've spoken with Norman a few times myself, but it appears I need to take it to the next level. Please let me know if anything else happens."

Later on Ken received another phone call from Norman on George's phone.

"Hello," Ken said, knowing it was Norman from the caller ID.

"Hi George, can I speak with Thelma?" Norman was not aware Ken still had the phone.

"Norman, this is Ken."

"Oh."

"Oh, is right. Listen Norman, you've left me no choice but to go to the police and request a restraining order."

"Ken, let's think about this. I promise I won't call anymore. Give me another chance." Norman had resorted to a pathetic begging tone.

"Again, I want to be perfectly clear with you. I am going to the police to have them issue a restraining order against you and this discussion is not open for negotiation." Norman abruptly disconnected.

Ken composed an official letter addressed to Norman, stating that any future contact would result in a restraining order from the Largo Police Department. He mailed a copy to Norman, left another copy with the front desk and kept a copy for his files.

When Stu and Elaine arrived at apartment 523 the following evening, they found Thelma in a sobbing heap on the couch. Elaine sat next to her while Stu caught up with George.

"Thelma," Elaine said. "Are you okay?" Elaine rubbed her back.

"Oooohh, I can't believe my own son would do this to me! How can my family be so cruel?" She wailed like a wounded bird.

"Thelma, what happened?"

"Oh, don't be naive, Elaine, you know exactly what happened. My son told Norman to stay away from me. What am I supposed to do now? We were so happy together, and now I just want to leave. I have to get out of this place." She sounded desperate.

"Thelma, everything Ken did is because he loves you and wants you to be safe. You know Norman was dangerous, right?" Elaine used the phrases Ken had suggested. Thelma picked her head up and stared at Elaine.

"Dangerous?"

"Yes, Thelma. He was becoming dangerous because he was trying to hurt people, and we do not want you hurt." Elaine remained calm and soft-spoken.

"Oh, he never tried to hurt me." Thelma sounded much less sure of herself now. Stu knew Elaine wanted to engage Thelma in a conversation of reason, a conversation Thelma was no longer capable of having.

"Let's head out to Applebee's for dinner," Stu suggested, trying to get his mother's focus off Norman. They managed to corral George and Thelma and were sitting in Applebee's less than forty minutes later. Thelma did not once mention Norman, nor did she ever mention him again.

Chapter 15 It's Upside Down

What do priests say to get rid of insects in the church?
Let us spray.

"Hey Elaine," Stu said. "Have you seen my dad's disability check for this month?" Stu was rummaging through piles of newspapers, magazines and candy wrappers strewn about the apartment.

"No, what do you bet they threw it away?"

"Why would they throw away a $3,000 check and keep all this other shit laying around?"

"You ask hard questions to which there are no answers," Elaine said.

"Dad?" Stu asked. "Have you seen your disability check lying around or in the mail recently?" Stu was becoming frustrated. He reopened every drawer, rechecked under every surface and even went through their trash, but to no avail.

"Dad, when these checks come, you need to make sure you give them to me right away, because it's a lot of money. Now I have to call and have them reissue the check." Stu looked at Elaine, who was reorganizing Thelma's clothes again.

Through clenched teeth and with a scrunched face Thelma hissed, "I hate it when she comes in here and takes over. These are my things! She has no right." Stu ignored his mother, because it was a circular discussion that went precisely nowhere.

"And where are my gold beads?" she snapped. "I know Elaine has my gold beads and I want them back."

"Mom, we have them at the house for safekeeping because we're afraid they might get stolen here. Any time you want to wear them, we'll bring them right over. Wouldn't you be sad if something happened to them?"

"I want my gold beads back." Stu and Elaine decided they had overstayed their welcome after only twenty minutes. They hugged and kissed George and Thelma goodbye, and debriefed walking to the elevator.

"Did you notice she didn't mention Norman once?" Elaine said.

"I guess that's progress, but now I've got to call and get that check reissued. I need to arrange it so they send it to me directly since I have the financial power of attorney. And Elaine, you should just bring those damn beads back here and if they get stolen, so what."

"Stu, they're a family heirloom, and your mother will hide them somewhere or they'll get stolen for real. It's crazy to let that happen."

"Elaine, just give them to her and you won't have to listen to her bitch about them anymore."

"All right, but I don't want to listen to her complain when they've been stolen or lost. It seems crazy to risk losing something so valuable."

They continued their conversation of issues surrounding George and Thelma, arriving at the conclusion that having two parents in assisted living together who reside in different universes was challenging, especially when there was no hope of improvement to the situation. George seemed to be checked out more and more, while Thelma was spiraling into an abyss of anger and craziness.

Ken and Stu stopped by for their weekly lunch outing, a task they now did more frequently because dinner had turned into a four-hour event. On a work night, it was just too much. They opted for Chili's as it was close and George could order his cheeseburger and fries. They were seated in a booth towards the back of the restaurant where the air conditioning was blowing directly down on them.

"Mom, you're shivering." Stu said, watching his mother hug herself with shaky arms.

"I'm freezing, I haven't been warm since I moved to Florida. Your father keeps the air conditioner set so low I have to open the balcony door and put sweaters on." It was true they were embattled in a temperature war in the apartment. Thelma turned the thermostat up to 80 degrees and then George turned it down to 60 degrees. Finally one of the boys taped a piece of cardboard over the device, out of sight, out of mind. It worked, but Thelma was still always cold due in large part to her increasing lack of body fat.

The group placed their order while George flirted with the waitress. She arrived with pints for everyone except Thelma who ordered Pepsi. Thelma grasped the straw in her gnarled hand, shakily unwrapping it by ripping small shards of paper off. By the time the plastic straw was revealed, a pile of paper resembling a mouse's handiwork lay on the table. The others were in conversation but quietly eyed Thelma as she struggled to place the straw in the icy Pepsi. She slowly lowered the straw, quivering as it neared the rim of the tumbler, somehow missing the glass every time by an inch. No lid covered the beverage, allowing her a four-inch opening for a bull's eye, but every time she closed in on success the straw veered off to the right. Ken and Stu made eye contact but said nothing, and George watched with a grin just under the surface. Thelma continued unsuccessfully for over twenty minutes, until finally with no apparent deviation from previous attempts, the straw slid into the glass. Thelma was unfazed and not the least bit frustrated.

Without missing a beat George said, "Hey Thel, the straw's upside down."

She immediately withdrew the straw in an attempt to insert it the opposite way. Stu and Ken howled with laughter, not at their mother's struggle but at George's quick wit. Thelma, oblivious to the entertainment she was supplying, continued on her mission for another ten minutes.

Ken and Stu were torn with emotion, because on one hand it was devastating to watch their mother grapple with the simplest of tasks, while on the other hand they were encouraged by their father's ability to be in the moment making jokes. Lunch proceeded with familiar patterns; Thelma ate two bites before announcing she was full, and George enjoyed two beers and polished off his entire burger and fries. Thelma discovered a second wind when the chocolate lava cake was placed in front of her.

Phone calls from Whispering Oaks were now a way of life for Stu, Ken and Elaine, however they were becoming more frequent and laced with an edge of desperation. Thelma was requiring more and more assistance with dressing, getting to the dining room and using the bathroom, but she was not the only one. George was having an increasingly difficult time walking, and real issues with making it to the bathroom on time and dressing. The monthly cost had gradually increased to nearly $10,000 with all the additional assistance. The manager informed Ken that George and Thelma had to move by month's end. This time she was serious.

Ken and Stu quickly ran research on moving their parents to *The 4th Floor*, better known as the memory unit, or moving them to a whole new facility. They soon discovered moving to *The 4th Floor* within Whispering Oaks would offer increased assistance while the cost would actually decrease. George and Thelma could stay together in a one-bedroom similar to their current apartment, but Thelma would no longer have the freedom to come and go unless escorted by someone else. George would be free to leave since he was not labeled a memory patient, and there was little fear he would wander off. Their meals would be served in the dining room on *The 4th Floor* and they would be required to eat at least one meal a day in the dining room. Family was welcome to take them out anytime or visit at any hour. Following a few phone calls to Karen and Sue, a decision was agreed upon by all four children. The move was scheduled for the following week.

"Thelma, you're moving to a new apartment," Elaine explained. "We'll have you and George hang out at our house for the day while we get everything moved and set up. No work for you guys, you can just relax on the porch or sit in the sun." Thelma nodded blankly. Only one year before Thelma was making comments about the crazies on *The 4th Floor* and now she was unaware of the significance of their impending relocation.

Stu, Elaine and Ken spent countless hours going through boxes stored in the closet, never unpacked from their previous move. There were boxes of entomological text books, antiquated science equipment from George's lab, boxes of old family bibles ranging in size from a cigarette pack to some the size of a cinder block. Among the treasures was the missing Oreck air filter along with an unused vacuum, boxes of old photographs, mounds of letters dating back to George's time in WWII and piles of clothes not worn in years. Purge, simplify and minimize was the goal, as much as humanly possible to reduce clutter around their new apartment. Clutter seemed to accumulate quicker than extra pounds at the holidays, but anything to keep their apartment cleaner, neater and more organized made life easier for Thelma.

The staff at Whispering Oaks moved all the large pieces of furniture, for a fee, while Ken, Elaine and Stu set up the new apartment to resemble their old. They hung the high school graduation photos of all the grandkids in the same arrangement, they placed George's recliner in a similar position to the television with his small end table to the left, and their bedroom was identical to their old one. They were amazed at how quickly the apartment came together, but then remembered just how experienced they were. It was time to retrieve George and Thelma.

"Do you remember the code to get off this thing?" Stu asked Ken under his breath as the elevator doors closed.

"Geez Stu, maybe you need to be moving to *The 4th Floor*. It's 4-1-1-1-4," Ken said. Whispering Oaks' answer to security was to code-protect the elevator doors on *The 4th Floor*. The doors would not open unless a special code was punched in, ensuring the safety of the residents. It really prevented residents from escaping. The doors opened to a cheerfully-painted lobby area with a receptionist who had eyes on the elevator. The hardwood floors spanned the wide hallways in three directions. Thelma and George were now living down to the right, past a glass-encased atrium, past their small dining room and down a carpeted hallway.

"What do you think Mom?" Stu asked. "Are you ready for your new place? You've been telling us you wanted to move and now you have!"

"Oh, I hate this place!" Thelma scowled. It was not Monkton, it was not life with their old friends, it was not a time when she was healthy and in control. Nothing would ever be okay again.

"Thelma! How are you sweetheart?" a nurse said as they passed in the hallway. Thelma did her best to smile, but it looked more like a scowl as she tried to say something but nothing came out. It was clear Thelma was known and well liked around Whispering Oaks.

"Here you go, Mom," Ken said, opening the door with a flourish to their new apartment. "Here's your new place with a view out to the front side of the building. You can watch all the action when you sit on the balcony."

"Yeah, great. Now we can watch the ambulances cart everyone away." Thelma stood in the middle of her new kitchen looking lost. "This looks like that other place we lived in."

George straggled behind, gripping his cane, insisting he could walk on his own. Stu walked in close proximity to him.

"Dad," Stu instructed. "Keep lifting your feet when you walk, you're dragging and you're going to end up tripping. Remember a fall is bad because if you break a hip, you'll end up in a nursing home," Stu reminded him of the ultimate threat.

Elaine arrived only a few minutes later, despite having made several stops along the way to pick up pizzas and Pepsi for dinner. Her arms were loaded with white plastic bags from Target filled with Depends, paper towels, chocolate, Cabot cheddar and bottled water. They all sat around the central coffee table eating pizza and doing their best to carry on a conversation.

"Dad, remember you can go downstairs to the main dining room for any of your meals, and you can take Mom with you." Stu was hoping George would take advantage of getting off *The 4th Floor*.

"Right," George said. "I'll be sure to do that."

Almost three weeks passed without a call from Whispering Oaks. When the call came, Elaine was just pulling out of her driveway on the way to work.

"Hi Elaine, this is Whispering Oaks and I'm calling about George and Thelma." Elaine waited.

"They need more Depends because there is a trail of urine from the bed to the bathroom every morning and the carpet is becoming difficult to clean that often." She waited for Elaine's response.

"Wow, I thought we just brought up a huge supply of Depends. What are they doing with them?" Elaine agreed to have a load delivered.

"And one more thing I'd like to discuss with you. You may or may not realize our rule is that all residents of assisted living are required to be continent. So if George or Thelma continue to have accidents on the floor and in the bed every night, they will have to move."

Ken stopped in the next day with a supply of Depends in XL for George and M for Thelma. As he was lugging the load down the corridor he approached the sunny atrium where Andy, a friendly young nurse, was facing off with a completely naked woman.

"GET OUT OF MY LIVING ROOM, who are you?" the naked lady yelled. "Get out of here right now or I'm calling the police." Andy calmly tried to speak with her.

"Dolores, it's me Andy, and I'm not going to hurt you. I'm here to help you."

"Don't touch me you creep!" she yelled. "Get out of my house."

Andy cooly stood his ground and acted as if this happened every day. Two staff members arrived to rescue Andy and deescalate the situation. They distracted Dolores by changing the subject and walking her back to her apartment. Ken shook his head as he continued down the hall, wondering how this place differed from an insane asylum.

The overwhelming odor of urine pierced Ken's nose upon entering the apartment and he looked at his parents both sitting quietly watching the television.

"Hey guys, it stinks like piss in here. You have to use your Depends, or they're going to make you move and it could be a move to a nursing home. Do you understand?"

"Oh Ken, it doesn't smell in here," said Thelma who suddenly turned her stink eye on Ken. "Who says we're having accidents? I hate these people, they're all liars. I need to get out of here. Your father and I are moving back up to that place, that other place. Umm, umm, you know that other place we lived at."

Ken took a deep breath as he sat on the couch next to his mother. He needed a minute to prepare for what he knew was going to be a very stressful hour. "You mean Champlain Waters?"

"Yes! That's it!" Thelma squinted her eyes and puckered her lips.

"So, you mean the place you hated, the place you referred to as a prison, a place you couldn't wait to get out of in a state where you were freezing all time?"

"Oh Ken, we didn't hate it there. We just need to make a few phone calls to umm, umm, what's his name and make arrangements and then we're leaving."

"Really? Okay, well make sure you call me when you get there, because I'll miss you." Ken was smiling knowing he was simply entertaining himself, he couldn't help it. In typical fashion George said nothing but was paying attention to the conversation.

"I'm curious though," asked Ken. "How are you guys going to get back up there?"

"We'll drive," snarled Thelma. Ken thought about the many things he could say but opted to remain silent. "Let's go downstairs to the dining room tonight," Ken suggested, needing to change the subject before they went down the rabbit hole.

"Oh, the food here is awful. I'm not hungry."

"Okay Dad, do you ever take Mom downstairs like we've suggested dozens of times?"

"No I haven't, but I will."

"Well, tonight I'll go down with both of you, and show you how to order off the menu or ask them to make any type of sandwich you want. You don't have to eat the special of the day if you don't like it, they'll make anything you want. You'll see lots of your friends down there too."

"We don't have any friends here!" Thelma growled. Ken wanted a drink but realized his parents did not keep whiskey in the apartment anymore.

Ken alerted the staff he was escorting both George and Thelma downstairs to the big dining room for dinner, and they would return afterward. Walking slowly down the hallway they passed a resident named Claire, who by most accounts looked normal but was not. She wandered up and down the hallways all day long. The instant she saw someone, she inched very close to them so you could feel her breath and know what she had for lunch. A true violation of personal space.

"Where is everyone?" Claire asked, looking all around. "Where is everyone going?"

"We're just heading down to dinner," Ken said, wishing his parents would pick up the pace. Thelma gave Claire the stink eye as they continued walking down the hall. Arriving at the elevators, they needed to wait for a staff member to unlock the elevators. There was no escaping from *The 4th Floor* without real effort. While waiting to be released, Ken glanced around and heard a group of residents singing *My Country 'Tis of Thee* in a parlor off the lobby. He watched as a woman clutched a baby doll to her chest, whispering softly to it as if it were her own infant. Ken really wanted a drink but would have to settle for cranberry juice.

Within the week Ken received a call from Whispering Oaks informing him George and Thelma could stay, but they would need to be moved across the hall to a new apartment outfitted with special laminate floors resembling hardwood. There would, of course, be a charge for the new flooring and the move, but Whispering Oaks was willing to handle the whole move in just a few hours. Ken and Stu decided it was in everyone's best interest to remove George and Thelma for the day to help minimize confusion. They really hoped this was the last move.

The new apartment was directly across the hall, still on *The 4th Floor*, and was set up exactly the same except the floorplan was flipped. Stu and Ken returned with their parents to show them the new apartment and help organize things to their satisfaction.

"This looks just like that other place we lived," Thelma said as she stepped off the elevator.

"I know, isn't it beautiful here?" asked Stu.

"Peeeuu, this place stinks." Thelma made a face and Stu's optimism vanished.

George and Thelma were given the grand tour of the apartment, but neither one showed much interest. The big difference were the new floors throughout, giving the apartment a more open feel. Ken suggested they head straight downstairs for dinner, because another outing off site might prove too much for one day. They agreed and headed down, a process not to be rushed. George walked down the long corridor at a markedly slower pace before reaching the elevators. Stu stayed with his father while Ken walked with his mother, who was still able to move on her own but was seriously hunched over.

"Oh, my back hurts so much," Thelma said.

"Try standing up straight," suggested Ken.

"Oh Ken, you don't understand what it feels like." George and Stu finally caught up just as the elevator doors opened. Two female residents were loitering near the elevator doors plotting their escape, but their hopes were dashed when told the elevator was heading in the opposite direction. It did not deter their focus on dreams of escape.

"Oh, this looks just like the place we lived before," Thelma said. "How did they get it to look just the same?"

"It is the same place, Mom, you just moved apartments," said Ken.

"But it looks exactly the same, how did they do it? I know what they're doing, they're trying to trick me and it's just a game!" Ken and Stu didn't know how to respond to this new revelation.

Entering the dining room they were greeted nonstop by old acquaintances inquiring into their recent whereabouts. Answers were vague, either because they could not articulate where they had been, or they were not admitting to living on *The 4th Floor.*

They sat at a table in the corner with a view of the entire room, a perk not appreciated. Ken and Stu directed them through the menu, again, and explained how they should come down here for meals at least once a day and order off the menu. George agreed but everyone knew it would never happen. They all ordered the Salisbury steak, a fancy name for a hamburger with gravy, baked potato, green beans and the requisite cranberry juice.

Thelma and George both looked forward to their dish of ice cream. Stu held George's dish of vanilla, because with only one working hand it was difficult to scoop the hard ice cream onto the spoon while the dish moved around with nothing to anchor it. Thelma faced a different problem; she had forgotten how to scoop her ice cream. Before Ken noticed her struggling, she had chocolate ice cream dripping between her fingers and a chocolate mustache. He quickly dabbed water onto a napkin and cleaned her up, just as a parent did for a toddler.

The transition was painfully slow as they moved from the dining room back upstairs, due to the traffic jam of scooters waiting for the elevator. Once in the elevator, Stu was proud of himself as he punched the secret code allowing them access to *The 4th Floor*. Thelma and George were oblivious to the code or that there even was a code. Halfway back down the corridor George needed to sit for a few minutes in one of the strategically placed chairs. Thelma was in her own world and kept on walking, so Ken stayed with her. Stu guided George, distressed by his father's slow, steady decline.

Chapter 16 Preparing for the End
Did you take a shower? I didn't know there was one missing.

Sue's thoughts vacillated between joy at seeing her parents again, and melancholy over the incredible slowness to the end of a wonderful life. They were not the people they had been only two years earlier because now there was no conversation, no reminiscing, no ability to play cards or go shopping, or do anything other than sit in the same room. Sue was thankful to have the time with them, but wondered why the process was so slow and painful for everyone involved. Lately every trip to Florida felt like it might be the last time she would see her parents. Ken always picked her up at the Tampa airport, with a pit stop at Whispering Oaks before heading to Stu's house.

Sue paused briefly in front of the apartment door to study the photos in the shadow box marking their apartment. Each apartment was identified by a shadow box filled with memories now faded from its occupant, but the hope was that seeing these familiar remnants might trigger a happy memory. George and Thelma's shadow box contained photos of their surprise 50th anniversary in 2003 aboard a train in Burlington, and you could see the joy on their faces. They had been told to dress up for a family photo since all the kids and grandkids were home for Thanksgiving. Once they arrived downtown they began to notice friends, realizing it was not a coincidence. They traveled on a private train from Burlington to Middlebury for four hours with an open bar, food, family and countless friends. There was nothing to do but socialize, and George was bestowed with the honor of driving the train for a while. He was in his glory.

Other photos included their four grown children, a group shot of all ten grandkids years earlier when they all appeared young and innocent. There was a photo of George and Thelma back in 1952 when they had taken a trip to Long Island, the weekend they became engaged. Another photograph highlighted the fashions of the 1970's with Thelma in a low-cut orange jumpsuit and George with longish hair. The smiles were genuine and happy.

"Hello?" Sue called, slowly pushing open the door. The apartment was dark, lit with only filtered sunlight struggling to push through dark storm clouds blowing in from the Gulf. Thelma stood.

"Oh, oh it's so good to see you honey!" Sue noticed her mother had not called her by name, and wondered if her mother still knew her name. As Thelma stood to greet her, she saw her mother donning only a pair of Depends, topped off with a floral shirt and sweater.

"Hey Mom, it's good to be here." Sue hugged her mother and bent over to kiss her father, who was naturally parked in his recliner. "Hey Mom, let's find you some pants to wear." Thelma looked confused but followed Sue into the bedroom, where they chose a pair of blue corduroy pants with an elastic waist. Sue helped her mother dress after noticing her just holding the pants, unsure what step came next.

Back in the living room they chatted– really a series of questions posed by Sue, who received one-syllable answers. She made a mental note to thank her brothers again for all they did every week. Sue knew sitting in their 4th-floor apartment all afternoon was going to be tough, so she made a list of items they needed at the store. Sue convinced her mother to come on an errand run with her, which turned into a two-and-a-half-hour excursion. Thelma now needed a walker, which doubled as a seat when she needed a rest.

"Mom, you need to put your hands on the grips like this," Sue demonstrated. Thelma was shaky and struggled to comprehend how to wrap her thumb around the rubber handles.

"Oh, my back is so sore. You just don't know what it's like. I hope you never have to go through this."

"Keep going Mom, you're doing great. The more you walk the better you'll feel." Sue continued to encourage her mother while hanging onto the walker to help steer and keep it moving forward. Just then Claire, the woman with no sense of personal space, wandered down the corridor when she spotted Thelma.

"Where are you going?" demanded Claire, getting very close to Thelma's face.

"Get away from me, you bitch!" yelled Thelma.

"Why did you call me a bitch?"

"I'm going to kill you!" Thelma gritted her teeth and flashed her crazy eyes at Claire. Sue tried to get her mother's attention away from Claire and focused on moving down the hallway. Claire quickly lost interest when she saw a young couple heading towards them.

"God, I hate it here. Oh, I can't walk any further. I need to rest." Thelma was now less angry, and they took a respite in the sunny atrium. Sue directed her mother to a chair situated directly in front of a window.

"I'm not sitting here."

"Why not? We'll just take a quick rest before we keep moving." Sue pulled up another chair, but had second thoughts about sitting when she noticed suspicious spots on the cushions. She decided to remain standing. Thelma sat down but was restless. "You should take walks down here every day, it will get you out of the apartment."

"Oh, I'm not coming out here. These people are nuts, I never leave my apartment." Sue let it drop because she knew it was pointless to argue—so instead she thought about a time when her mother lived for socializing. Thelma had two best buddies, Catherine and Jane, with whom she spent countless hours. They occasionally took road trips to visit their grown daughters and one visit brought them to Boston where Sue was living. The three friends arrived wearing wigs, laughing and ready to party. It was a rare day when Thelma didn't talk with at least one of them on the phone.

"Thelma," said a passing nurse. "It's great to see you out walking." Thelma made a face at her as she passed, and then stuck out her tongue.

"Mom! What was that?" Sue was concerned with her mother's lack of civility.

"These people are always telling me what to do. It's my apartment, they don't have any right. It's disgusting what they do."

"What do they do?" Sue had no idea what her mother was talking about.

"Oh, they wipe me down there, it's disgusting. They act like I don't even know how to use the bathroom." She was getting angry again.

"Mom, they're just trying to help you and keep you clean. No one is trying to hurt you."

"It's disgusting. I'm getting out of here as soon as we call that other place." And the circular conversation began again. The shopping trip happened. When they returned, George was napping in his chair, and Sue made her goodbyes before heading to Stu's house. It was cocktail hour.

Stu and Elaine had a houseful with Karen arriving shortly, and that was how they liked it. Everyone sat around the living room, kitchen and porch just catching up and swapping George and Thelma stories. Everyone was in pain, good pain, from laughing too much. It felt good.

The conversation then turned to the reality of the future for George and Thelma. The kids took a realistic view of the situation, able to discuss issues head on.

"Since we're all sitting in the same room, let's talk about DNR orders for Mom and Dad," Stu said. "Do we all agree if either one of them suffers a serious health issue like heart attack, stroke, cancer or something catastrophic, we do nothing invasive?" Stu waited for agreement from the group. Everyone shook their heads but they were weighing different scenarios which might complicate a DNR.

"What if they suffer a bout of pneumonia or if one of them breaks a bone?" Sue wondered.

"Well, I think we want to treat those types of issues, but I don't think we should have them undergo any surgery or radical treatment," Ken said.

"I completely agree," said Karen. Stu double-checked with everyone to confirm they were all on the same page, and agreed to have a DNR put in place at Whispering Oaks.

"It just doesn't make sense to artificially keep them alive longer, when they're miserable and their quality of life has completely diminished." Ken looked at his siblings and continued. "Dad has repeatedly told us not to put him in a nursing home, so that supports the idea of a DNR for him—and Mom is on a runaway train and the brakes have failed."

"We're all on the train," Karen said. "The only difference is which stop we get off."

"This is not how they envisioned the end of their lives," Stu said. "It's too bad Dad didn't just roll the John Deere on himself back in Monkton. He would have died happy."

"This may sound cold, but maybe we should start writing their obituaries while we're all together," Ken suggested.

They spent the next hour compiling a timeline of their parents' lives with dates and milestones. Oddly, it was a gratifying and laugh-filled experience to remember their parents with whole minds and bodies. Many of their friends were horrified at the thought of writing obituaries before their parents had passed. Some of their friends viewed it as inviting death, and others just flat-out refused to talk about death with their families.

Before Sue flew home to Maine, she stopped by Whispering Oaks to say goodbye. Again she wondered if this was the last time she would see her parents, and it made the goodbye bittersweet. She sat quietly on the couch with her mother, watching as both parents bobbed their heads in sleep. She was ready to leave the claustrophobic apartment and gently rubbed her mother's back to wake her. Thelma startled, confused, before registering Sue's face.

"Mom, I have to leave now. It was so good to see you guys, and I'll be back in a few months, not sure exactly when but I'll be back. Be good and try to behave!"

"What else can we do here?" Thelma said with a curled lip.

"Well, cause some trouble, Mom. Keep things hopping!"

"Oh no, I don't need trouble, I just need to get out of here." Sue kissed her father and headed for the door, when her mother started crying.

"What is it, Mom?"

"I don't want you to leave. I'm scared and I hate it here." Sue went to her mother, held her hand and hugged her.

"Do you want to walk me down to the elevator?" Sue asked.

"Why don't you have your mother go downstairs with you," George suggested from his recliner. "Have her sit out front, and I'll go down in a few minutes to get her." Sue knew there was no chance he would remember to go get her in a few minutes. Not to mention, he could barely walk anymore and he would never make it all the way out front without help.

"I'll just have her walk me to the elevators, Dad." Sue kissed her father again and walked slowly down the corridor with her mother. As they approached the elevators, Thelma began sobbing, gasping sobs with tears. Sue hugged her mother again, and knew she couldn't leave her mother just standing there alone. Sue found an attendant and explained the situation. The attendant gently guided Thelma back towards the apartment while Sue boarded the elevator, and she watched with tears as her mother was escorted away. Her throat burned and her chest was tight. This was not getting easier.

The following week Ken and Stu arrived simultaneously at Whispering Oaks to take George and Thelma out to dinner.

"Stu, wouldn't it just be easier to bring them food, rather than dealing with dragging them out?" Ken asked. "And it'll be a hell of a lot quicker." They were signing in at the front desk and attached the *FAMILY* badges to their shirts. Ken remembered the substantial collection of *FAMILY* badges littering his car that he kept neglecting to return.

"Ken, it's the only time they get out, and how much longer do you think we're going to be able to do it?" Stu was not willing to give up yet.

"Yeah, well we've been wondering that for a few years now!" Ken knew it was important to Stu, and went along without further argument. They entered the apartment to find it dark in the late afternoon and quiet because the television sat idle. Stu flicked on a lamp, illuminating his napping parents.

"Hello, sleepy heads," Ken said as he unwrapped several pieces of chocolate sitting in a large bowl on the counter. The bowl had been full of chocolate a few days earlier. "You guys were supposed to be ready for our dinner out tonight," Stu said. "Instead we find you asleep on the job. Tonight we're going to Olive Garden, okay?" Stu did not really expect any valid input. "You two need to get ready."

"Dad," Ken said, "Let's get a clean shirt, because you have cigar crap all over the one you're wearing." George grinned. Ken rummaged through George's bureau, retrieving a new polo shirt with the tags still attached. He opened a kitchen drawer looking for scissors and discovered a rather large collection of chocolate wrappers. There were thirty to forty wrappers, and he knew his father had not gotten out of his chair to hide wrappers. That left only one person with a chocolate addiction who liked to squirrel things away.

"Hey Stu, check this out." Stu shook his head, gathering all the wrappers and tossing them in the trash.

The process of taking George and Thelma out to dinner was daunting. Stu took George, who needed to be transferred to a wheelchair now because he could not walk the distance to the elevators, to the car or to the restaurant. Ken situated Thelma with her walker, giving instructions yet again on how to hold the handles. She followed Ken out of the apartment but crashed into the wall as she tried to make a left turn. Ken grabbed the walker and straightened her out, but in the process she let go and had to be reinstructed on the proper grip.

Forty-five minutes later they were seated at the Olive Garden waiting for their cocktails or in Thelma's case, her Pepsi. Dinner went smoothly until the check arrived.

"Oooh, oooh, I think I need to use the bathroom," Thelma announced. Another new behavior. Ken and Stu looked at each other with horror as they realized there were no other females in the group. No way could Thelma manage the bathroom on her own.

"Do you have to go number one or number two?" Ken asked. Stu laughed, a nervous laugh.

"Oh, it's just number one." She wasn't even embarrassed.

"Good," said Ken. "You have a Depends on, just use that for now." Ken was serious. "Come on Stu, we need to leave now before the situation gets any more disturbing." They paid and made their departure.

As Ken and Stu were leaving Whispering Oaks, they again discussed the increasingly difficult task of taking George and Thelma anywhere. They voiced the misery of taking them out and how in the not too distant future it might prove impossible due to bathroom and mobility issues. They both felt a profound sadness that their parents' lives were getting more and more restrictive, with less and less quality.

"Hello," answered Elaine into her phone as she cleaned up the kitchen before heading out to work.

"Is this Elaine MacCollom?" she mumbled a yes. "This is Whispering Oaks, and we tried to reach Ken and Stu first but neither picked up their phone. George is having difficulty breathing so we called 911. He's on his way to Gulfshore Medical, and Thelma is safe in the apartment."

"Why didn't you call us before calling 911? He has a DNR."

"Well," the nurse said, a bit taken aback. "He was struggling to breathe, and our policy is to call 911 for assistance."

"Okay, of course, sorry. Where is he again?" Elaine jotted down information. "We'll be up there as soon as we can and I'll get in touch with Stu and Ken." She dialed Ken.

"Hey Ken, it's Elaine. Your dad is being transported to Gulfshore Medical right now because he had trouble breathing. We need to get up there immediately to make sure they don't do anything invasive, but I can't make the decisions. You guys have to. Stu's tied up with patients now."

"Wow, okay, thanks Elaine. I'll call Karen and Sue while I'm driving to double-check we're all still on the same page regarding the DNR. Thank God we discussed this very scenario a few weeks ago." He successfully reached his sisters and they were still in agreement. Within ten minutes of the initial call from Whispering Oaks both Ken and Elaine were walking into the hospital.

"Hey Elaine, the fun never ends, does it?" Ken joked, but knew this visit was getting more serious.

"Ken, did you reach everyone? You need to talk with the doctor and advise him about the DNR before they start treating him."

Entering the hospital room they saw a group huddled around a frail George lying in the bed hooked up to an IV and oxygen. Ken chatted with the doctor, who delivered the news that George was suffering from congestive heart failure. Ken shared the family's, and George's, wishes regarding the DNR.

"Ken," the doctor began explaining. "We've already given George a dose of Lasix—a diuretic to help flush his system of excess fluids—because if we hadn't, he would drown in his own fluids in a matter of days." The doctor looked from George to Ken and Elaine. "This was not some crazy measure to keep him alive. A DNR simply means we cannot administer CPR if his heart stops."

Elaine and Ken gave the doctor a look of confusion and he continued.

"There is another directive called *comfort measures only,* but that differs from a DNR, and your father's advanced directive only stated the standard DNR."

Elaine and Ken shared their frustration over being ten minutes too late, and now realizing they needed to amend George and Thelma's living wills. Their eyes fell on George laying in bed struggling to breathe, and promised no more trips to the hospital. George hated hospitals, despised being trapped in a failing body, and truly wanted to die in Vermont. They stayed with George for another hour before heading back to work, but promised to return later in the afternoon.

The following day Ken entered the hospital room noticing George's arms were held down with restraints. "What the hell is this all about?" Ken asked the nurse, who was milling about the room.

"Well, George tried and succeeded several times last night in pulling out all his IV lines, so this is the only way to prevent him from doing it again." Ken's heart was heavy seeing his father strapped down in bed like a psych ward patient. He vowed to put an end to this.

"Hey Dad, I'll be right back. I'm going to get you something." He returned a few minutes later, toting the familiar white pastry box from Frida's filled with a dozen fresh jelly donuts. Just as Ken was pulling out the first donut, the nurse entered the room. With a look of disgust she announced, "Oh no, I'm sorry but George cannot be eating donuts, he has congestive heart failure."

Ken glared at her. "Listen, my father is lying here being tortured by you people who offer him rubbery hormone-injected chicken, and I have brought him a jelly donut. If he wants a jelly donut at this point in his life, he is going to have a jelly donut!" Ken took a breath and continued, "I hardly think a jelly donut is going to jeopardize his health. In fact it will most assuredly improve his attitude."

The nurse relented and quickly retreated from the room. George grinned. Ken had already unstrapped his father, who was no longer trying to rip out his IV line. George consumed his donut with immense pleasure.

Ken tracked down the doctor, who explained in detail that congestive heart failure is a chronic condition requiring George to be on drugs to control the buildup of fluid. Congestive heart failure patients slowly drown from the buildup of fluid in their lungs, causing a painful struggle for breath. Ken felt another serious conversation with his siblings was in order.

Through a series of phone calls and texts, they discussed the need to call hospice, because no one was able to predict how much time George had left. It might be a few weeks or it could be months. Hospice provides emotional, spiritual and limited medical support to patients who are suffering from a terminal disease and their families. The goal of hospice is not to prolong life, but rather make the end of life more peaceful and improve the quality of the patient's remaining days—something the medical profession lacked the ability to do. A six-month window of life is the typical parameter for hospice to be activated, but a doctor's order is also required. Hospice sends a team of pastors, nurses and social workers to the patient's home or hospice facility.

George was released from the hospital a few days later back to Whispering Oaks, where he required two people to transfer him to the toilet, to the bed and to his wheelchair. Thelma had zero recollection that George had been in the hospital, or was even gone for a few nights. They both now spent their days sitting in the living room with the television on, and a slow-motion trip down the corridor with assistance for meals three times a day. Hospice made their initial evaluation, determining George was not upon death's door, but scheduled weekly visits to monitor the situation. If George's condition worsened, they promised to come immediately.

"Hey Mom, what's for lunch today?" Stu asked as he approached his parents sitting in the dining room with another male resident. Management preferred to keep the males together as their numbers were rather low compared to the female population.

"Oh, it's disgusting," Thelma started. "I can't…eat this food. I…getting out of here. These people are…awful. You can't believe what they do to me." Her words skipped like an old LP. All of her conversations now revolved around her wretched treatment and their dire circumstances.

"Well, Mom, you guys can leave anytime you want–but you'll have to make all the arrangements yourselves." Stu said this half jokingly and half serious. "Be sure to call us when you get there, wherever that is." Thelma had no response, because somewhere deep down she knew it wouldn't and couldn't happen.

Out of the blue George started telling a story to his lunchmates.

One day when we were playing volleyball during lunch when I worked at CSIRO in Canberra, a group of American tourists walked by. They watched us for a few minutes when one of them yelled out, "You Australians sure do like to play volleyball."

"Yes we do," I replied.

And they yelled back, "Hey, you're not Australian, you're from Boston!"

George had always been proud of his Boston heritage. His story had nothing to do with their lunch conversation, and Stu recently noticed his father just blurting out stories as if he were watching a running clip of his life, sharing random tidbits.

Stu paid close attention to George's ability to move as he escorted them back to their apartment and helped transfer him to the recliner. It was not promising. Stu was concerned because if his father wasn't in danger of passing away within a matter of weeks, Whispering Oaks would not allow him to stay, due to the rule for this assisted living memory unit. The rule stated residents must be able to transfer without help unless hospice was involved, or they would be transferred to a nursing home or skilled nursing facility. If hospice was involved and determined the end was imminent, he could stay. Stu was uneasy because George did not want to go to a nursing home. It was becoming a delicate ballet between managing a failing body, respecting the wishes of a loved one and obeying the law.

Karen and Sue were both notified of their father's worsening condition with Ken and Stu's weekly updates. Both girls felt guilty about not calling their parents more often, but it took a certain mindset to have an exchange with them. Conversations with their father lasted maybe thirty seconds with the same questions each time: *How is the truck running for Henry? Does Charlie like UMass? Tell him to check out the Stockbridge building. Has Katie finished med school yet?*, plus a few others. The phone was then passed to Thelma who complained, complained and cried, or complained some more, but there was no conversation. Without the ability to go visit them in person, phone calls were exhausting and every phone call was identical. Sue being the furthest away, felt the need to get to Florida in case it was the last time she saw her father. Karen also made a quick trip down to see him.

Ken once again picked Sue up at Tampa International and delivered her to Whispering Oaks for the afternoon, where she appropriated the Explorer for the duration of her visit. Entering the apartment, she was assaulted by the scent of urine despite the new laminate floors and daily cleaning. George and Thelma sat quietly with the television off, where they both were napping but awoke upon Sue's arrival.

"Oohh, hi honey. It's so good to see you…I've been having a hard time." Sue hugged her mother with a heavy heart. "They're awful here. We need to get out of here!" Their world was egocentric and Sue long ago stopped expecting any inquiries regarding herself or the family.

"Hey Mom, hey Dad." She bent over and hugged her father in his chair. Glancing around the apartment she saw the evidence of a life in decline with wheelchairs, walkers, packages of Depends, dozens of photos of grandkids and dwindling prized possessions. Ken ran in to say hello but needed to get back to his office, not to mention he made multiple trips to *The 4th Floor* each week.

Sue and her parents shared a Cuban sandwich she picked up on the way over. George balanced his plate on the right arm of the chair, making it easier to grab with his right hand. Parts of his lunch inevitably landed in the cracks of the recliner. Thelma struggled to figure out how to hold the sandwich as she squeezed it until her fingertips shook and it approached her mouth. It was hard to watch. The food became wedged under her fingernails from the deathgrip. Following lunch Sue wiped her mother's hands with a wet cloth, noticing the ragged remnants of a manicure and a week's worth of food stuck underneath the nails.

"Mom, how about we get manicures this afternoon?" Sue needed a reason to get out of the apartment. "Dad can stay here and hold down the fort. How does that sound?"

"Oh that's wonderful," Thelma said. Sue wasn't sure if her mother comprehended the whole thing, but it really didn't matter because a change of scenery was good for everyone. "Oh, I need to use the bathroom before I go."

"OK, go ahead. I'll be right here when you're ready!" Thelma just stood there in the middle of the living room not moving, looking worried. "Mom, are you OK?"

"I...I...I don't know where the bathroom is." Sue was unsure how to respond, but remembered Ken's story of their mother getting lost in the kitchen—the kitchen attached to the living room.

"You have two bathrooms here, Mom."

"Well, I've never used them before, and I've never seen them!"

"Look, there's one right here, or you can use the one off your bedroom." Sue pointed out both options, and Thelma made her move towards the bathroom off the living room. She entered and stopped.

"What...do I do...now?" Thelma asked as she stared at the closed toilet seat. Sue watched and channeled patience. Sue wondered just how long this downward spiral might last, and prayed her own life never end like this.

"Here, Mom, let me help you," Sue said entering the bathroom. She raised the toilet seat and began lifting Thelma's shirt to find the waistband. As Sue fiddled with the elastic, she noticed something dark and protruding from just above the waistband on the side of her mother's abdomen. She lifted the shirt a little further to inspect the growth and realized it was a nipple!

"Oh my God," Sue said under her breath. Her mother's breasts were hanging all the way down, and for a petite small-breasted woman that was quite a feat. Sue guessed at some point you just stop wearing underwear, and those birthday cards where the woman's boobs hang down to her knees were sadly accurate. They finished in the bathroom and headed out for a manicure.

The petite Asian girl who gave Thelma her manicure approached Sue and quietly explained in a thick accent she had gently cleaned underneath Thelma's fingernails with a toothbrush in an attempt to remove particles of food. Sue thanked the girl and made a note to tip her well. Sue sat reading a book while glancing over in her mother's direction every few minutes. The next time she looked up she saw the familiar head bob. Perfect, maybe her mother would find a few minutes of peace.

Back at Stu's house later in the afternoon, Ken arrived following work. Cameron was in and out working on his latest entrepreneurial endeavor and Elaine was performing at least fifteen different tasks at once. The three siblings debated about their parents.

"I asked the nurses," Ken said. "About stopping all medications for both of them—but I discovered it pretty much takes an act of God."

Elaine piped in from the kitchen, "It's ridiculous because your mother isn't getting any of her respiratory meds because she can't inhale properly, and the memory drugs are clearly not working. With George, why keep giving him drugs to prolong his life when he can't even use the toilet by himself?" No one argued with her.

"The pharmaceutical companies," Ken added, "have a multi-billion-dollar boondoggle keeping people alive long past life expectancy with little to no quality of life."

"But it's okay to drug them," Stu said, "and raid their life savings. But it's not okay to let them die naturally and assist them at the end." Ken promised to dig a little further in an effort to see what they might be able to accomplish in regard to stopping medications.

As if on cue, a few weeks later when the boys were visiting Whispering Oaks, a nurse approached wearing a look of concern.

"Oh boy, I wonder what news she's about to deliver?" Ken wondered aloud.

"Maybe Mom has found another boyfriend," Stu guessed.

"Or quite possibly we're about to receive notice of their eviction."

Stu shrugged, "It might just be that they're out of Depends."

The nurse looked at them almost afraid to deliver her message. "Neither of your parents will take their medications, they are both refusing everything."

Ken and Stu suppressed a laugh and gave a high five, understanding this would be misinterpreted as callous. Ken jumped in. "You know, it's okay. We want you to respect their wishes, and if they refuse their meds, so be it." They couldn't believe how simple the solution turned out to be, although they wondered how long this might last. For now, at least, things were happening in a natural progression. The nurse gave an almost imperceptible nod but it was clear she understood.

George had reached a point where he was well aware the end was imminent and they suspected he consciously stopped taking his meds, whereas Thelma was just angry and following George's lead. Ken and Stu received a few more phone calls from concerned staff over the refusal of meds and Thelma's increasing agitation. Stu reassured the staff it was okay, but suggested they slip her some Ativan in a cup of hot chocolate to help calm her.

Things limped along for another couple weeks before the next phone call from Whispering Oaks. This time they meant business.

"Hello Ken?"

"Yes, speaking."

"This is Whispering Oaks," Ken took a deep calming breath. "Your father has declined to the point of requiring more assistance than we can offer. As you know, we have allowed him to stay on since his hospitalization, thinking his time might be short, but we can no longer service him here at Whispering Oaks." Ken continued his deep slow breathing while listening. "You are welcome to transfer him to Cypress Oaks across the way, which is our skilled nursing facility, but Thelma would not be an appropriate resident there. She could remain here on *The 4th Floor*. I'm so sorry to deliver this news to you. It's the 20th of October today, so we will give you until the end of this month to make a decision."

Ken reeled. They could not separate their parents after the last five years of existing together in the same room and nearly sixty years of marriage. Ken also refused to place his father in a *skilled nursing unit,* simply a euphemism for nursing home. Ken immediately called Elaine, who was capable of getting things done and quickly. There were less than two weeks to figure it out, and they knew how lucky they were George and Thelma had a nice retirement income and money in the bank, affording them options. Ken called Cypress Oaks to check on the cost and availability to have a starting point.

From her end, Elaine made numerous phone calls to facilities, setting up appointments to visit within the next few days. Elaine figured between herself, Ken and Stu they could knock them all out in a matter of days and make a decision. It was Ken and Elaine who made the bulk of the visits, leaving them depressed at seeing the endless number of elderly people wasting away in wheelchairs abandoned in hallways, bodies slumped, minds nothing but mush, few visitors in sight, and the melancholy odor of disinfectant and urine with a hint of mustiness.

The last visit of the day brought them to a facility called Cabot Manor, situated halfway between Stu and Ken. Cabot Manor was a much smaller facility than Whispering Oaks and it was privately owned by the same owner for all twelve years of its existence. The facility was housed in one building, with a separate memory unit. The most attractive feature was their willingness to allow George and Thelma to remain together until the end. No more moves and no threats of a nursing home. Elaine's friend was able to make things happen quickly. Within the week, George and Thelma were moved again. No one dared declare this the last move, they'd said it too many times.

Chapter 17 Cabot Manor

A goose walks into a bar.
Too bad it didn't duck.

This next move required George and Thelma to downsize from their rather spacious one- bedroom apartment to a generic studio. The studio apartment included a handicapped accessible bathroom, a mini fridge and a small sink. There was just enough room to house two hospital beds, George's nasty recliner, Thelma's slightly smaller pink recliner, two bureaus and a large screen TV. A hastily written note on the back of a piece of paper was taped to the screen, warning anyone daring to touch the TV had best choose between Fox News or the History Channel. The facility did not allow residents to hang pictures on the wall, which left their collection of family photos and prized Civil War prints piled askew on bureau tops.

Elaine trucked home more boxes belonging to George and Thelma, where they joined dozens of other boxes in Allie's old bedroom. Elaine was a good sport but she finally put her foot down at any extra furniture that didn't fit in the studio apartment. Elaine had no use for it and absolutely no desire to move it again. Karen's daughter Christina gladly took possession of the dining table and chairs, while other pieces were doled out to nieces or nephews who were starting out and in need of furniture. Anywhere but Elaine's house, and she was happy.

"Hey Mom, do you like your new place?" Stu inquired after the first night, hoping for a miracle but not expecting it.

"I...I...I...I am getting out of this place. They are awful," she continued, but her speech was now a string of gibberish impossible to understand. No one knew if in her head she knew what she was saying, but the ability to form words and say them was rapidly disappearing. Her face balled up in anger, and her eyes conveyed displeasure with life. Stu noticed whenever she became excited or agitated, her speech worsened. But on good days she occasionally strung together a couple of sentences. George sat slumped in his recliner with the television blaring, acknowledging Stu's arrival with a grin and a mumbled wisecrack.

Stu noticed his father was no longer chewing cigars and chalked it up to another sign the end was near. Their desire to engage and be present was fading at an alarming speed, but when they thought about it, they realized it actually was a painfully slow progression. Ken likened Thelma's brain to Swiss cheese becoming more like baked brie.

Ken popped into Cabot Manor late one afternoon before heading home. The visits were taking a toll on Ken, leaving him depressed and drained because there were no conversations, the room smelled like old people and his parents were on a journey with no hope. Both Ken and Stu struggled after their visits.

"Hi Mom," Ken called out, trying his best to sound upbeat. "Want to go for a stroll around the lobby? You can check out all the handsome dudes playing balloon volleyball."

"Oh,...I...I...hate..." and what followed was a string of unintelligible sounds. Ken observed a large bruise on her forearm and went to inquire with the nurse on duty.

"Well," the nurse started. "Your mother was extremely combative last night and her arm bumped against the side of the wheelchair when she thrashed around." Ken had no reason to believe the bruises were a result of neglect or abuse on the part of the facility, but wanted them to be aware he was watching. He knew all too well how Thelma was when she angered; just another reason he felt drained after visits. His mother was no longer the kind, gentle woman who raised him. Sitting before him was a shrinking angry woman, unable to communicate, with venom in her eyes.

"Okay, Mom," Ken said. "We're going for a walk around this joint, so you just need to sit back and relax." She glanced at George, not wanting to leave his side, but Ken kept wheeling.

"Why...why...why...are...the coloreds all looking...at me?" Thelma blurted out in earshot of several black members of the staff. Ken was horrified. He quickly glanced at the nurses and aides with a shoulder shrug and silent apology. To their credit, they smiled in acknowledgement of Ken's uncomfortable situation.

"Mom! What the hell was that?"

"Oh...they...all just...stare at...me. They hate...me...and...they talk...about ...me."

"Geez Mom, you wonder why? You can't just go around saying things like that." Ken was honestly shocked, because she had never shown racist tendencies, ever. This behavior was from left field. Ken wheeled his mother around the second floor lobby several times before returning to their room. George was napping and Thelma was out of conversation.

Ken and Stu discussed the possibility of bringing their parents to Stu's house for Thanksgiving dinner, but understood the incredible difficulty of the situation. Stu realized with profound sadness that having his parents to his house was no longer possible. Even if he was willing to do the heavy lifting and spend the two hours transporting, it would not be good for them.

So Ken, Stu and Elaine made a pilgrimage to Cabot Manor for Thanksgiving dinner. And to their amazement the food was edible, even palatable, with all the trimmings and an impressive array of pecan, apple and coconut cream pies for dessert. The dinner conversation consisted of Ken, Stu and Elaine chatting and arguing amongst themselves about everything from the Tampa Bay Lightning, the demise of our government to the best vodka on the market. George and Thelma were silent throughout dinner, aside from when a direct question was presented and ample time allowed for a response. An hour at dinner pushed everyone's limits.

"Dad isn't doing very well," Ken explained to Sue. "He just sits in his chair, refuses to go downstairs for meals and needs assistance for everything, everything. Hospice is now coming every few days but honestly, I don't give him much time."

Sue, Norm and Charlie planned to head down for Christmas, expecting it might be the last time. Sue prayed her dad would not pass before then. Charlie's girlfriend Jess was also flying down from UMass to meet Charlie, and then they were going scuba diving in Key Largo.

Over the next month George's condition did not change, and Ken reported hospice was now visiting daily but end-of-life care had not yet commenced. George's breathing was labored; he napped, slumped in his chair and rarely interacted with anyone. Ken forewarned Sue and Norm.

"Hey Mom, hey Dad," Sue greeted as she took in her parents' new accommodations. It was not the Ritz, it wasn't even Whispering Oaks, but for what it was, it was okay. But it really wasn't okay. Sue knew this was not how they envisioned the end of their life; in a cramped room with side-by-side hospital beds. There were clothes strewn about the room, piles of papers and greeting cards everywhere and a rank odor. It was not okay.

Thelma looked up at Sue with a hint of recognition and was able to stutter a few oohs as Sue, Norm and Charlie hugged her and planted kisses on her gnarled cheek. Her ability to retrieve names had vanished but there was a glimmer in her eyes. After not seeing them for a few months, Sue and Norm were surprised by how shrunken she appeared, as though the recliner had swallowed her. Her arms were covered with bulging veins and deep purple marks showing through her papery skin. George briefly opened his eyes and mumbled a few incomprehensible words. Sue and Norm made brief eye contact conveying sadness.

Back at Stu's house they discussed the inevitable end of life and when it might happen. Considering the current state of George's health, the prospect for the end was near. They located the "blue folder" of information George provided years earlier with a prearranged funeral director, cemetery plots at the Veterans Cemetery in Randolph, Vermont and a very basic will. It was not like George to plan, but the kids were happy to have this information and a place to start when the end arrived.

The week passed quickly and they made the visit to Cabot Manor for their goodbyes, perhaps the final goodbye. Entering the room, they heard the TV before they saw George sitting up in his wheelchair, alert, smiling and eating peanuts directly from the can.

"What the fuck?" Ken said. "Yesterday he was on death's doorstep, and today he's chowing down a can of Planters." Ken looked around at the others to verify they felt the same. This was not the first time they'd witnessed this strange vacillation between lucidity and near death. With George feeling better and the room claustrophobic, they opted to venture downstairs to the front porch for some fresh air.

"Oooohhh, ooohhh, ooohhh," was all Thelma managed to get out as Sue pushed her wheelchair towards the elevator. George grabbed a newspaper as he wheeled past, rolled it up and whacked Stu with it. George was now sporting his famous grin, and the others shook their heads in bewilderment.

George continued to rally for several weeks, but by no means was he up and walking around. He was alert, awake and responsive whenever someone entered the room or spoke to him. He continued to refuse the dining room for meals, continued to take frequent naps and still needed assistance with the bathroom.

By mid-March, a few months later, George was not even making the trek from his bed to the recliner; he remained prone in his bed.

"George, Geeeoorr, Ge, dahhdau, deedagob," Thelma sputtered as she wandered close to George's bed. She was visibly concerned about her husband but was unable to communicate. The two were rarely out of each other's sight. Hospice was a constant as they prepared George and the family for death.

Ken took it upon himself to call his sisters, as death was still a tender wound for Stu. Karen made plans to drive down to St Pete by the weekend but Sue had commitments in Maine leaving her with palpable guilt. Ken assured her she had seen their father numerous times over the last few years and promised daily updates.

This time there were no rebounds and it seemed George had made his peace. Thelma hovered around George like a mother bird tending her nest, and was annoyed with hospice who had invaded her space. Not so long ago, everything George did seemed to irk her, but now as their world was crumbling, she refused to leave his sight.

By the end of the week everyone knew it was only a matter of hours. The kind woman from hospice explained how the final hours typically go. He would continue to struggle to breathe but was receiving morphine to minimize any pain from a buildup of fluids in his lungs. He had stopped eating and drinking and was slipping into a deeper sleep.

When loved ones sat with him and talked, he would at times squeeze their hands and utter a soft sound from his fading soul. George was still in his bed, in his room at Cabot Manor and not a hospital. Stu and Ken had at least seen to that. He didn't want to die in a facility but there was no other way short of shipping his ailing body to Vermont and laying him in his beloved orchard to pass. George certainly would have been good with that, but the authorities and new owners of Monkton Valley Orchard may not have been so thrilled.

Ken brought his boys, Connor and Duncan, to say a final goodbye to their grandfather. They were unsure what to do as thirteen- and fourteen-year-olds with scarce experience saying goodbye to a loved one. Ken nudged them to move closer and whispered to them to hold their grandfather's hand. Elaine scooted over a couple of chairs for the boys to sit in while they glanced at each other, both uncomfortable but deep down they knew this was an important moment. Ken had prepped them and suggested talking about their memories from the orchard. Duncan scanned the crowd of family members before returning his gaze to his dying grandfather.

"Hey Gramps, it's Duncan here." Again he glanced up and looked to Ken for support, who silently motioned with his hand to keep talking. "I remember how we got to drive the go-cart all around the orchard. Dad says it helped prepare me for when I get my real license in a few years. I think I'll be a better driver than my dad, my mom and my brother because I pay attention. I feel the motion of the car. One of my favorite things I did with you was shoot your gun at the coffee can. Grandma and mom were nervous we were going to shoot ourselves!"

"Gramps, it's Connor. I have to disagree with Duncan about the driving part, because I think I remember him crashing the go-cart into the birch tree. I never crashed and I recorded the fastest lap around the orchard. I still remember when you let us help you with the huge brush fire, the flames were almost higher than the house. It was awesome and you could feel the heat on your face. It was so much fun to throw stuff on it and just stare at the flames."

The boys lost their awkwardness and continued reminiscing for another half hour. Ken motioned it was time to go and both boys, without prompting, leaned in and kissed their grandfather one last time. They exited the room in silence.

Cameron arrived a few minutes after his cousins left. Cameron idolized his grandfather and needed to make his final goodbye, something he had not been able to do with his brother. Cameron did not hesitate as he approached his grandfather's side and grabbed his hand.

"Gramps, Cam here!" Cam immediately felt a squeeze from his grandfather. "I'm working on a few projects and I think I'm gonna be really successful. And you know what I need to tell you? That's right Gramps, trust me! Trust me to make great business decisions and do the right thing." Cam laughed despite himself. "I do want to bring up a bone of contention while I'm here. Do you remember when Henry and I were visiting you up at Whispering Oaks? My parents sent us over to review tax documents you needed to sign. I guess I fell asleep on the couch and you told Henry to draw on my face. Evidently Henry grabbed a Sharpie and asked if he should draw a penis or a mustache, and you said a dick! So Henry drew this big-ass dick on my face, and I had no idea. Then when we were heading downstairs, the big black orderly guarding the elevator was looking at me weird, and people in the elevator looked horrified and some were laughing at me. I had no idea! Of course Henry was laughing. Then I get to the car and see myself in the mirror. Thanks for egging Henry on, Gramps." Cam spent the good part of an hour laughing with his grandfather.

Karen called to notify her brothers she was en route. Karen always had a special bond with her father, as was the eldest and this was a tough goodbye. She spent the time recounting stories of her hijinks and his reaction to them. She spent several hours rubbing his arm, holding his hand and chatting quietly. She lingered, torn between letting go of her father who was clearly ready to leave this life, and letting go of her childhood. Her hand dropped and released her father's wrinkled limp hand and moved to kiss her mother goodbye. She wondered if this was also the end for her mother. Karen stopped, taking in the room before taking a long slow breath and walking away.

"Hey Sue, it's Elaine." Sue was working at school but snatched her phone as soon as she saw it was Elaine. "The end is near and when you get a chance, call my phone and I'll put the phone up to your dad's ear." Thirty minutes later Sue had a lunch break and found a quiet corner in the school library to make the final call.

"Dad, I wish I was with you to hold your hand and give you a kiss, but I'm up in Maine. I love you. You know you've been the best father ever, you gave us such a fun childhood, made sure we experienced as many things as possible, taught us education was important and taught us through your actions not to sweat the small stuff." She paused waiting for a response which never came. She took a breath trying to prevent herself from crying but it was too late, silent tears stained her face. The lump in her throat burned but she plowed on, with news about Norm and the boys. After a few minutes she needed to wrap it up as she heard the rumbling of students approaching.

"Dad, I love you. You know you'll be with Keith soon, and he's waiting to have a game of Hearts with you. Bye, Dad." She wiped away the tears and felt so isolated, knowing her siblings were all together to support each other. She was alone, tucked away in the back corner of a school library. Elaine got back on the phone.

"Sue, I just want you to know your dad tried to speak to you but he was too weak to form the words. He heard you." Elaine had been a godsend and pillar of strength through the entire ordeal, considering it wasn't even her parents and that she had already endured the loss of a child.

Sue quickly placed a call to Henry and Charlie. Unbelievably, she reached both of them on the first try and advised them to call their grandfather to say goodbye. This was outside their comfort zone, but neither one hesitated on making the call; a decision they never regretted.

"Ooohhh…it's …gflee…adjooml…goodlne," Thelma tried to say the next morning when Stu arrived to sit with his father. Although Thelma was unable to communicate, she was visibly upset by George's declining health. She wandered the room circling George's bed, looking at him and touching him with shaking hands. This routine continued throughout the day as Stu, Ken and Elaine sat in shifts waiting for the inevitable. Finally about 11 pm on Saturday night, Ken was the lone holdout when he decided to call it a night. He briefly watched his parents peacefully sleeping. He exited the room and left his parents in the hands of the capable hospice worker.

"Hello," Ken answered. He had been home less than an hour, relaxing on the couch with a low-budget horror movie. A phone call at midnight could not be good news.

"Ken? This is Gretchen, the hospice nurse with your dad. I think you should get over here right now, because the end is very near."

"I'm on my way and I'll call my brother Stu. Thanks." Ken took a few minutes to inform Marie and get himself back together when the phone rang again.

"Hello?" Ken said, expecting the worst.

"Ken, it's Gretchen again. There's no need for you to come over, your dad has passed. I'm so sorry for your loss. I want you to know your father passed very peacefully with your mother sound asleep in the bed right next to him."

"Thank you for calling me right away, and I'll take care of calling the others. This may sound like an odd question, but what happens to my dad's body at this point?"

"It's not an odd question at all, Ken. We notify emergency services, who will come right over and take your dad to the funeral home. We have all the information here, and George's final wishes have been well handled by the family."

"What about Mom? Is she still sleeping? Will she be there when Dad is removed?" Ken asked, feeling slightly uncomfortable with this line of questioning, but he needed to know.

"Your mother is a very sound sleeper and we think it best if we let her sleep while all this takes place. If we try to wake her now it could be very upsetting for her, and as you know she can be combative when upset or confused. We'll make sure someone stays with her so she'll not wake up alone to find George gone. You and your siblings will have to make a decision about her next steps, but we'll stay with her through the night."

"Okay, thank you Gretchen," Ken said absently into the phone. Although it was a moment Ken fully expected, had even mentally prepared for, the news still felt like a body blow. His father was gone. He called Stu and Elaine, who were not shocked by the late phone call but were once again reminded of their other immense loss. They were at a point in their marriage and grieving process where a simple look between them was all they needed. They both felt the impenetrable bond of the last few years. George's passing was almost a relief but also a sad reminder; it was Easter weekend all over again.

Although everyone was sad George passed, they all felt overdue solace because he was no longer trapped in a failed body and struggling to cope with a mind strangled by stroke. He was now free of his earthly shackles. Thelma, on the other hand, continued as a prisoner here on earth while her brain slowly dissolved. Over the previous six years, since the night of the stroke, Thelma and George had been an inseparable entity. A void was now present in Thelma's world, her life partner of over fifty-five years was gone.

Chapter 18 Evergreen
Everything will be okay in the end; if it's not okay, it's not the end.

"Whhhhhhss wheerre is George?" Thelma demanded immediately upon awakening next to an empty stripped bed. Gretchen was still sitting unobtrusively in the room during the early morning hours of Easter Sunday, well before the sun was due to make an appearance.

"Thelma?" Gretchen said, cradling Thelma's hand in her own. "Would you like a glass of water?" She rubbed Thelma's hand and forearm waiting to see where Thelma's thought process was headed.

"Wwwhherres Ggggrg?" she grunted. A slow deep breath bought Gretchen a few seconds to think before having to speak. This was not her first deathbed experience, but it did not make it any easier.

"Thelma, George is gone. He passed away." Gretchen spoke gently without ever stopping the soft caress of Thelma's hand. Human contact was crucial here, perhaps the most important part of the delivery. Thelma stared at Gretchen, slowly blinking her eyes trying to digest the words. The empty bed next Thelma was in sight, and a lone tear rolled down her cheek.

Stu and Ken arrived back at Cabot Manor early the next morning to sit with their mother. Gretchen filled them in on Thelma's state of mind before making her goodbyes and giving her a hug. The first order of business was to remove the empty bed sitting there as a constant reminder. Stu offered to take Thelma outside away from the room while Ken quickly arranged for the bed removal.

"So Mom, how are you feeling this morning?" Stu asked, attempting to make conversation where there wasn't any. He bounced between bringing up George or ignoring the whole situation. Without the means to communicate, Stu opted for benign small talk instead. An eerie quiet enveloped Thelma with no episodes of frustration, no spurts of gibberish and no expressions of discontent. Stu finally settled on a seat at the end of a row of porch chairs. He parked his mother next to his chair and held her hand, while rambling on with stories about Elaine, Allison and Cameron. Stu watched as an old man pushed the handicap button on the front doors before ambling clumsily with his walker and settling in the seat next to him. Thelma did not even throw him a dirty look.

After a few hours at Cabot Manor, Ken and Stu were on emotional overload. They had a growing list of things to do and their mother was nodding off in her chair. A perfect exit plan after returning her upstairs.

"So what's first on the list?" Ken asked as they made their way to the parking lot.

"We have to submit an obituary to the paper," Stu said. "We need to contact relatives and whatever friends they have left, we need to talk with the funeral home about cremation and we need to figure out what we want to do about a service. Stu ran his fingers through his hair and sighed. "I can take care of calling the agencies because I've been dealing with them for the last few years and I have all the information."

"Okay," said Ken. "I'll contact the funeral home to see what they need from us. I'll call Sue and Karen to work out what else needs to be done. I'll call you later." Ken was about to hang up when he needed to ask a question. "How long do you think Mom is going to hang on?"

"Geez Ken, I don't see it being very long. I can't imagine she can last more than a month or so, what do you think?"

"Yeah, I'm with you Stu," Ken acknowledged. They embraced in the parking lot before heading off to deal with the societal tasks of death.

Sitting in his car strategically parked under the shade of a large oak tree, Ken made phone calls. Karen and Sue were first on the list. He filled his sisters in on all the details of the morning and the to-do list.

"So Ken," Sue said. "What are we going to do about a service?"

"Stu and I were talking about that, and we think it might be best to wait and see what happens with mom. We don't think she's going to last much longer and then we can have a service for both of them at one time." Ken waited and asked, "What do you think?"

"I completely agree," Sue said. "But we definitely need to have the service in Vermont because that's where they lived their life. Their church meant a lot to them. So how long do we wait?" Sue waited for Ken's response, because it felt awkward talking so casually about their parents' funerals.

"How long do we wait?" Ken repeated. "Good question. It's the end of March now and realistically can Mom last through the summer? I think we should take a *wait and see* attitude so we can have a joint service. You know, like a two for one! Let's face it, if we plan something right now for Dad, I guarantee you Mom will pass away the following week."

Stu and Elaine attacked their list with vengeance. Each organization seemed to have different requirements and different hoops to jump through. Elaine was a master at phone warfare. Ken contacted UVM, the church and the funeral home who agreed to hold the remains until the family was ready for them.

Submitting the obituary would be the easy part since they had it written ahead of time. The *Burlington Free Press* obit desk was only open for limited hours, but contact was made. Feeling good about the prepared obit, Sue was shocked that obituaries cost $30 for the first three lines and $3 for every line afterward. Obituaries were narrow strips of text and George's lengthy obituary totalled $584. Profiting from death.

GEORGE BUTTERICK MACCOLLOM-SOUTH BURLINGTON
George Butterick MacCollom, 87, of South Burlington died March 30, 2013 in St Petersburg, FL. George was born in Roslindale, MA on June 10, 1925 to parents Welby

Henry MacCollom and Florence Hattie Butterick. George grew up in Roslindale with his brother Welby Francis MacCollom, but spent time in Sterling, MA during the Depression with his grandmother. Sunday school and scouting were a large part of George's early life. A pivotal day for George arrived on June 10, 1943 when he turned 18, graduated from Roslindale High School and enlisted in the ASTP (Aptitude Specialist Training Program). He studied at both Princeton and Yale for a semester before joining the 104th Infantry Division of the Timberwolves. He fought in WWII where he earned the Bronze Star for action in Holland and the Purple Heart after he was wounded in Pier, Germany. After returning from the war, George attended the University of Massachusetts on the GI bill where he earned his bachelor's in entomology. He thoroughly enjoyed his time at UMass with his fraternity brothers in Sigma Alpha Epsilon (SAE). He then earned his doctorate at Cornell, where he met his wife, Thelma Forsyth. They were married December 5, 1953 in Ithaca, NY and relocated to Burlington, VT in 1954 when George became a professor and chairman of the entomology department at the University of Vermont. He taught, researched and worked with the US Extension Service advising fruit growers in the Champlain Valley. In 1969, George embarked on a year long sabbatical with his family to Canberra, Australia studying the Australian fruit fly at CSIRO. He retired in 1996 as Professor Emeritus from UVM. George and Thelma made South Burlington their home where they raised four children and enjoyed a blessed life. In 1988 they made the decision to move to Monkton, VT realizing his life-long dream of becoming a gentleman farmer. He developed the Monkton Valley Orchard, a non-organic orchard, growing a variety of apples and blueberries. His grandchildren logged hundreds of miles on the property riding go-carts, lawn mowers and tractors. George was well known for his annual Goose Dinners where invitees were either placed on the A List or B List depending on their attitude regarding his hunting abilities. George spent many lunch hours playing handball and many hours on the weekends duck hunting or fly fishing at the Lake Mansfield Trout Club. There were many competitive games of croquet played on his regulation sized court in Monkton with family and friends. George will forever be remembered for his endless jokes and jovial attitude towards life. George was predeceased by his grandson Keith MacCollom in April 2009. He is survived by his wife Thelma; daughter Karen MacCollom Theoktisto and husband Phil Theoktisto of Melrose, FL; son Stuart MacCollom and wife Elaine of Seminole, FL; daughter Susan MacCollom Richard and husband Normand of Georgetown, ME; son Kenneth MacCollom and wife Marie of St Petersburg, FL. He is also survived by his grandchildren: Anna Theoktisto Camardese, Katie Theoktisto, Allison MacCollom West, Henry Richard, Cameron MacCollom, Christina Theoktisto Blanchard, Charles Richard, Connor MacCollom and Duncan MacCollom. Plans for a memorial service will be announced later.

The death felt anticlimactic, in part because there was no service or funeral planned for the immediate future and Thelma was still hanging in there. They also understood and firmly believed George was now at peace. The kids knew a service was crucial to putting closure on George's passing, but Thelma was the looming question.

By the following evening everyone was processing George's passing in their own way. Thelma remained mute since waking to George's empty bed, and the staff suspected she understood what had happened, at least to some degree.

"Hello," Stu answered quickly, checking the caller ID. *CABOT MANOR CALLING.* His stomach was in knots.

"Stu, this is Sheila at Cabot Manor. Your mom has had an extremely difficult night." She went on to explain the real reason for the call was Thelma had taken a fall and they were concerned she broke her hip. The facility needed guidance from the family in light of the DNR. Stu rubbed his face before answering.

"Sheila, I'll need to confer with my siblings before any decision can be made. So what happened?"

"Well, your mom went to sleep about the usual time and she had been rather subdued since George passed. She must have awoken in the middle of the night because an attendant found her wandering at the top of the staircase screaming for George." Sheila reported how the attendants tried to calm Thelma but when steering her away from the staircase, she became combative and fell.

"Okay," Stu said. "Well I guess I'll call my siblings right now. Is she in pain? If her hip is broken, what happens then?"

"If her hip is broken she will either need surgery or rehab. As for pain, we gave her anxiety meds to help her sleep because they were on the *okay to administer* list."

"Wow," Stu sighed. "A lot to consider, but I think we need to understand what's going on with her hip first."

"Right, so you need to speak with the family, and then we can make a decision tomorrow. I'm so sorry, Stu."

When Stu arrived at Cabot Manor a few hours later he found his mother in the fetal position in the middle of her bed, not moving. For a moment he worried she had willed herself to join George; the way you hear about couples who have been married forever and then both pass away within hours of each other. He approached the bed like a small child might approach a snake in the driveway. He gently placed his hand on her back and felt warmth but no perceptible movement. He breathed easier, because dealing with another death this soon was too much right now. But then he thought how poignant and how much easier it might be. He felt ashamed for such thoughts. He sat with his mother for several minutes before searching for Sheila.

She brought him up to date, although there was nothing new to report. Thelma had remained in a fetal position for hours. Sheila assured Stu they were checking on his mother every fifteen minutes, but needed direction on what to do next. Stu had spoken with his siblings again and the unanimous decision was to have an x-ray and if the hip was broken, they could not allow it to go untreated. That would constitute cruel treatment and cause her undue pain and suffering. The question hanging in the balance was if her hip was broken, would she go to rehab? Would she have surgery or just remain at Cabot Manor? Surgery was an unlikely option because she was virtually immobile now and rehabbing was out of the question for her. Perhaps they could just manage the pain. The x-ray was needed.

An hour later the mobile x-ray technician performed magic, capturing three different angles of Thelma's hip with zero cooperation from the patient. Still she remained in the fetal position but screamed whenever anyone touched her. The poor x-ray tech looked relieved when his task was complete. The results were conveyed back to Cabot Manor within the hour with good news, no broken hip.

Stu and Ken sat with Sheila hidden in her office tucked away behind the front desk.

"This place always reminds me of the Eagles song, *Hotel California*," Ken said.

> *Last thing I remember,*
> *I was running for the door*
> *I had to find the passage back*
> *To the place I was before*
> *"Relax", said the nightman,*
> *"We are programmed to receive.*
> *You can check out anytime you like,*
> *But you can never leave."*
>
> *Eagles 1976*

"Ken, Stu," Sheila began. "Again, I'm so sorry about your dad, and now your mom. The good news is her hip is not broken, but we do have an issue to discuss. Due to her condition of being unresponsive and no longer able to assist with her transitions, we feel her placement on the assisted floor is no longer an appropriate level of care. We are recommending Thelma move down to the *Evergreen* unit on the first floor, where she can receive the care she needs. We are quite concerned about her welfare since the fall and she doesn't appear to have the ability to stand on her own anymore."

"When do you see this happening?" Ken asked.

"Well, we do have an open spot now and could make the move sometime today if you are agreeable."

"OK," Stu said. "What's the difference in cost and what's the difference in care?"

"There will be an increase in cost simply due to the increased level of care, which I can calculate for you right now." Sheila played around on her computer for a few minutes. "As for the difference in care, *Evergreen* is our memory unit and is locked 24/7 so your mother will not run the risk of wandering and falling. There are attendants and a nurse with the residents at all times. Your mother will have help dressing, toileting, bathing and eating everyday. She will be able to remain on *Evergreen* indefinitely, with no worries about another transfer."

Ken and Stu just looked at each other. They huddled, called the girls and made the decision. The one bit of good news was Cabot Manor took complete control of the move while they took their mother downstairs for a wheel around the property. Thelma remained collapsed in her wheelchair and flinched if anyone touched her. Within the hour the move was complete.

Evergreen was located on the first floor and was protected by a keypad. Anyone wishing to enter or leave was required to key in a code, a protection for the residents.

And Thelma was wheeled into yet another new home. Ken was given the code to enter *Evergreen;* it took him a few tries to get it right. Upon entering, there was a small room supervised by an attendant, and then a half wall into the main unit. The attendant buzzed them through. Ken supposed it was an extra layer of protection for those residents who wanted to make a run for it.

"Hello, you must be Thelma," the attendant chirped.

"The one and only," Ken said. Ken and Stu glanced around, taking in the memory unit and seeing it for what it was. In the main room a large-screen TV blared an old black-and-white Fred Astaire movie. There were several chairs for ambulatory residents but the majority of seating consisted of parked wheelchairs with slumped bodies.

"This is Mom's worst nightmare," Ken said.

"What other options do we have?" Stu asked. A nurse escorted them down the hallway to Thelma's new room. Entering the room they saw two beds, one empty and one occupied by a very still woman lying prone under a cotton blanket. She looked dead. There were two bureaus, and two uncomfortable chairs situated next to each bed and a bathroom. Bare-bones accommodations. Thelma was quiet and made no comment, she remained still as Stu and Ken jabbered on about the surroundings. The nurse helped Thelma into her bed and she screamed in pain from her hip injury. Once she was finally comfortable, her sons sat vigil with her for about an hour. Thelma slept and they left.

"I don't give her much time," Ken said as they exited the facility. "I think we can realistically wait until summer before we plan their memorial."

"I guess we'll just have to wait and see," Stu said quietly.

Life in *Evergreen* didn't change much from day to day. Residents were assisted with dressing and bathing before being delivered to the dining room for breakfast. They were assigned seats, as some residents did not get along. A few residents were able to feed themselves, while others had to be spoon-fed by an attendant. Following their meal they were wheeled over or walked over to the TV viewing area. The underlying chatter of residents talking to themselves filled the room. Those not talking were slouched over in sleep at angles sure to cause neck pain.

For several months Ken, Stu and Elaine continued the tag-team approach to visits while Thelma remained the same. Watching Thelma shrink to 80 pounds was distressing, but not as much as the lack of interaction, the lack of recognition of her own children and her disinterest in chocolate.

Trips to Florida became less frequent but the need to see her mother prompted Sue to make the visit with impending sadness.

Entering the *Evergreen* unit was downright depressing. Nothing changed. Sue spotted her mother at the end of a row of wheelchairs and gently kissed her mother's cheek. Thelma opened her eyes glancing at Sue with the faintest glimmer of recognition but no words.

"Hi Mom, it's good to see you." Sue rambled, not knowing how to make this visit something other than hearing herself talk for an hour.

"Let's go out back and walk around the path." With no protest from her mother, Sue fiddled with the locked brakes before maneuvering the wheelchair to the back garden. A two- inch lip on the threshold had to be scaled, causing the wheelchair to bump.

"Ooooo…Oooooo," was Thelma's reaction. Sue continued talking to her mother as they circled the short concrete path in one direction for six painstakingly slow laps. Figuring it was good for the brain to go in opposite directions, Sue reversed course for another six laps. Sue tried to carry on the one-sided conversation, but the stroll fell into silence.

Just as they were finishing a lap, a female resident approached them, seriously invading their personal space. The resident was mobile, albeit with a cane, and emitted a crazy aura.

"I'm Queen Shit of Turd Mountain!" the resident yelled, as she grinned at Thelma and Sue. A belly laugh escaped Sue despite herself. Thelma was oblivious. Pushing her mother away from the crazy lady they made one more lap, giving Sue the opportunity to lean into her mother's ear.

"Mom, you know it's okay to go. Dad is waiting for you, and your friends have a Crown Royal Manhattan with your name on it." There was no response from her mother. After an hour at *Evergreen* Sue returned her mother to the row of wheelchairs parked in front of a Bing Crosby movie, kissed her and left.

Back at Stu's house the time for decisions had arrived. The four kids sat together for a hard conversation.

"Well," said Ken. "It's now September and Mom is still here with no real change. We need to do something for Dad, because at this rate Mom could go on for a few more years."

"We're heading into the holidays," Sue said. "If we don't do something before Thanksgiving, it won't happen this year with all of us needing to travel to Vermont. I suggest late October or early November."

They all concurred and made a plan to divide and conquer the lengthy list of funeral tasks. Within a week they had secured the College Street Congregational Church, George and Thelma's church for over 50 years, and they had managed to schedule George's burial for earlier the same morning at the Veterans Cemetery in Randolph, Vermont. A block of hotel rooms was secured and the widow of George's best friend offered her home for the party afterwards. Leading up to the memorial service things fell into place, until the week before.

"Hello," Sue croaked into her phone. Seeing Ken's name on her phone in the middle of a work day caused her stomach to twist.

"Hey Sue, sorry to bother you at work, but something has happened."

"What? Is Mom okay?"

"Yeah, Mom is fine. Well fine might be an exaggeration, but it's not about Mom. The church just burned."

"What? The Congregational Church? What happened?"

"Some 24-year-old asshole said he heard voices telling him there was treasure in the steeple and he went up there and set it on fire."

"Did the whole church burn? What about Dad's service next week!?" Sue asked.

"That's the reason I'm calling, we can't use the church. The steeple is destroyed, the main part of the church will be okay, but the church is currently unusable."

In the spirit of community, the other Congregational Church in town immediately offered their building for George's memorial service. The family coordinated plans to all arrive at the Hampton Inn in Colchester, Vermont on the night of October 31. Upon entering the hotel lobby, an odd assortment of costumed characters milled about.

"What the hell?" asked Ken who had also just arrived.

"It's Halloween, Ken," said Sue.

"No, this is something else." Ken raised his eyebrows and nodded his head to the left. "Check out the 6' 3" kitty cat with the black patent leather skin-tight bodysuit. That is no female kitty."

"OMG you guys," said one of the nieces. "This is most definitely an Anime Convention."

"And what the hell is an Anime convention?" asked Ken. They were quickly brought up to speed on anime, a form of Japanese animation. At the conventions anime fans dress up as characters and cosplay or stay in character throughout the convention.

"Well, it's just bizarre," said Ken.

After everyone settled in their rooms they ran a few errands in preparation for the events the following day. They needed finger food and non-alcoholic drinks for the reception at the church, they needed supplies to create the photo boards to display, and they needed alcohol for the real party at Barb McDowell's house after the memorial service. They ordered several trays of food from Bove's, George's favorite Italian restaurant, for the party. Following dinner at a farm-to-table restaurant in Burlington, they reconvened in Ken's hotel room to assemble the pictures and hang out as a family.

"So what did you decide to put Dad's ashes in?" Karen inquired.

"I'm so glad you asked," Ken said. With a grin he fumbled in a large bag before pulling out a plastic pesticide sprayer. The room erupted in laughter. They all knew their father would have loved the joke and would have given a thumbs-up.

"I think we need to embellish it a little," Karen said. "Like maybe a Boston Red Sox sticker." Everyone nodded their agreement.

"And we should definitely place a pack of White Owl Miniatures next to the 'urn'," Stu added. The teenagers offered to run the errands for the Red Sox sticker and cigars. The others organized, reminisced and created a board with the photographs everyone contributed.

Ken relaxed on one of the beds while composing his part of the eulogy. Suddenly he jumped off the bed, grabbed a glass from the bureau and held it up to the wall of the adjoining room.

"Oh my God," he mouthed. "You're not going to believe this, anime characters actually procreate! God help us." By midnight their sides hurt from laughing and they all headed to their own rooms to sleep before the long day ahead.

The caravan of cars traveled down interstate 89 to Randolph Vermont for the burial before meandering down a country road to the Veterans Cemetery. Nestled in a valley of the Green Mountains, the cemetery was idyllic, despite it being late fall with little foliage left. During summer months family members were encouraged to cut flowers for their loved ones from the cutting garden. Most gravestones, or rather plaques, had in-ground vases for the fresh cut flowers. Plastic flowers were prohibited.

With a crowd of mostly family members at the graveside, the blue skies gave way to steel gray, and a cold rain commenced. Everyone scrambled to cover up with hoods and jackets, but a lucky few had umbrellas.

"I do believe this is Dad talking to us," Ken announced. "First the church burns, and we all know what a pyro he was. And now he sends the rain." A chuckle ran through the crowd, because they all felt the same.

The memorial service proceeded with military honors despite the rain. As the two soldiers approached the graveside in perfect formation, they gave a momentary hesitation when they saw the pesticide sprayer sitting there with a pack of White Owl Miniatures, but they managed to refrain from smiling and the flag was presented to

Charlie. Fifteen minutes later the small crowd was heading back into Burlington for the memorial service in a few hours.

At the First Congregational Church, the four kids and the grandchildren able to attend all pitched in to set up tables for the reception immediately following the service. A spread with an assortment of Cabot cheeses, crackers, hummus, chips and cookies filled several tables. Sue made a large tray of one of George's favorites, whoopie pies. Once things were set up and the picture boards set out, they made their way to the sanctuary. A bagpiper played in honor of George as the kids watched in amazement at the number of people filing into the church. The four children and their families were seated in the front pews, but there was a clear vacancy.

There had been discussion about bringing Thelma to the funeral, but the idea was readily vetoed. Thelma was in no condition to travel, plus she would not have understood what was happening. The kids also understood the last thing their mother would have wanted was for her friends to see her languishing in the late stages of Alzheimer's.

As funerals go, this was actually a celebration of George. Being a protestant service meant it would be short and family members were free to speak. Hugh, George's good friend, shared a few stories, before Norm offered a heartfelt remembrance of his father-in-law. Then each of the four kids, in order of age, took the pulpit.

Karen's special relationship with her father shined through with her words. Stu was emotional, serious and heartfelt. Sue prepared a list of thank-you notes to her father in the manner of Jimmy Fallon, starting with humor and ending with tears.

Mom always instilled in me the importance of Thank You Notes, these are for you Dad.

Thank you for always having our safety at the forefront; like the time you asked Ken and I to inventory the pesticide shed at the Hort Farm. You issued us WWII era respirators whose condition was questionable. I think we told you we finished the job but the truth is, we made an executive decision to live.

Thank you for the many lessons in semantics and vocabulary. We were reminded often that they were not BUGS, they were insects. The only creatures worthy of being called bugs were Lady Bugs, June Bugs and Bed Bugs.

Thank you for teaching me the best metric conversion trick when I was ten. We were living in Australia and you were convinced the US would convert to the metric system and you wanted us prepared.
*0 degrees C = 32 degrees F
*Frosty Fives

*Tingly Teens
*Temperate Twenties
*Thirsty Thirties
*Frying Forties

Thank you for clarifying the difference between clean dirt and dirt. I'm not sure you ever convinced Mom but I bought it and believe it. Clean dirt are all those things you might track in but aren't germy and disgusting like garden soil, beach sand, grass clippings and saw dust. Gross dirt are things like tractor oil, cow manure, dog poo, garbage and pond scum.

Thank you for being such an influential role for both my boys. You would be so proud of them both. Henry and you made a special connection when he took you to DC to visit the WWII Memorial. He has now joined the army, no other branch was worthy. Charlie has just graduated from UMass, your alma mater and wants to pursue a graduate degree in the sciences. He has even connected with your former graduate student Carol who has taken him under her wing. I know you've had a hand in it.

Thank you for showing us what trust is. It is a powerful thing. When we were teenagers and heading out for the night, you asked us where we were going and we said OUT. Then you asked us when we'd be home and we said LATER. You knew we weren't angels but we never ended up in jail, at least I never ended up in jail. I hope I've passed that on to Henry and Charlie because being trusted makes moving forward possible. Thanks Dad.

Bringing up the rear was Ken, for which the others were thankful, because he was by far the most skilled orator and the funniest. Ken was delivering a humorous story about the time when he was driving home to the house on Laurel Hill when he saw an immense amount of smoke rising from behind the house. Approaching the house, he noticed his father outside fully engaged in controlling a grass fire out of control.

Just as Ken finished recanting the story a roar of sirens passed the church drowning out Ken's voice. The coincidence was not lost on the congregation.

For the hour or so following the service everyone chatted among relatives they rarely saw, cousins who they promised to stay in touch with and old friends from Burlington. The party continued at Barb McDowell's house for anyone who wanted to attend, where they were regaled with stories of George and countless toasts made in his honor. A few of George's ashes had been held in reserve to be spread under his apple trees in Monkton. Stu and Elaine made the trek to Monkton, and quietly spread the ashes underneath a MacIntosh tree. The last few days offered a welcome closure for the family.

Routines and normalcy returned. Thelma's tortured daily existence remained unchanged despite the family offering nightly prayers for her peaceful end. Henry went to see his grandmother during a visit south and found her wheeled up to the assigned table for the lunchtime meal.

"Hi Gram," Henry said as he bent over to kiss her shriveled cheek.

"Ooo." She flinched and stared at Henry.

"Gram, it's me Henry. You know, your favorite grandson!" If he had been expecting a reaction, he was disappointed. Pulling a chair next to his grandmother, he sat, glanced around the table and absorbed the scene. Three other wheelchair-bound residents sat poking at their food in silence. Henry carried on an uncomfortable one-sided conversation for a few minutes before giving up. It had been a while since he'd seen his grandmother and the change was staggering. In the time since he'd last seen her, she had lost 20 pounds and the ability to walk or communicate. He thought she resembled a shrunken dried-apple doll with puckered cheeks and wrinkled skin, like the kind he had made in fifth grade when studying Colonial times. He had one trick up his sleeve.

"Hey Gram, guess what I brought for you?" He pulled out a package of plain M&Ms and poured a few onto a napkin in front of her. Her eyes widened and she reached for an M&M with her arthritically disfigured fingers. Suddenly one of the women at the table reached over to take some M&Ms but Thelma was not having it. With one stealthy move no one knew she was capable of, she snatched her fork and tried to stab the woman. Thelma growled something unintelligible as the fork narrowly missed the woman's hand. Henry smiled at the entertainment, but felt heavy-hearted watching his beloved grandmother in her current condition.

6 Months Later

There was little discernible change to Thelma's plight. The family was informed by the memory doctor that an Alzheimer's patient's worst enemy was a healthy heart. She was now down to a skeletal 70 pounds, with hollows between her clavicle and neck large enough to hold a cup of water. She was spending more and more time sleeping while eating less and less. The family continued to visit several times a week, along with frequent prayers for an end to the suffering. Finally, a year and a half after George's passing, Thelma was released from her prolonged but valiant fight with the insidious disease.

"Hello?" Ken answered his phone simultaneously, glancing to see it was Cabot Manor calling and hitting mute on the NASCAR race he was watching. He was now numb and immune to the spikes in emotion whenever the facility called.

"Hi Ken, I'm so sorry to deliver this message, your mother has passed. She passed peacefully in her sleep within the last hour. You and the family are welcome to come see her and say goodbye. The funeral home will be picking her up later this morning."

"Wow, okay, thanks for calling, and I'll let my siblings know." Ken was surprised at the wave of sadness, despite an overwhelming sense of relief for his mother.

Unlike with George's passing, the family never had that moment to make their final goodbyes to Thelma. Alzheimer's is often called the "Long Goodbye," but she had essentially left them months ago if not years, robbing them of a meaningful goodbye. Plans now had to be made for Thelma's memorial service.

"At this point," Sue began processing with her siblings. "We can't really do anything this month because it's December, and again we all have to fly up to Vermont."

"And not to mention," Stu added. "The Veterans Cemetery won't hold any services until the spring when the ground has thawed."

"That's fine," Karen said. "It'll give us time to figure out what we want to do for the service and hopefully the church will be back open."

Once again the kids divided up the tasks of informing relatives and friends, checking on dates with the VA and the church, running the obituary and figuring out an urn. Sue offered to take care of the obituary, feeling relieved and comforted they had written it a few years earlier.

THELMA FORSYTH MACCOLLOM-St Petersburg, FL. Thelma Forsyth MacCollom, 83, of South Burlington VT died December 1, 2014 in St Petersburg, FL following a valiant struggle with Alzheimer's which she handled with incredible grace and candor.

Thelma was born in Milton MA on August 8, 1931 to her parents Wallace Whitelaw Forsyth and Dorothy Ross Hadenstrom during the early years of the Depression. The family soon relocated to Ithaca NY where her father found employment at the Gas & Electric Company.

Thelma graduated from Ithaca High School in 1949 where she played violin in the orchestra. She then attended Rochester Business Institute honing her secretarial skills she used at Cornell University.

It was at Cornell she met her husband George Butterick MacCollom whom she married on December 5, 1953 in Ithaca. The following year Thelma and George moved to Burlington VT where George became a professor of entomology at UVM for over forty *years. South Burlington became their home where they raised four children and enjoyed a blessed life.*

Thelma was actively involved with Home Arts, bridge clubs, the Women of UVM and raising her children. Thelma worked as the church secretary at the College Street Congregational Church where they were lifelong members. In 1988, Thelma and George moved out to Monkton to pursue the dream of starting an orchard.

During these years in Vermont, Thelma was the consummate hostess who loved entertaining, playing bridge, knitting and walking with friends even through sub zero temperatures. In 2009 they migrated to Largo, FL in order to be closer to family and enjoy warmer weather.

Thelma was predeceased by her husband George B MacCollom in March 2013 and her grandson Keith MacCollom in April 2009. She is survived by her daughter Karen MacCollom Theoktisto and husband Phil Theoktisto of Melrose FL; son Stuart MacCollom and wife Elaine of Seminole FL; daughter Susan MacCollom Richard and husband Normand of Georgetown ME; and son Ken MacCollom and wife Marie of St Petersburg FL. She is also survived by her grandchildren Anna Theoktisto Camardese, Katie Theoktisto, Allison MacCollom West, Henry Richard, Cameron MacCollom, Christina Theoktisto Blanchard, Charles Richard, Connor MacCollom and Duncan MacCollom. Her four siblings also survive her: Richard Forsyth, Phyllis Montana, Patricia Peters and Diane Ingersoll.

Thelma was a loving and caring wife, mother and friend who will be sorely missed by many.

By early June plans were in place for Thelma's memorial service later in the month. The church was back in working order and the cemetery was scheduled but no decision had been made regarding the urn.

"I think we should place Mom's ashes in a purple Crown Royal bag," Sue suggested.

"Brilliant," Ken agreed but Karen was not on board.

"I don't think that's right," Karen said. "It just seems a bit gauche, I think we need to have Mom in a proper urn." Sue offered to have a green marble urn made for Thelma, and in the spirit of compromise decided to place her mother's ashes in a Crown Royal bag inside the urn. Everyone was happy.

The family began to arrive in Burlington on Wednesday afternoon, at which time they would connect for drinks and dinner. All four kids, some of their spouses and several grandkids made the trek to Vermont for the final chapter. Henry was in the Army not able to take leave, Katie was in med school and cousins Cam and Charlie encountered serious car trouble in the middle of the country. Thursday was dedicated to all the last-minute details such as speaking with the minister who was not acquainted with Thelma, procuring flowers for the church and refreshments for the reception immediately following Thelma's celebration of life.

It was a déjà vu moment for the family as they cruised down Interstate 89 towards the Veterans Cemetery for Thelma's graveside service. This time, however, the sun was shining through the pleasant June air. Several cousins from Massachusetts were in attendance as Thelma was laid to rest next to George.

Back at the College Street Congregational Church the organist played several of Thelma's beloved hymns, including *Amazing Grace* and *Holy, Holy, Holy* as people filtered in. As with George's service, each of the kids spoke in order of birth. None of them had conferred with each other as to what they would say, it was better not to confuse their own thoughts. Tears were followed by chuckles, and then more tears, as they paid tribute to their mother. Sue decided to compose thank-you notes similar to those she wrote for her father.

Thank you Mom for teaching me there are exceptions to the rule. You did not like swearing and we were reprimanded if any four letter words spewed from our mouths. However, whenever you dropped something or someone cut in front of you while driving, we always knew there was an "Oh Shit" coming.

Thank you for demonstrating your entire life, how to be social and how to entertain. You had numerous groups of friends and were never as happy as when you were planning a dinner party. You showed us that you didn't need lots of money, you just needed to invite friends and share a meal.

Thank you for sharing your love of cooking. Because of you, all your kids and I think most of your grandkids enjoy cooking too. Both my boys like to cook so much they asked me to put together a binder of recipes from Gram. So, of course, I had to include whoopie pies, scotch-a-roos, your famous meatballs, quiche, Bavarian beef and party chicken.

Thank you for sharing the importance of tradition. Every Christmas we had your Christmas bread, went to church and were allowed to open one present. On our birthdays, you always let us choose our birthday meal and you always remembered our favorite cake. Mine was German chocolate and in Ken's case, it was raspberry pie.

Thank you for giving the best advice. One time when I was new to driving, I hooked bumpers with another car in the Martins parking lot and I was so scared to tell you I had damaged the bumper. When I finally found the courage to tell you, you said, "was anyone hurt?" I told you no and you said, "great, just don't do it again". You also told me to always be myself, never try to be somebody I'm not. That message has stayed with me and has made me very happy.

Thank you for being the best mom.

A guitarist played two of Thelma's favorite contemporary songs *You Can Close Your Eyes* by James Taylor and *Tears in Heaven* by Eric Clapton. The minister gave an impressive eulogy considering he had never met Thelma, prayers were offered and the family sighed a collective relief.

At the reception in the Perkins room of the church, the kids caught up with many of George and Thelma's friends who were able to attend. In the eyes of the old friends the kids were suddenly Stuey, Susie and Kenny again—but Karen being the oldest had always been Karen. The kids struggled to connect the aged faces with names, but eventually it all came back.

After wrapping things up at the church, the party moved over to the hotel which graciously agreed to allow a gathering in their lobby. The only stipulation was that any alcohol being consumed must be in discrete containers. A makeshift bar was assembled in Sue and Norm's room with the door propped ajar for easy access. The gathering in the lobby consisted primarily of immediate family, a smattering of cousins and a few friends of the kids. George and Thelma's friends were limited in number these days and those still around had paid their respects back at the church.

A buffet of Bove's specialties were laid out including lasagna, Thelma's favorite; spaghetti and meatballs, bread and salad. Sue had made a large batch of Scotcharoos, a decadent dessert of Rice Krispies, peanut butter and sugar with a frosting of melted chocolate and butterscotch chips. Thelma had been well known for her Scotcharoos.

"Anyone have a hacksaw?" Ken asked. "These things are as hard as rock."

"Ugh," Sue was clearly disappointed this batch was not her best, realizing the stress of the week had taken its toll. That did not stop the abuse from her siblings and cousins.

The party migrated up to the room with the bar where the siblings and their kids hung out into the early morning hours reminiscing, laughing and pondering what was next.

"You know," Sue said. "With both our parents gone, we're next in line."

"Well," Ken said. "Mom has honestly been gone a long time—but I know what you're saying."

"And even though they were ready to go," Stu started. "It's hard losing a parent. There's a finality to it."

"Well," Karen said. "I don't want to put my girls through this when the time comes. I'm a nurse and Katie's a doctor, so I'll be having myself a special little cocktail when the time comes."

"That's assuming you haven't lost your mind and can remember you want to have that cocktail," someone chimed in. They spent the good part of an hour discussing ways to end their lives if it came to prolonged stays in a memory unit. As morbid as it all sounded, they laughed and became very silly.

Conversation drifted away from the topic of death towards pleasant stories from their childhood.

"What was that ridiculous story Dad used to recite?" Karen asked.

"Oh yeah," Stu said. "I forgot about that. Wasn't it the Nutt Family?"

"I think I remember the beginning," Ken said. "Did you ever hear the story of the family called Nutt? Or something like that."

"Yeah, yeah, yeah," Sue said. "There was something about Johnny Nutt and hickory nuts.

"I remember something about one of them kissing a cow," Stu added.

"One of the little nuts ate too much yeast and blew up," said Karen.

"And at the end," Ken said. "Someone fell in a pool of shit."

Sue pulled out her phone to Google it while the others started piecing it together bit by bit. It took them about an hour or two to recall the lyrics to the poem, if it could be called a poem. George used to recite *The Nutt Family* word for word. Between the support of Google– which was not much help–and aging memories, they were able to cobble together the poem, which turned out to be rather disturbing.

The Nutt Family

Did you ever hear the story of the family called Nutt?

There's father Nutt and Mother Nutt and all the little Nutts. There's Johnny Nutt and Billy Nutt and Patsy Nutt and Pete. The parrot goat and yellow dog will make this complete. There's hazel nuts and hickory nuts and nuts from far Brazil, doughnuts, coconuts and filberts to your fill. Yet you'll agree that these are nothing but just nuts, chestnuts as you will see.

Johnny was a drinker at the early age of six and he'd beat his father drinking beer or gin and whiskey mixed. One night he drank a pint of yeast and expected to get up the next day at six, such was the rumor, but the yeast got in its work and so he rose an hour sooner.

Billy Nutt had an appetite, it made no difference whether he had good food or oats or straw or even leather. One day he held a neighbor's horse. They thought it safe of course, but Billy getting hungry ate the harness from the horse. They took him to the hospital, the stomach pumps supplied and an X-ray to his back applied to find the harness. Then they tried and peered with anxious faces, but they couldn't even find a bit or discover any traces.

Peter Nutt was always known as absent minded Peter. He certainly was a careless and absent minded creature. One night he clean forgot to shut the cow shed door. That night the mercury went down as it never had before. Oh strange it now may seem, it froze that poor old cow so stiff that when they milked her all they had for breakfast was ice cream.

Patsy was a brakeman on the New York night express. He led a terribly fast life but was slow I guess, he reached far out to kiss his wife when he went by one day. He went so fast that he kissed a cow about a mile away. Patsy had a little boy they called "red head Willy." He was a lamp for them at night, a stove when they felt chilly. One day he wanted to get six eggs, he put them in his hat and when he reached home those eggs were fried. Now what do you think of that?

Old Father Nutt began to think his sons were a disgrace. First he went on a tear and rent the air and everyone defied and then he jumped in a cess pool and attempted suicide. They fished for him at length and when they pulled him out, they found that it had been a terrible drain upon his strength, and then he drank a quart of benzene and hasn't been seen since.

"Holy shit," Ken said. "What the hell kind of story is that?" They were all perplexed, but laughed despite themselves.

"Yeah, well I'm pretty sure I won't be sharing that poem with my 4th grade class!" Sue said.

As the reminiscing continued, the stories jumped around, but it brought comfort and a sense of closure to the kids.

Remember Mom didn't want us to know she had chocolate in the house so she would place a Milky Way bar in her apron pocket, go in the living room and vacuum so we couldn't hear her opening the candy.

Remember when Dad would start spraying the birch trees on Laurel Hill and we all knew that distinct pesticide odor and we'd run to shut the windows before the toxic fumes overtook the house.

Remember when Roger Murray brought Dad a pill bottle marked "Smart Pills" and Dad looked at it and said, "This is rabbit shit!"
Roger answered, "See you're already getting smarter."

The gathering broke up in favor of sleep. The next day the family scattered with some headed home while others headed up to the Trout Club for a few days of respite. This was the new phase of life without their parents, without the constant worry about what was going to happen to their parents, without the anxiety-inducing phone calls from the facility, and with the knowledge they were truly blessed to have had such a normal loving and supportive childhood. George and Thelma's kids had grown closer through their parents' journey despite the challenges, and this would have made George and Thelma happy.

The End

Acknowledgements

I want to thank my siblings: Karen, Stu and Ken for supporting me through this process and feeding me notes about their experiences as they were happening with a special nod to my brother Ken. He has been my cheerleader and brought humor to the process. I also want to thank my husband, Norm, for also being my cheerleader and only offering advice when solicited. I began this project when my parents were still alive because the material was just too important (and crazy) but I had to put it on the back burner for a few years as life got in the way. Once I retired I was able to focus, find motivation from my writing group and had the time to finish. I also want to thank Joyce Hendley and Gail David for helping me with the editing process.

Made in United States
North Haven, CT
27 January 2023

31702045R00098